The Singing Irish

The Singing Irish

A HISTORY OF THE NOTRE DAME GLEE CLUB

MICHAEL ALAN ANDERSON

FOREWORD BY DANIEL STOWE

University of Notre Dame Press

Notre Dame, Indiana

Printed in Canada by Friesens Corporation

Joey Coleman ('95) was creative editor for this project.

Library of Congress Cataloging-in-Publication Data

Anderson, Michael Alan, 1975–
The Singing Irish : a history of the Notre Dame Glee Club /
Michael Alan Anderson.
pages   cm
Includes bibliographical references and index.
ISBN 978-0-268-02045-3 (hardcover : alk. paper)
ISBN 0-268-02045-0 (hardcover : alk. paper)
1. University of Notre Dame. Glee Club—History. 2. Glee clubs—Indiana—
Notre Dame—History. I. Title.
ML28.N66U554   2015
782.4206'077289—dc23

                                    2015017668

∞ *The paper in this book meets the guidelines for permanence and durability
of the Committee on Production Guidelines for Book Longevity of the
Council on Library Resources.*

The author and the University of Notre Dame Press thank Glee Club alumnus

ROBERT S. "BOB" OPPOLD ('73)

whose generous financial support of this volume is made in memory of his parents.

In Memoriam
Robert L. and Patricia J. Oppold

Thank you, Mom and Dad.

Your loving son,

Bob

Contents

Foreword

DANIEL STOWE

When I arrived on the Notre Dame campus in August of 1993, I had just an inkling of the dynamic of a men's glee club. Having spent a year as graduate assistant for the Cornell Glee Club, I had witnessed social and musical bonds and the commitment of alumni also characteristic of our group, but I was unprepared for the singular intensity of the Glee Club experience as manifested here at Notre Dame. Now, as I reflect on the nature of that experience as we enter our centennial year, it strikes me that it might be a product of the many simultaneous journeys, many arcs, in our group's life, ranging in length from a single day to the entire century-long span of the Glee Club's continuous existence.

The kernel of our journey together is the single rehearsal. Every weekday afternoon, for an hour, we gather together, sharing in the mysterious cycle of departure, challenge, and ultimate arrival at a new destination that define any voyage. I find the fact that we meet on a daily basis to be the core reason for the strength of our unity. Immersed in the details of ensemble music, we clean up muddy passages, trying to sculpt and refine our performance. Alongside our musical work, there is the day-to-day management of the group, tended to principally by the Club officers. These are the daily acts of trimming the sails, of staying the course, while we keep our focus on our longer-range goals.

An academic term has its own trajectory, as we aim for our two major concert events each semester. The initial meetings of the fall, first with returning members before classes begin and then the first rehearsal with the new members, pulse with anticipation of the adventure of building a new group. We set off together, focusing on the core "rookie" material, using it to demonstrate the technical principles common to all the music we'll encounter. We find ourselves addressing problems that have crept into our performance, and it's here where the truly gifted members begin to emerge. I am particularly delighted when a new singer points out an error of long standing, hitherto unnoticed by any of us. After a few weeks, and about a month out from our fall break tour, new folders appear in the rack and we apply our newly won skills to the pieces on our fall program. The plan is always to learn the new music methodically, but sometimes our measured (if rapid) pace devolves into more of a sprint in the final push before the trip, particularly if a gig requiring new, individualized material pops up.

We certainly can also hit the doldrums. About four weeks into a term, the newness has worn off somewhat; as academic demands increase, absences tend to rise. At that point, my job is to try to make every rehearsal worth the time for each Clubber: "if you miss, you miss out." Dangling the carrot, I plead, "the more you come, the less we all have to rehearse." I realize I am echoing a universal lament from the conductor's podium.

Intensity always increases as mid-semester approaches with telescoping academic tasks and the approach of our tour. Then we depart: with equal parts excitement and relief, we start a real road trip set within our metaphorical journey together. Musical growth between each tour concert seems like a week of rehearsal. New members learn the expectations of musical professionalism, and they experience a new degree of fraternal camaraderie. We unfailingly receive tremendous hospitality on the road, and I am continually amazed at the size of our audiences. The strength of the university's name gives us an audience base unmatched among collegiate choruses, a fact I never allow us to take for granted or accept as routine. The fatigue of long days and long nights can weigh us down toward the end, but the young men always finish strong. We return to campus, perhaps not rested, but still recharged, and there is the chance for us to present our handiwork in a performance at Leighton Concert Hall. Of late, I have tried to suggest that while singing for a home audience is a precious opportunity, we will give a looser performance if we approach it a bit more clinically, channeling our excitement through the lens of the professionalism we developed on the road.

Each term, fall or spring, has its own particularities, and the differences between them are inscribed in a larger arc, that of the entire academic year. The rhythm of our fall is of course inextricably linked with the season on the gridiron, which helps sustain the energy through any mid-semester ebb; in the spring, the prospect of warmer days ahead can serve the same purpose. The impending Christmas season provides a new burst of wind in the sails. (Scarcely after the final note of the fall concert is sung, the guys serenade the departing crowd in the lobby with holiday tunes.) Then, in late fall, the seniors receive my voting request for Commencement Concert music, perhaps their first realization that the conclusion of their own Notre Dame journey draws nigh. Throughout the fall, their "lasts" pile up: last hayride, last "ND in Revue," last caroling, last Christmas Concert . . .

In the spring, after the tour and the campus concert, the pace is more leisurely; this is the best time of year for an orchestral collaboration. Offstage, Glee Club life peaks with the formal in late April. Finally, senior week:

the time between the end of the academic year and Commencement exercises. This is as close to a summer camp environment as the Glee Club gets. Rehearsal in the morning, activities in the afternoon; bonds that will last a lifetime deepen, and at last we bid farewell on stage to our graduates Saturday evening, singing the music they've chosen. They invariably choose well, shaping an eclectic program of challenging works and old favorites, a testament to their sophistication as musicians and performers.

Where did those graduates begin? Here traces another arc, that of each individual Clubber. Some come fully formed, as it were, with their capacity for musical and administrative leadership immediately apparent. Others begin more timidly and gradually unfurl as they gain confidence and discover their gifts. It's hard to say which type is more gratifying to observe—we couldn't function without the former group, but to see a mousy rookie metamorphose into a senior soloist and concert-announcement raconteur is nothing less than thrilling. Of course, these arcs are common tropes for the university experience in general, but I think the unique opportunities that the Glee Club provides for personal growth propel all of us to a higher trajectory of achievement.

And on to the largest arc, that of the Club itself as a student organization with more than a century of history, from the initial meetings through the moments of brilliance under Samuel Ward Perrott and each of his successors. In my short time at the helm, we've literally had a new keel laid beneath us: our move to the DeBartolo Performing Arts Center ten years ago provided a propulsive boost that has scarcely faded. We'll continue to push forward, trying to keep our Club a destination where young men can deepen their awareness of aesthetic beauty, unlock their own talents, and be part of a larger whole. Glee Clubber and chaplain James Foster ('77) beautifully terms this last item a core spiritual need for all of us:

> There are few basic desires of the human heart: the desire to love others and be loved by others, the desire to blossom and to grow into the best persons we can possibly become, and the desire to belong to something much bigger than just ourselves. Those desires are at the core of who we are as persons. Every priest has one homily, and this is mine. (Author correspondence with Fr. James Foster '77, 29 August 2014)

And so tomorrow, the next day, and beyond, the current members and their director will return to the task of stewardship of the Glee Club. The Club does not belong to us. It is a ship, a safe place in a stormy sea, in the same sense that the word "nave" is used to describe the central hall of a church. As its stewards, our task is to guide our vessel safely to its next destination, to keep it seaworthy, indeed to ensure that it is delivered to its next occupants in better shape than that in which we found it.

I'm grateful daily that I've had the opportunity to share in the journey.

Preface

A historical project of this scope would be impossible to accomplish without the help of a large team of individuals committed to its success. Harv Humphrey from the University of Notre Dame Press showed confidence in this book about the Notre Dame Glee Club from the beginning, and I am also grateful to Matthew Dowd and Wendy McMillen for stewarding a vision for the volume that pushed the boundaries of the press. Charles Lamb, Elizabeth Hogan, and Erik Dix in the Notre Dame Archives have facilitated the process of gathering valuable print and digital materials for the book. Also, Kathleen Smith from my home city of Rochester was kind enough to read through some chapters in the early writing stages and offer editorial feedback. Jim Farrington and Jared Case, also from Rochester, helped me sort through bibliographic and cataloguing questions.

A circle of alumni and friends of the Glee Club interested in piecing together the history of the ensemble formed in the summer of 2014. They assisted me as a kind of focus group against which I could calibrate trends. John E. Fisher, James Foster, C.S.C., George Hammer, David Clark Isele, Charles "Chuck" Lennon, Richard Leonhardt, Robert Meffe, Tom Nessinger, Mark Pilkinton, Brian McLinden, Dorothy Pedtke, Rudy Reyes, Doris Stam, Aaron Trulley, and Doon Wintz were quick to respond to my queries and unveiled details that appear in this book that I simply could not have known without their help.

This group of informants was matched by a smaller core team of Glee Club alumni who not only delivered feedback but also put in hours of work ensuring the work's timely completion and accuracy in detail. Pat Revord volunteered time to compile a database of Club repertoire. John Moe freely shared resources and memorabilia in his possession. Mark Torma, Joseph Mulligan, and Brian Scully were invaluable helpers "on the ground" in South Bend to aid in the retrieval of information and images from the Notre Dame Archives. Besides his outstanding contribution to the preparation of this book, Joey Coleman has been a tireless cheerleader for the commemorative volume and the centennial celebration more broadly. His confidence in my work and his wisdom with handling a range of creative and design issues helped propel the project, especially in the final stages.

The current director of the Notre Dame Glee Club, Daniel Stowe, has been an inspiration ever since he put the music of Josquin des Prez in front of me in the fall of 1993. I have been in awe of the heights to which he has taken the Club musically, to say nothing of the remarkable places to which the group has traveled under his direction. Not only has Dan led the choir for almost a quarter of its history, but his clear memories and his ability to see both forests and trees in Glee Club culture have been an asset to me in the writing process. I am thankful for his genuine interest not just in this project, but also in my career as a musician and scholar after I graduated from Notre Dame. His friendship is something I will always cherish. I hope this book will serve as a small token of my appreciation to this venerable steward of the Glee Club enterprise.

In many ways, Patrick Scott is the guardian of the Glee Club legacy. While a student at Notre Dame, Pat wrote a senior thesis in 1976 on the history of the Glee Club, from its inception through the year 1958. This paper provided an important starting point for my work. But this is just a fraction of his contribution to this book. Pat has quickly responded to hundreds of questions large and small that have arisen over the past two years. He has also been kind enough to read the entire manuscript, offering careful edits and setting the record straight numerous times. Countless stories and colorful details in this book have come directly from Pat. For this, I am indebted.

My parents, David and Virginia Anderson, gave me the opportunity to attend the University of Notre Dame in the fall of 1993. While I was in college, they were great supporters of the Glee Club, frequently driving to South Bend from the Chicago suburbs to catch pre-game revues and other concert events during the year. It made me happy that my fellow singers knew my parents and liked them. My mom and dad have also demonstrated the importance of giving back to Notre Dame, which I hope to have done with this commemorative volume. It is to them that I dedicate this book.

ONE

Introduction

"I thought I could write a book of the things I can recall, but after talking to some of the alumni at the reunion, I found myself a listener."[1] In the Notre Dame Glee Club's inaugural alumni newsletter of 1963, Daniel H. ("Dean") Pedtke wrote of his delight in reuniting with former singers at a celebration marking his twenty-fifth year as the group's director. He also mentioned his idea to write a book about what had transpired during his time as conductor of the Glee Club, the distinguished all-male chorus of the university. Having led the ensemble for more than half of its history to that point, Pedtke was in an excellent position to compile his memories. But such a volume did not materialize.

Pedtke's wish to collect his reminiscences of the Glee Club was not the only call to tell a history of musical life at Notre Dame. In 1928, Father James Connerton, C.S.C. ('20), then director of the Moreau Seminary Choir, former member of the Notre Dame Glee Club, and later president of King's College in Pennsylvania, remarked that "hidden behind that veil of modesty which naturally envelopes all the arts, the history of music at the University of Notre Dame is practically lost to the modern world."[2] Perhaps the origins of a music program at Notre Dame were shrouded, but the early history of music at the university, including that of the Glee Club, does survive in fragments and deserves to be articulated. While several American universities had established men's glee clubs in the later nineteenth century (Harvard was earliest at 1858), Notre Dame struggled to sustain a male chorus until the turn of the twentieth century, and even then there were breaks in continuity. Considering the

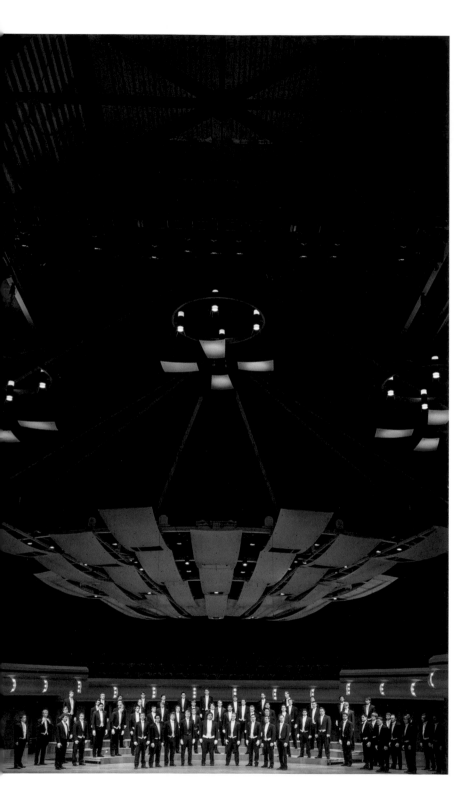

Glee Club has now reached its centennial as a student organization, it is high time that the veil of modesty was lifted from the university's chief choral ambassador.

According to the constitution of the group, "the function of the Notre Dame Glee Club is twofold: a) to represent the University in vocal performances on and off campus and b) to provide social activities."[3] But this generic statement could be said of any collegiate chorus. This book endeavors to showcase that which makes the Notre Dame Glee Club distinctive among American college choirs. Chapter 2 explains the slow rise of the university's all-male chorus, charting some of the events and personalities that secured its footing as an organization in 1915. Although director Samuel Ward Perrott was no doubt a pivotal figure in the formation of a stable Glee Club, the activities of the group appear scattered in various contexts before Perrott's arrival. Perrott's musical standards and ambition for the group ensured its viability for the long term.

Following an account of the early history of the group, the book proceeds topically instead of chronologically, emphasizing a contextual frame for prominent aspects of Glee Club history rather than a strict timeline of key moments in its evolution. Chapter 3 examines membership in the Glee Club from a broad perspective, noting trends in enrollment, the role of the officers, and some special "Clubbers" who have been cited repeatedly for their contributions in the surviving documentation. The next two chapters focus on the gentlemen who took the podium and led the ensemble over the last century. A centerpiece of this study is the impact of longtime director Dean Pedtke, who guided the Glee Club for thirty-five years—over one-third of its history. Joseph Casasanta and Daniel Stowe, who have also conducted for substantial periods of time, offered valuable contributions that have shaped the programs that today's audiences encounter on stage. Though other directors have had shorter tenures, each has nevertheless strengthened the ensemble in demonstrable ways.

Concert activity occupies the next major portion of this commemorative volume. Chapter 6 explores the performances that took place at Notre Dame and in South Bend more generally, while chapter 7 provides a perspective on the extensive travels of the ensemble away from the campus, both domestically and internationally. While European travel began rather late, in 1971, the Glee Club has embarked on tours to other parts of the globe in the last two decades that most collegiate ensembles will never match. The music that the Glee Club sings and its broad circulation in media are the subjects of chapters 8 and 9, respectively. The former chapter focuses on some of the greatest hits one is sure to encounter in Glee Club performances and the evolution of programs across the century. Chapter 9 is particularly crucial, as it demonstrates how the group's music was disseminated publicly not only through recordings but also through frequent national radio broadcasts and an unparalleled set of consecutive annual appearances on Ed Sullivan's *Toast of the Town* from 1949 to 1955.

This account of the Glee Club's history wraps up with three chapters on the social aspects of the group, beginning with the relationship of the ensemble to Notre Dame's football enterprise (chapter 10), from its appearances in the stadium to its pre- and post-game concerts offered for the spirited fan base of the university. In any endeavor at the University of Notre Dame, it is difficult to escape the long shadow of the football program. From its inception, the Glee Club has been closely linked to the team on the gridiron. The nickname "Singing Irish," in fact, was part of an analogy that was invoked from the late 1920s through the mid-1980s to illustrate that the athletic prowess of the football team (the "Fighting Irish") was paralleled in song by the Glee Club. A description of the 1985 Commencement activities in the *Dome* yearbook uses the label "Singing Irish" even before the words "Glee Club" are mentioned: "The evening provided an opportunity to hear the 'Singing Irish' as a near-capacity crowd filled Stepan Center to hear the Glee Club one last time."[4] Concert programs and group biographies were peppered with the moniker "Singing Irish," and although this term is no longer in use in Glee Club culture, the name persisted for a good part of its history.

The subject of football yields to an overview of a variety of traditions and rituals that have formed within the ensemble, whether visible to the public or closely guarded by Club members (chapter 11). The vast array of activities undertaken outside of the rehearsal room and the concert hall fosters a brotherhood that is unmatched among campus organizations. Finally, the fraternal nature of the group is turned on its head in chapter 12, as the role of women in and around the organization is considered. Female movie stars, women soloists, and women's choirs have figured prominently in Glee Club life since the 1920s. It would be a mistake to let these contributions go unmentioned.

Preparing a history of the Glee Club has required patience and selectivity; there are simply too many stories, countless traditions, and hundreds of tour stops that will not receive attention in this volume. It is easy to focus on the group's present culture or on one's own memories, but this would make for a shallow and unbalanced narrative. What follows is an attempt to highlight major trends of the Club while also capturing its incomparable spirit at select moments in time, without privileging any particular decade. Inspired by Dean Pedtke, I too have found myself a listener—a fortunate witness to the voices of present students, to the stories of dozens of Glee Club alumni going back to the 1940s, to friends of the ensemble, to the sound of live and studio recordings, and, yes, to a wealth of documents that detail the activities undertaken and impressions made by Notre Dame's foremost musical enterprise.

TWO

Traces of a Glee Club

As early as 1871, there were calls for a choral fraternity at Notre Dame. By late 1874, two professors, Staley and Gillespie, promoted the organization of a "glee club" at the university, while the student weekly magazine *Scholastic* declared, "A glee club will be organized tomorrow. Professor Paul will be the leader."[1] Within two years, the fledgling club was considered on par with the university band, orchestra, and liturgical choir, and the music building was expanded to accommodate the growth in the university's musical offerings.[2] In June 1880, the ensemble performed at the annual Commencement ceremony alongside the band, now the oldest active college band in the United States.[3] A campus-wide glee club seems to have unraveled by the mid-1880s, and yet there was a performance in 1888 described as "annual." The group, whatever its circumstances, refused to die, sporadically rearing its head in performances.

Evidence of sustained activity is no clearer as one approaches the turn of the century. On one hand, yearly calls to organize a campus glee club persisted, while performances in Washington Hall by this group continued to be documented. In the late 1880s and '90s a certain Prof. Frederick Liscombe is mentioned as leading the university's Glee Club.[4] Some of his choral programming was informed by variety shows, popular at that time. Skits, comic patter, and even dance were the stuff of glee club concert events. But Liscombe occasionally slated more serious repertoire, such as the choral arrangement of Sir Arthur Sullivan's "The Lost Chord," mentioned in connection with one program. Liscombe also prepared his glee club to perform in the campus opera in 1889.[5]

With its ups and downs in the late nineteenth century, a glee club at Notre Dame was slow to crystallize, in part because of the steady success of another type of glee club—that cultivated in individual residence halls. Theoretically the training ground for a young man's potential promotion to the university-level chorus, the hall glee clubs attracted considerable attention in the early period, and two halls in particular deserve mention. The Brownson Glee Club may be singled out for its practice of electing officers, as well as for its joint performances with that hall's literary society. Meanwhile at Corby Hall, a glee club existed within the Corby Literary Society along with that dorm's mandolin and guitar club. The Corby Hall Glee Club, directed by one "Mr. Smith" in 1907, had nightly rehearsals in the residents' smoke-room and apparently had the means to organize an annual banquet, despite its lack of officers. Tellingly, the glee club of Corby Hall was considered by some to be the university's only "genuine" glee club.[6] Only by the mid- to late 1920s was it evident that hall glee clubs were truly the minor leagues of campus musical activity and that an all-male university ensemble was the choral jewel.

THE dream of many an old student and many a faculty member became a reality this year when the first Glee Club of Notre Dame was formed under the direction of S. Ward Perrot, Law '16. From the start the new organization was successful and the showing made by the enthusiastic men this year proves that the club will not end with the scholastic year of '15 and '16; but that it will become a permanent part of the Notre Dame calendar of activities.

The year 1899 was typical of both the promising prospects of a university glee club and the subsequent failure to sustain any momentum. A director, Prof. McLaughlin, and four officers were in place as rehearsals commenced in January, a characteristically late start in those years. The club's lackluster performance at the celebration of George Washington's birthday in Washington Hall—a major annual event at Notre Dame—was followed by rampant defections by members of the ensemble. Whatever the number of singers who began the year, only a handful remained at Commencement.[7] Yet in May, McLaughlin could be found coaching his Glee Club in choruses to be sung as part of a Greek play at the university.[8] The following academic year, there were more calls to establish a robust male chorus of at least fifty members, now under the university's band director, Mr. Roche.[9] In 1903, hope for a revived Glee Club appeared to rest with a new set of named officers and yet another band director, Carl Petersen, who, by 1909, was conducting the Varsity Orchestra and the South Bend Symphony, in addition to the Glee Club.[10]

While Petersen was not mentioned at the helm of the Glee Club for most of the first decade of the twentieth century, the choral fraternity seemed to be inching toward firmer ground. There were several documented appearances of the Club between 1906 and 1909.[11] Three different leaders are mentioned in this interval: (1) a voice teacher, Prof. Milton B. Griffith, (2) J. Ludwig Frank, and (3) Rev. Michael J. Shea, a 1905 graduate best known for setting music to Notre Dame's "Victory March," with words written by his younger brother Jack.[12] Shea's Glee Club had more than fifty members, and he recommended strongly that the hall glee club system act as a stepping stone to the university male chorus.[13]

The year 1911 is notable for two reasons. On November 17 of that year, the Glee Club allegedly became a "permanent organization," with James Wasson serving as president and J.C. Wildgen as secretary of the group. Officers were nothing new, of course. At the same time, we learn that Carl Petersen was back on the podium "as usual."[14] His resumed tenure can be dated with confidence to 1909, a year in which the *Dome* yearbook noted that the Club had "numerous appearances before the public."[15] Petersen had been directing the singers in vaudeville performances on campus, and the repertoire was fittingly droll and overly sentimental.[16] The shreds of evidence indicate that the Glee Club survived the roller-coaster ride of the twentieth century's first decade, when the ensemble's status sometimes seemed shaky.

Whether the Club somehow lay dormant in 1913 is an open question. The annual plea went out for singers—especially for first tenors—to join the Glee Club. The group was then under the direction of a "Professor Bender." *Scholastic* reported,

> Professor Bender, who has charge of vocal training at the University this year, is organizing a Glee Club. The club meets every Wednesday afternoon at four o'clock. The attendance at the first practice was satisfactory, although there was a scarcity of first tenors. Every singer in the University should report for practice. Notre Dame can and should produce a Glee Club that will rival those of other universities. We have the material and the opportunity. All that is needed is "pep."[17]

That Bender was organizing *a* glee club at Notre Dame, rather than *the* Glee Club, might give us pause as to the status of the ensemble, especially in conjunction with the charge that the university "can and should" produce a glee club. But clearly this was the same glee club that had become a "permanent organization" two years earlier. Bender's first performance with the club took place in February of 1914, and the group was tapped later that spring to perform in a vaudeville show in Washington Hall.[18]

Next in the parade of early and short-lived Glee Club directors was Samuel Ward Perrott, the son of an Indianapolis police superintendent and a student at Notre Dame from 1912 to 1914. Wishing to attend law school, Perrott enrolled at Harvard University for the 1914–15 academic year and joined the Harvard Glee Club as a first tenor. It was during his short stint in Cambridge, Massachusetts, that Perrott "got the idea of how a club should be run."[19] What the young man absorbed was the repertoire and choral standards of Archibald T. Davison, director of the Harvard Glee Club and that university's chapel choir. Davidson is credited with transforming the glee club's musical fare from mostly lighter songs to classic choral masterpieces (by Palestrina, Bach, et al.) arranged for male chorus.[20] Perrott imported the Harvard Glee Club model to South Bend when he returned to Notre Dame as a senior law student in the fall of 1915.

When students began the 1915–16 academic year, the usual call for singers circulated around Notre Dame, pleading in *Scholastic*, "It is not necessary to be a Caruso!" Fifty singers were sought for the year, on par with the numbers that Michael Shea reportedly corralled in 1907, and an initial meeting was organized after Sunday Mass on October 10, 1915, in the Sorin Law Room.[21] Some one hundred prospective singers attended the gathering, which was visited by university president John W. Cavanaugh.[22] At this inaugural meeting, Cavanaugh was made an honorary president of the Glee Club, likely a reflection of his deep engagement with the musical arts and drama both on campus and around the country.[23] The new honorary president appointed that year's officers and its new director, Perrott, who was eager to promote a Glee Club of a different sort.[24] Fifty-three men formed Perrott's Glee Club—sixteen voices in both the Tenor II and Bass I sections, ten first tenors (Tenor I), nine assigned to the Bass II part, and two accompanists, a luxury for a men's chorus then or now.[25]

The young Perrott revitalized the Club culture with new energy and repertoire that emulated the Harvard archetype. The rehearsal schedule was ambitious, with members required to attend five practices per week, including two per day on Tuesdays and Thursdays (12:20 pm in Washington Hall and 6:20 pm in the Sorin Law Room).[26] Perrott's first concert on December 11, 1915, was unsurprisingly lauded for its success with musical repertoire of "high seriousness."[27] The concert program survives from that day, and one quickly sees that the entertainment was shared with the university orchestra and mandolin club, the latter group being quite common on college campuses in the early twentieth century.[28] The Glee Club cleared the high bar set by Perrott that evening, even though the group sang just four pieces: the Irish folk song "Bendemeer's Stream," Franz Joseph Haydn's "Serenade," "On the Road to Mandalay" (by Oley Speaks), and an unidentified "Notre Dame Song," sung to the melody of a Netherlandish folk song.

Perrott's two years with the Glee Club constitute the basis of an "origins" legend of the Notre Dame Glee Club. Like all legends, the story of Perrott's success with the Glee Club contains some truth and no small amount of fiction. It is true that he was a transfer law student with ambitious goals for a university men's chorus, but it cannot be said that he founded the group, which was apparently established as a permanent organization in 1911 and existed in various guises since the later nineteenth century. It has also been repeated over time that the original Notre Dame Glee Club had just twelve members, when it is clear that more than fifty began the year, and many were turned away. That the university president was so heavily involved with the 1915–16 Glee Club might have provided some validation to the legend. The extensive coverage in the 1916 *Dome* would also lead many to think that this group had begun a very different singing enterprise, but the yearbook also recog-

nized that Perrott was leading the "best Notre Dame Glee Club in years."[29] Besides the fact that it launched a period of unbroken history for the Glee Club, Perrott's squad was the first to venture beyond the campus limits and tour locally, which distinguished the group from its predecessors.

Father Cavanaugh was instrumental in securing the Glee Club's first journey away from South Bend, arranging a concert in Indianapolis on May 7, 1916. Sponsored by the Notre Dame Alumni Association and presented at the city's Minat Theater, the Club's program drew over two thousand in attendance, including Indiana's Governor (and later Senator) Samuel M. Ralston, the mayor of Indianapolis, Joseph Bell, and the bishop of Indianapolis, Joseph Chartrand.[30] Strong publicity followed, and more tours were on the horizon. The Notre Dame Glee Club, once struggling for members and continuity as an organization, was firmly in place and poised to take its show on the road.

1916 Glee Club

1917 Glee Club

1918 Glee Club

THREE

Membership and the Privileged

Even if the claim that Samuel Ward Perrott founded the Notre Dame Glee Club has been cast into doubt, his contribution catalyzed a group of singers that had an uneven presence on the university music scene into an organic whole. The core of twelve men is another spurious detail from the legend, but the question of how membership was cultivated in the enterprise is an important one, both in its early days and for the balance of the twentieth century. This chapter broadly examines the "human capital" of the Singing Irish, the more than two thousand choral singers who have joined its ranks. The dynamics of auditions, the fluctuations in membership, and the special roles taken up by students within the organization all contributed to the Club's position as a musical gem of the university and one of the esteemed all-male choruses in the country.

AUDITIONS, CUTS, AND NUMBERS

Auditioning potential members of a vocal ensemble is generally an uncomplicated, if grueling, process. The candidate often prepares a song of appropriate difficulty, performs some vocal exercises to determine range, sings from a mystery musical excerpt, and displays aural skills. This procedure describes to some extent how the Notre Dame Glee Club was auditioned for most of its history. An article from the middle of the director Dean Pedtke's years suggested that "test[s] of range, quality, musicianship, and experience" were central to a Glee Club audition.[1] There is evidence in the preceding era under Joseph Casasanta that an intermediate step was part of the tryout process: the individual audition was followed by a quartet audition. After whittling down his group to seventy-five men in early 1931, the director heard "quartette try-outs" and auditions for "solo and novelty numbers."[2] It is not clear whether a quartet tryout involved a group of prospective students or whether it concerned one candidate in the company of three veterans. It is evident, however, that the small ensemble trial was no informal, rubber-stamping step: it was a critical process for selecting the year's final personnel. In 1934, Casasanta "brought to a close . . . the period for tryouts" and subsequently "announced that individual quartet tryouts will be held very shortly."[3] Director Pedtke signaled the intense competition at that stage, noting that the singers "work as hard for quartet tryouts as for an exam."[4]

Thousands of students have auditioned for the Glee Club over the last one hundred years. The clearest records—and most substantial number—of singers trying out for the group come from the Casasanta years, when an annual audition drew 175 men on average. The director's first year (1926) featured 220 auditions. The pre-

ceding years under director J. Lewis Browne were also robust, attracting about 125 students annually. The number of auditions from Pedtke's term seems in line with that from Browne's tenure, despite less surviving evidence. Of the seven years of data available in Pedtke's thirty-five-year stint, roughly 130 per year auditioned for the Glee Club.[5] As the Club competed with more campus groups for attention in the 1960s and onward, information on annual auditions was less publicized. Director Daniel Stowe noted that forty singers, on average, have auditioned each of the last four years, and about half are accepted into the roster.

Glee Club directors have upheld the high standards of musicianship required of auditioning singers, but prospective members also needed to demonstrate that they were socially fit to be part of the chorus. By the 1960s, a tradition developed in which applicants would be subject to an informal interview with Club officers following their musical hearing.[6] The interview with current members, it was thought, was a true measure of character and gave the candidate a taste of the fraternity and the droll nature of the group. Tim Kenny, president of the Glee Club in 1989–90, explained that candidates were peppered with ridiculous questions such as "If you had to choose to be one kind of fruit, which kind would it be and why?" Prospective members were also asked, for example, to fill in maps of the United States and answer irrelevant questions about the country's geography.[7] The more the interviewee played along with the antics, the more honorable he was judged by the veterans. These closed-door interviews produced countless hysterical stories that have been retained in the social memory of the group through the years.[8] Though it is not clear how much the social interview ever mattered in the director's roster decisions, occasionally the officers prevailed in their recommendation that a singer be accepted whose musicianship was below the standard.

After auditions, the candidate was left in a state of sometimes-nervous anticipation while the director developed a roster for the Glee Club. Some were told right away that they would not make the coveted list of new members. In 1941, campus writer Frank King quipped that many were informed that they might be more useful on the football team than in the Glee Club.[9] Others waited to see their names posted on the bulletin board outside of the director's office. Inevitably, the director could not supply all voice parts with equal numbers, and indeed there were sometimes calls for more singers—first tenors especially—after auditions had formally concluded.[10] In the Casasanta and Pedtke years, rosters tended to be whittled down across the academic year with less than forty members chosen for the annual spring tour. For more than a generation, though, the Glee Club has secured new members in time for the first week of classes, and directors have not trimmed the size of the group as a matter of course.

Detailed figures from campus periodicals and yearbooks, together with records kept by directors, permit a brief analysis of trends in annual membership and auditions heard. Membership in the Glee Club during the past century fluctuated dramatically at times. The Great Depression and World War II affected membership levels to some degree, but recording opportunities, television appearances, and tours often boosted successive rosters. Even a single year could show great variation. The 1933–34 Glee Club may serve as an example. In a depression year that started with a core of twenty singers returning from an unprecedented summer tour, some 150 students auditioned for the group in September, and fifty-six new members were added to the Club within a month.[11] By the end of October, the group's size ballooned to ninety-five singers, but by mid-January 1934, Casasanta had shrunk what was known as the "concert club" membership to fifty-eight, according to his "elimination policy."[12] Six weeks later, the director sidelined more members to arrive at the touring group of forty-two students,

Membership and the Privileged

"following a semester of hard work and keen competition."[13] Over one hundred singers can be counted on rosters from each of the years 1946 until 1956.

In its hundred-year history, the Glee Club has averaged seventy members per year, but the numbers require qualification. One can see the growth of the ensemble through 1929, when Casasanta fielded a group of eighty-one singers. The size of the Glee Club (and the university's student population as a whole) receded during the Great Depression of the 1930s, but rose again after the directorship of the band and Glee Club was divided in 1938 and as the economy recovered in the next decade.

World War II had a profound impact on the size of the ensemble. A depleted ensemble of sixty was reported in 1943, but 90 percent were new recruits for the group—a mix of Marines, Naval Reserve Officers Training Corps, and those disqualified from military service.[14] The civilian Glee Club roster was cut in half from its pre-war levels by early 1944. A paltry twenty-three members were listed as performing in the spring concerts that year, including the annual concert associated with the university's Commencement exercises.[15] This marked rock bottom for the size of the group. In the fall semester, Scholastic cheered the growth of the Singing Irish to forty voices, and by November tryouts from the NROTC ranks had boosted the number of singers to eighty-six.[16] Two years later, new opportunities afforded by the G.I. Bill brought tens of thousands of war veterans back to college campuses, and Notre Dame was no exception. Glee Club membership rebounded accordingly.

With the volume of students auditioning early in his directorship, Pedtke had the idea to form a junior varsity squad of Glee Clubbers. In the tenure of director Browne, students rejected from the audition (of any class) formed a chorus that rehearsed apart from the Glee Club and—at least in 1924—was subsequently scheduled to perform in a spring choral festival.[17] Pedtke's reinstitution of this idea had a positive impact on recruitment. This new "B Team"—directed by Fr. John Daniel Gallagher after music graduate student Cletus Schommer left with a master's degree in 1940—grew out of Pedtke's desire to give a second chance to those who stumbled in the audition, ensuring that no quality voices would be lost forever if they had simply been turned away that one time.[18] His junior squad was generally confined to freshmen, and during the 1942–43 academic year, it convened daily in the late afternoon because of class conflicts in freshman schedules that prevented rehearsal with the varsity group at 12:30 pm.[19] Testimony from the mid-1950s confirms that the freshmen were being diverted into the junior varsity glee club, and accounts from the early 1960s highlight the activities of the alternative group. In one case, they combined with the St. Mary's freshman glee club for a concert, and, on another occasion, the group spelled the regular Glee Club from a concert appearance during Junior Parents Weekend.[20] After two years under the leadership of William Cole (1963–65), the "B team" was folded back into the larger group for rehearsals.[21] It is clear, however, that the freshman club did not materialize every year; it was entertained only when Pedtke had an assistant to lead it and when the rehearsal room was overflowing.

The 1952–53 Glee Club fielded its largest membership with 160 students, but most of the singers were evidently held in reserve in the younger squad. Only 52 members are listed in the yearbook for that year, and a characteristic group of 36 toured with the group in the spring. The numbers would fall steadily through the next half century, particularly in the twilight of director Pedtke's term. The Notre Dame Glee Club averaged 64 members during the Isele, Belland, and Stam years, a time when male choruses around the country either foundered or were converted into mixed choruses. After a precipitous drop to 41 singers during Mark Ring's two-year stint as director, the ensemble was rebuilt by Daniel Stowe, who expanded the group to 81 by the fall of 1997, which was "too many, really, given the talent pool."[22] The Glee Club was down to 75 singers at the dawn of the twenty-first century, and the director has maintained the corps at that size in recent years. In contrast to the early groups that set the touring roster between 36 and 40 singers, the most recent generation of Glee Club members have all been given the opportunity to tour with the group from the start, an expensive endeavor to be sure when the traveling roster exceeds 60 students.

TAKING OFFICE

Perrott's 1915 Glee Club was the first to establish a constitution to guide its activities as a student organization. The charter prescribed that the group's operations were to be administered by a "governing board" of nine members. In addition to the director, the constitution called for a president, vice president, and secretary, plus a senior, two juniors, one sophomore, and one freshman to serve as class representatives. The full slate of officers was installed on December 13, 1915, at a meeting in Washington Hall.[23] The number of officers fluctuated at the outset according to the needs of the ensemble. A treasurer and business manager were soon added to the club's administration, as were the positions of assistant business manager, publicity manager, and librarian.

Though the top officers were generally elected, the business manager was an appointed position, charged with the crucial responsibility of organizing and negotiating tour schedules behind the scenes.[24] By the late 1940s, the business manager had several assistants, reflective of the unusual intensity of this job.[25] In conjunction with the president of the Glee Club, the business manager undertook letter-writing campaigns to alumni clubs and Knights of Columbus councils, establishing initial contacts for performances. The most anticipated annual event was the spring tour, but winter trips and fall weekend tours were additional options to fill. Extensive records reveal the business manager's role in arranging transportation and lodging for the touring members, including the director and the chaplain. Finances were strictly overseen by the university because the tours, budgeted in 1956 at $12,000 for example, were to be covered by local sponsoring organizations.[26] Some of the Glee Club tours before 1920 incurred losses, causing finger-pointing among the officers and prompting revisions to the constitution.[27] And while many business managers developed reputations of frugality under the constraints of the university-imposed budgets, Dean Pedtke recalled that Anthony Trigiani ('54) greatly expanded Glee Club revenues by both overcharging host cities and reselling for profit a large number of seats he had intentionally overbooked on the train ride to the East Coast, actions that cost him his position.[28]

The role of assistant director or student director of the Glee Club is a curious one. His chief responsibility was to lead the group in song in the director's absence, which could be quite often, given the number of informal concerts

the Glee Club offers in a given year. Although they were not considered officers, student directors played a guiding role with the group throughout its history. Joseph Casasanta, who studied music at Notre Dame, was the Glee Club's first assistant director, shouldering a heavy load of concert appearances in the J. Lewis Browne years (1923–26), just after Casasanta's graduation. In 1957, the Glee Club's president, John Fitzhenry, was also its student director, notably leading the choir in a joint performance with the St. Mary's Glee Club.[29] Between 1959 and 1961, John Oliver served as both student director and accompanist for the Glee Club, a good use of his skills as a music major.[30] And after director Pedtke suffered a stroke in 1973, Howard Bathon ('74) admirably stepped in to conduct, taking the Club on a four-day tour to Iowa and leading the annual Commencement concert in Stepan Center.

THE VARSITY QUARTET AND THE SMALL GROUP PHENOMENON

For most members of the Glee Club, attending rehearsals and appearing in dozens of concerts each year is rigorous enough. For others, there is even more music to be explored, rehearsal energy to expend, and smaller concerts to perform. With a willing group of motivated singers, quartets and other small groups were formed to supplement and enhance their experience in the all-male choir. A "glee club quartet" and a "university quartette"

are mentioned in 1899 and 1912, respectively, and became a fixture on Glee Club programs and tours after the 1915 reorganization. By 1925, the quartet had risen to become "one of the most prominent organizations" on campus.[31] Variously called the "Varsity Four," "Happy Four," and "Quartette," the early Glee Club quartets had separate auditions from the larger chorus and were sometimes appointed by the director.[32] Through the 1950s, records indicate that the quartet often provided entertainment during intermission of Glee Club concerts to make for an uninterrupted musical experience for audiences.[33] The quartet also appeared in place of the full chorus when campus and civic organizations requested musical entertainment. Most often chronicled in the 1920s and '30s are the Glee Club quartet's engagements at Knights of Columbus events, but other gigs included banquets of the Rotary Club and the South Bend University Club, vaudeville shows, homecoming parties, class balls, and alumni events.[34]

This subset of Glee Club star singers did not always amount to a quartet. In 1917, a Rotary banquet featured the full male chorus plus the "university quintet," which sang a number of state songs, and in 1929, the Glee Club and the "varsity trio" were part of the entertainment at a football banquet.[35] Director Pedtke developed an octet during his tenure, "formed to take care of smaller concerts" when the scheduling demands on the Club became too great.[36]

But the quartet had staying power above all. While on tour in 1949, the Club sent a quartet to appear on Ed Sullivan's fledgling television show, *Toast of the Town*. Quartets also were featured more than once in the campus social events following home football games known as "victory dances."[37] These types of concerts by the foursome garnered a good deal of press, and the group received numerous requests to perform at civic events, on radio programs, and for student dances. At least twice, the group was dispatched for carnival festivities, once at St. Mary's College.[38] In all of these events, the repertoire was tailored to audience needs and often mimicked the variety one finds in official Glee Club concerts. For instance, the set list for a 1954 performance at a Knights of Columbus event included songs titled "Ave Maria," "Blue Moon," "Clancy Lowered the Boom," and "Sophomore Philosophy."[39]

In addition to an official Glee Club quartet or octet, other small groups have come and gone from the ranks of the chorus. In 1942, Glee Club vice president Kevin O'Toole (a tenor) formed the eponymous Kevin O'Toole Octet, which included the Glee Club's president, bass Reggie Flynn. This short-lived ensemble was documented at Central High School and at St. Patrick Church in South Bend. They were also the entertainment at a St. Mary's–Notre Dame freshmen dance.[40]

Dean Pedtke found variety in musical theater hits and small skits, growing eventually to include full Gilbert and Sullivan operetta scenes. In comic skits, the full ensemble backed a smaller troupe on stage, as in "Let Us Gather at the Goal Line," from Ed Cashman's 1946 musical comedy *Toplitsky of Notre Dame*, and his mock cantata *The Archangel Mike* (1948). Aside from these and other isolated cases, the vogue for small group musical comedy did not reach Notre Dame for much of its history, as it had done, for example, at Yale University with the famous Whiffenpoofs, active since 1909. Director David Clark Isele composed music for a small group of Clubbers, who sang his operetta *Red Hot Riding Hood* in 1975, and director Douglas Belland likewise composed music for various nameless small groups to sing during concerts on tour and on campus.

The latest generation of Glee Clubbers, though, has been drawn to top-40 arrangements for its small groups, no doubt spurred by the impact of the Contemporary A Cappella Society of America (CASA), established in 1991. With names such as the Quadraphonics, the J's, and Fifth Harmonic, these groups often appeared in Glee Club concerts, but they also maintained some independence from the larger ensemble. The model was taken to a new level with the creation of the Undertones in 1996, a twelve-man group launched by freshman Patrick Quigley. Releasing eight albums, performing their own concerts on campus, and touring nationally on school breaks, the Undertones have achieved sustainability that the other small groups could not reach, and they continue to be in high demand among those who desire a popular take on male *a cappella* repertoire that the Glee Club does not traditionally offer. The Club officers and director monitor the state of these groups, and the current constitution of the ensemble stipulates rules by which small groups must abide, including a "finder's fee" arrangement for mini-concerts that the large Club doles out to the satellite ensembles.[41] All of these small groups, of course, share a Glee Club heritage and have never been afraid to borrow freely from those traditions in concert.

GOING SOLO

One of the most surprising qualities of the Glee Club is that, historically, only a small fraction of its members studied music formally in their years on campus. The extensive auditions of the ensemble across its history expose, on one hand, the substantial vocal talent available to the Glee Club. But a group of strong singers did not necessarily equate to a roster of trained musicians. In 1959 for instance, an article remarked that, among the Club's incoming singers, "only the minority can read music."[42] In 1974, there was not a single music major in the Glee Club. Tim Kenny, president of the group in 1989, gave this frank assessment of the overall musical caliber: "We only have two music majors all together. There are several fantastic individual singers, but on the whole, we have average individual talent. We do work and sing well together, though."[43] Director Daniel Stowe has been known to turn this apparent deficiency into a recruiting tool, highlighting in concerts the large percentage of those who are able to perform with the group while pursuing majors *other* than music.[44]

For most choral singers, their director is their voice coach. Daily musical drills and instruction on individual pieces have the power to transform untrained voices into a group of conscientious and self-aware singers. In the Glee Club as in any choir, there have always been some individual voices, however, that the directors were proud to promote. Far more visible than music majors was the position of the "soloist" in Glee Club history. It is no exaggeration to say that the soloists were the dominant presence at Glee Club concerts for at least half of its history, and it was not uncommon to have a handful of solos (sometimes more than ten!) in a single concert, some of them earning encores.[45] As the number of solo works in the concert repertoire dropped over the years, the auditioned role of standing soloist was phased out before 1970 in favor of assigning soloists only for particular songs. In its time, though, the Glee Club soloist was an esteemed member of the group, attracting much attention in the press and in general overviews of the organization.[46] These select, talented singers were often pulled into campus musicals or into the entertainment troupe known as the Linnets, founded by director Casasanta. They too could be farmed out for gigs not fit for the full ensemble, such as school balls, class proms, and local alumni club events.

It is impossible to catalog the soloists through the years, but a few names consistently appear with glowing reviews. In the late 1920s, tenor Anthony Kopecky ('29) was a Glee Club soloist for each of his four years in the

Anthony Kopecky

ensemble, in addition to being in the Varsity Quartet for three years and senior class president in his final year.[47] A crooner of Slovak descent from Riverside, Illinois, Kopecky could be found singing well outside the orbit of the Singing Irish. It was reported that he had recorded an album with Chicago-based songwriter and orchestra leader Wayne King and had also sung at Chicago's Oriental Theater with the Paul Asch Orchestra.[48] He was also a regular vocal presence at major campus events, including the then-popular commemorations for George Washington's birthday. After graduation, Kopecky made a name for himself in the Chicago area, singing at numerous weddings and funerals of city politicians and other local elites.[49]

While Anthony Kopecky was a "natural," untrained soloist, other soloists came to the Glee Club with rigorous preparation or left it for high-powered musical pursuits. Joseph Pawlowski ('41) was a soloist in 1935–36 and scholarship student in voice at Notre Dame, before returning to Poland to study voice at the University of Warsaw. As a drum major of the band under Casasanta, Pawlowski had been heard as a soloist on CBS and NBC radio networks during his time in the United States.[50] Baritone soloist Donald Tiedemann ('41) likewise achieved impressive musical heights during his college years at Notre Dame, having passed up a conservatory education at the highly selective Juilliard School. President of the Glee Club in his senior year, Tiedemann sang for three summers with the prestigious Chautauqua Opera Company in western New York, a program that nurtures promising young vocalists and remains the nation's oldest active summer opera company.[51] His most visible moments as a marquee singer on campus came on the gridiron. During his freshman year, Tiedemann sang "When Irish Eyes Are Smiling" when Notre Dame played Navy, and he belted out "God Bless America" at halftime when the Irish hosted Georgia Tech in 1940.[52]

Other Glee Club soloists arrived at Notre Dame with significant professional backgrounds in music. Before singing with the Glee Club, tenor soloist Anthony Donadio ('42) studied at the Peabody Conservatory and had experience singing on radio and live for Baltimore audiences.[53] A decade later, tenor soloist John Noland ('53) came to Notre Dame having studied piano at the College of Music in Cincinnati.[54] Rudolph "Rudy" Pruden ('57, '62MA) was the baritone soloist from 1955 to 1957 and the first Glee Clubber of color. He studied for one summer at the prestigious Eastman School of Music in Rochester, New York, before coming to Notre Dame and further sang with the De Paur Infantry Chorus, a professional glee club under the direction of African American composer and arranger Leonard de Paur.[55] With the title of "Glee Club soloist" now long removed from the ensemble's lexicon, the dozens who have assumed this role in concerts of the last three decades have nevertheless been selected with the same kind of care by their directors. Daniel Stowe recalled several outstanding soloists in his time, including Patrick Quigley ('00), Sean Osman ('02), Michael Holderer ('03), John Fister ('08), Dominic Go ('10), and Jamie Towey ('15).[56] Often it is their raw musical qualities, not unlike that of Kopecky in the 1920s, that connect most immediately with Glee Club audiences.

Rudolph "Rudy" Pruden

Membership and the Privileged

MOST HONORABLE MENTION

As a footnote to this chapter on membership, there are several individuals who deserve special mention. First are the three Clubbers that served as the mascot of the university—the esteemed Notre Dame Leprechaun. Although the leprechaun was not recognized as the official mascot until 1965, Glee Club member Ralph Thorson ('48) was noted as the "Forgotten Irishman . . . under the green hat and pantaloons" in 1946, the first leprechaun in Notre Dame's history.[57] Two Clubbers from the 1990s also led the university as its mascot, Bryan Liptak ('92) and Andrew Budzinski ('95). Since Glee Clubbers are well accustomed to projecting their voices and entertaining large audiences, they are good candidates to be the leprechaun, charged with whipping up the crowds to cheer on the Fighting Irish.

In addition to these extraordinary performers, there is a group of official honorary members of the Notre Dame Glee Club that must be acknowledged here. In 1986, the Glee Club made its first honorary member the ever-vibrant Charles "Chuck" Lennon ('61, '62MA, DL H'11), who served for thirty years as executive director

Ralph Thorson

Chuck Lennon and Lou Holtz

of the University of Notre Dame Alumni Association. One of the Glee Club's biggest proponents, Lennon unfailingly joined the chorus on the risers when alumni were invited to sing the final three songs of the Club's concerts, no matter the venue. The skip in his step was unmistakable: "Being able to come up at the end of every concert and sing with [the Glee Club] is one of the greatest memories of my Notre Dame experience." Lennon also remembers playing Glee Club recordings in the van he drove around the country visiting alumni clubs. "By 1984, I could sing all of the [Glee Club's] songs—a bit 'off key'—but I would belt them out in the privacy of the van as I drove from place to place."[58] Truth be known, he also dressed up as Santa Claus for Glee Club Christmas concerts. Having an ally in the Alumni Association benefitted the Club directly. Each year, the Alumni Association bought special Notre Dame neckties for new members of the group to wear with their blazers.

Father Theodore Hesburgh, C.S.C., was bestowed with the honorary status in 1989; the former president of the university spoke at numerous ceremonies that were accompanied by the strains of the Glee Club. He said of the group, "I never cease to be edified by their spirit and wonderful presentation."[59] Perhaps the most memorable experience with Hesburgh was when the Club sang for him on his eightieth birthday at the Tantur Ecumenical Institute in Jerusalem overlooking the city of Bethlehem, when the group was on a tour of Israel for performances with the Jerusalem Symphony in 1997. Former Notre Dame football coach Lou Holtz, former Joyce Center crowd control supervisor James J. Murphy, and alumnus Harry Durkin ('53)—a host of at least fifteen tour concerts spanning decades—are other worthy recipients of honorary Glee Club membership status.[60] Like the Glee Club itself, these honorary members radiate the spirit of the university and spread far its mission as faithful stewards in different ways.

Father Theodore Hesburgh, C.S.C.

FOUR

Shaping the Sound I

SETTING THE STANDARDS

Across the one hundred years of unbroken Glee Club history, more than two-thirds of those years took place under the leadership of just three men—Dean Pedtke (35 years), Daniel Stowe (22 and counting), and Joseph Casasanta (12). Others serving shorter stints did not necessarily have less impact on the choir, but the established culture of the Glee Club in many ways rests with these three directors. This chapter reviews the contributions of all of the conductors who took the podium from the group's earliest days through the present era under Stowe, reflecting on how their respective tenures affected the Glee Club and sharing highlights of their biographies and anecdotes that reveal their distinct personalities.

GESTATIONAL YEARS

Liscombe, McLaughlin, Roche, Shea, Griffith, Webster, Petersen, and Bender. These names mean little or nothing to living Glee Club alumni, but they were mentioned, at one point or another, as leaders of—or strongly associated with—the all-male chorus that was notoriously "on-again, off-again" in the late nineteenth century and the first decade of the twentieth century. Professors Frederick Liscombe and James McLaughlin are credited several times in the years leading up to 1900. Both directed the men's chorus in concerts celebrating Washington's birthday. In 1891, Liscombe's club was commended for "exquisite" singing and "remarkable proficiency" in the program, with repertoire that included John Liptrot Hatton's "Tar's Song."[1] McLaughlin's 1899 Glee Club sang its first concert of the year on Washington's birthday, which *Scholastic* deemed a "creditable performance."[2] That same year, McLaughlin was noted as both the director and the president of the Glee Club, an unusual dual role that reveals the flimsy nature of the enterprise.[3] Considering the annual pleas for singers that have survived from that time, the Glee Club's inability to sustain itself during this era comes as no surprise.

It is unclear from surviving records whether 1905 graduate Rev. Michael Shea directed the university's glee club in academic year 1907–08, but he received mention for advocating a choral environment at Notre Dame that emphasized the hall glee club system as a ladder to the advanced men's ensemble.[4] Shea's major achievement in the school's history, instead, was his setting of the words of the school's "Victory March" to music in 1908, the text having been written by his younger brother, Jack. In the first decade of the twentieth century, only Professor Carl Petersen's contribution to the Glee Club received attention in extant sources. Serving as director of the varsity orchestra and South Bend Symphony in addition to the Glee Club in 1909, Petersen conducted a group of between twenty-five and thirty members that rehearsed twice per week in Washington Hall and did not perform much in public. He was praised, however, for his work in preparing the Glee Club for spring vaudeville shows during the years 1909 to 1911.[5] Although the Glee Club reportedly was established as a permanent organization in 1911, only "Professor Bender" is mentioned—and scarcely at that—as leading the chorus in the years leading up to 1915. Meantime, the group had regressed to one rehearsal per week.[6] The organization was due for an upgrade in leadership, and this came with the arrival of a Harvard law student eager to reshape the Glee Club into a first-rate choral organization.

PERROTT, PARKER, AND A NEW PROTOTYPE

Samuel Ward Perrott

The century of uninterrupted continuity for the Notre Dame Glee Club began under the leadership of a student, Samuel Ward Perrott. Perrott was enrolled at the university for two years before transferring to Harvard Law School. In 1915, he returned to Notre Dame to complete his law degree.[7] As described in chapter 2, his experience in the Harvard Glee Club under Archibald T. Davison proved valuable for the model he would introduce in South Bend. Known as "Ward," but also referred to in the campus press as "Sammy," "Mr. Director," and "The Hoosier Tenor" (because of his Indiana roots), Perrott established a prototype for Glee Club operations that have survived to this day, such as tuxedo dress, touring, balanced repertoire, and intensive daily rehearsals. Although the organization was forever changed, Perrott left the university before finishing his degree in 1916, taking a job in the legal department of the Tractional Terminal Company of Indianapolis.[8] He had not, however, finished his work with the Glee Club.

Despite his day job, Perrott refused to let the momentum of the Club be stifled in the academic year 1916–17. He commuted weekly to South Bend for Saturday rehearsals and kept in close contact with Notre Dame president John W. Cavanaugh. The nonresident director was concerned that the group continue under capable leadership, and, to that end, he suggested to Cavanaugh that seminarian and future president of Notre Dame J. Hugh O'Donnell ('16) conduct the Glee Club in the fall of 1916. Cavanaugh originally balked at Perrott's idea, writing "what you propose is almost as impossible as to arrange to have one of the brothers go to town to give dancing lessons every day."[9] The president relented, however, and O'Donnell took the podium, continuing the daily noontime rehearsals for the opening semester. The new director was extolled in the season's fall concert; according to a review in *Scholastic*, the choir "responded beautifully to his chironomy [conducting gestures]." The same article noted that Perrott, the "real director," attended the performance.[10]

O'Donnell resigned his post by the beginning of 1917, and Glee Club accompanist Howard Parker assumed the conductorship, again with the approval of Perrott. Dubbed the "busiest man on campus," Parker edited *Scholastic* magazine and directed the Mandolin Club, which performed often with the Glee Club; he also led the university's orchestra.[11] Parker was spotted conducting at banquets for the Rotary Club and the Knights of Columbus that semester, but it was Perrott who directed the Glee Club's first tour concert on Easter Monday (April 9) to a full house at Orchestra Hall in Chicago.[12] Perrott returned to direct just a few weeks later when the fledgling club journeyed to Indianapolis and Logansport. He later joined the U.S. Army as World War I escalated in 1917, but he pleaded with Fr. Cavanaugh to maintain a commitment to the Glee Club.[13] Though Perrott's model was established, leadership continuity was in short supply.

J. Hugh O'Donnell   Howard Parker

Mandolin Club, 1917

PROFESSIONALS AT THE HELM

For the next eight years, consummate professional musicians took center stage. Professor John J. Becker, head of a very small Department of Music at Notre Dame since the fall of 1917, took the reins of the male chorus in that same year. Trained at Cincinnati's Krueger Conservatory, Becker received a doctoral degree in composition from the Wisconsin Conservatory in 1923, while he was working in South Bend. He would continue in music administration at the College of St. Mary of the Springs in Columbus, Ohio (1928–29); the College of St. Thomas in St. Paul, Minnesota (1929–33); and Barat College in Lake Forest, Illinois (1943–57). He was also the state director of the Work Projects Administration's Federal Music Project in Minnesota from 1935 to 1941.

In his ten years at Notre Dame, Becker sought to reconfigure the music department with programs of study in piano and violin, while developing the university's orchestral program.[14] He further worked to attract talented artists who were performing in the Chicago area to South Bend to give concerts, including his former organ teacher Wilhelm Middelschulte and renowned Irish tenor John McCormack.[15] Where Becker seems to have made his mark with the Glee Club was in the realm of repertoire. He strongly pushed for the singers to perform the "masterworks" that he himself had studied and to not sell themselves short with lighter musical offerings. The overly fraternal nature of the group, though, became an obstacle to Becker's plans in the early 1920s, and he stated his misgivings about glee clubs in general after departing South Bend.[16]

Becker's term with the Glee Club ended in 1923, though he remained at Notre Dame until 1927. After he left the university, Becker's career as a composer began to take flight. Along with Charles Ives, Carl Ruggles, and Henry Cowell, Becker is considered to be one of the leading sources of avant-garde music in the United States in the second quarter of the twentieth century, though much of his work remains unpublished. He penned substantial stage works, as well as pieces for orchestra, chamber ensembles, chorus, and solo voice. In his first year with the Glee Club, Becker wrote the wartime commemoration "Rouge Bouquet" on a text by American poet Joyce Kilmer for the choir to sing with trumpet and piano. He believed his finest work, however, to be *A Marriage with Space* (1935), a ballet with speaking chorus developed in partnership with Chicago poet Mark Turbyfill.[17]

One of the talented performers that Becker brought to South Bend was his teacher, organist J. Lewis Browne. Browne would succeed Becker as Glee Club director in 1923, though the former left the university before his student.[18] Born in London in 1864, Browne emigrated to the United States with his family in 1873. He played organ recitals around the country and directed music at a church in St. Paul, Minnesota, before relocating to Atlanta by 1903.[19] In 1907, Browne was thrown in jail after shooting at a priest through the window of the rectory at Sacred Heart Roman Catholic Church where he had just been asked to resign because of his "neglect of duty."[20] Telling the press he had

John J. Becker

no memory of the event, he seems to have escaped the attention by moving to Philadelphia and working there between 1908 and 1910. He played more than five hundred recitals on the Austin organs in the Egyptian and Greek Halls, the main auditoriums at the Wanamaker's department store. Though John Wanamaker once called Browne "the premier organist of the world," the latter suffered from alcoholism and was let go before the installation of the enormous "Grand Court" organ, still in operation today.[21] Browne left Philadelphia for Chicago to help design the Medinah Temple organ and to serve as music director at Old St. Patrick's Church there. He remained in the city for the rest of his life, maintaining an organ studio for students and also heading the theory department at the city's Fine Arts Conservatory of Music.[22] Commuting weekly to Notre Dame after 1923, Browne directed not only the Glee Club but also the orchestra, the choir of St. Patrick Church in South Bend, and later the Moreau Seminary Choir.[23]

Browne clearly was pulled in many directions when splitting his time between Chicago and Notre Dame. Fortunately, Joseph Casasanta, the accompanist and student director for the Glee Club, was being groomed to take the position when Browne's commute to Indiana and the directorships became too burdensome. Browne was confident in his assistant's ability to lead the Glee Club, orchestra, and the band, expressing as much to Notre Dame's president, Fr. Matthew Walsh, in a letter from 1926.[24] Although the torch was passed to a young man with nothing of the high-profile professional musical experience of his two most recent predecessors, the Notre Dame Glee Club had settled on a conductor who would vault the ensemble into the national spotlight.

J. Lewis Browne

MARCHING TOWARD NEW HORIZONS

If Perrott, Becker, and Browne gave the Glee Club roots, Joseph Casasanta gave it wings—and some marches to sing as well. As a Glee Club member and frequent conductor of the group during Browne's tenure, Casasanta was already entrenched in the culture of the ensemble when he took the podium. He was a known quantity on campus and already collegial with the singers. Casasanta also had led the university band since 1921 and reportedly received Notre Dame's first Bachelor of Music degree in 1923, and a master's degree the following year.[25] Though he would make great strides with enhancing the visibility of the Singing Irish, Casasanta was most loyal to the marching band, which garnered the lion's share of university funding as a musical organization.[26]

Joseph Casasanta's lasting contribution to the university was the music he composed and the public face he put on the Glee Club and the band. Shortly after his graduation, he realized that the university needed a stable

Joseph Casasanta

of pep songs that could supplement the popular but increasingly overexposed "Victory March." In a seven-year stretch, Casasanta penned four school songs, not one of which has been retired from the Glee Club or band repertoire to this day. Any Notre Dame devotee will have encountered Casasanta's compositions. In 1924, the director wrote "Hike, Notre Dame" with his brother-in-law and Notre Dame professor of architecture Vincent Fagan. It was a march that captured the campus-wide fervor around one of Coach Knute Rockne's new formations on offense. "Hike, Notre Dame" became a staple of Glee Club concerts and often drew encores. Casasanta followed up this smash hit with another march, "(On) Down the Line," in 1926.[27]

Casasanta was not finished writing music. While on a train to the Notre Dame–Army football game in New York City in 1929, professor of English Fr. Eugene Burke asked the Glee Club director why he had not written more school songs, to which Casasanta replied, "I thought they didn't want any more." Burke offered to write words for a new school song if his colleague could set them to music. Less than a week after their return from New York, the collaboration resulted in "When Irish Backs Go Marching By," which was as eagerly absorbed by the Notre Dame public as the other marches.[28] Casasanta's fourth and final song to enter the university's musical canon was not a march, but rather its alma mater, "Notre Dame, Our Mother," written in 1931, following Knute Rockne's untimely death.[29] Casasanta composed and arranged other works as well. For instance, he was commissioned by St. Thomas Military Academy in St. Paul, Minnesota, to write an alma mater for the school in 1932. Above all, his arrangement of the "Victory March" is still in use by the marching band and glee club. It was lauded by the song's composer Michael Shea as "good work admirably done for the best University in the land."[30]

Speaking about the Singing Irish under Casasanta, campus reporter James Carmody (himself a second tenor in the Glee Club) noted, "Under his guidance it has known a fame that is nationwide."[31] This was no exaggeration: the Glee Club had drawn the country's attention with high-profile tours, widely distributed recordings, and a robust presence on radio airwaves. In his first full year as director, Casasanta and Glee Club business manager Andrew Mulreany staged an exhilarating two-week winter tour that included performances and radio appearances in Boston, New York, and Philadelphia, capped by a visit to Washington, DC, where they met President Calvin Coolidge and performed a concert attended by three U.S. senators and Supreme Court Justice Pierce Butler.[32] Meanwhile, Glee Club recordings from the Victor and Brunswick labels made in the late 1920s (to be discussed in chapter 9) impressed Americans with the group's sound and further spread the pep songs composed by its director.

Just as J. Lewis Browne was pulled away from South Bend for musical endeavors in Chicago, Casasanta was pulled in many directions too, conducting several other musical activities on campus—the Jugglers, the Linnets, and the Collegians—that surely sapped any spare time he could find beyond his work with the Glee Club and band, to say nothing of his academic teaching load. The Jugglers were a popular on-campus orchestra organized in 1927 that recorded the "Victory March" and "(On) Down the Line" for Columbia in that same year.[33] The Linnets performed light musical revues under Casasanta's direction beginning in 1933; meanwhile, the Collegians—in place since 1920 and originally directed by Glee Club accompanist Harry Denny ('20)—were a dance band that specialized in modern works. Both organizations collaborated regularly with the Glee Club in the 1930s, putting Casasanta's fabled showmanship on full display.[34]

Casasanta's stock ostensibly was high by the mid-1930s. He had his finger on the pulse of most musical endeavors on campus and was one of the early members of the American Bandmasters Association.[35] If Casasanta had an Achilles' heel, it was his relationship with the increasingly conservative university administration. Notre Dame president Fr. John O'Hara was concerned about the direction of the Glee Club in particular and had higher hopes for a student orchestra, which had only reached thirty-five members in 1935.[36] The serious repertoire that the previous directors cultivated had all but vanished from Glee Club programs; pressure from the administration signaled an imminent changing of the guard.

DEAN DELIVERS

Just as outside professional musicians Becker and Browne replaced Perrott and other directors of the Glee Club from the ranks of the student body, so too did the administration trade

During his tenure at Notre Dame, the university honored Joseph Casasanta at the 1932 Commencement exercises. Shortly after the ceremony, Casasanta wrote these words to university president Charles O'Donnell: "Whatever I have done, I owe all to Notre Dame. She has always been, and will always be, the source of all my inspiration, love, and joy."

Daniel Pedtke

the years under the wonder-student Casasanta for a credentialed professional, the unflappable Daniel Pedtke. Pedtke was born in Chicago in 1906 and began his prodigious performing career as a pianist, counting acclaimed pianists Sergei Tarnowski and Alexander Raab among his teachers.[37] He also took up the organ in his teenage years and studied under Wilhelm Middelschulte (director Becker's teacher) and former Glee Club director J. Lewis Browne. After obtaining the Bachelor of Music from DePaul University, he passed the most stringent performance and written examinations of the American Guild of Organists and was elected a fellow in June 1936.[38] Pedtke played the organ at different Chicago-area churches in his early career (most notably at Our Lady of Mount Carmel) and also served at the Cathedral of St. Andrew in Grand Rapids, Michigan.[39]

In 1932, Pedtke entered the academic world, becoming head of the music department at the all-women's College of St. Teresa in Winona, Minnesota, where his musical responsibilities were wide-ranging. He taught music theory courses, liturgical music, piano, and organ; he also directed two choirs and the orchestra. Pedtke further produced various musical events for each class: a Gilbert and Sullivan opera by the freshmen, a Lenten sacred cantata by the sophomores, and so forth.[40] Following his colleague and close friend from St. Teresa, Willis D. Nutting, who had just been hired at Notre Dame, Pedtke was set to become an organ instructor there, commencing his work in the summer of 1936. But in August, he received a generous offer for a faculty position at his alma mater, DePaul University, for the 1936–37 academic year. No doubt seeing the chance to advance the state of the music department at Notre Dame, president John O'Hara matched DePaul's offer, ensuring Pedtke the position of head of the music department, the same title he had held in Winona.[41]

Daniel Pedtke would chair the music department at Notre Dame for nearly two decades beginning in 1937, eventually coming to be known popularly as "Dean." His first order of business was the reorganization of the university's symphony orchestra, which had taken hiatus in 1936–37 after less than desirable results under Casasanta. Pedtke vowed to present the symphonic classics with this group and rehearse them twice per week in Washington Hall. In September 1937, he instituted a freshman-only choral ensemble, which would represent a breeding ground for future varsity Glee Club talent. First called the "Choral Club," this training ensemble of some forty voices practiced twice per week under Pedtke and three times per week the following year under graduate assistant Cletus Schommer.[42]

Still, Dean had his eye, and ear, on Casasanta's Glee Club. An NBC recording of the April 1938 national broadcast of Universal Notre Dame Night activities reveals how the singing had deteriorated since the recordings of the late 1920s. Pedtke would not criticize Casasanta directly, but he observed many years later that Casasanta's group had two ways of singing—"loud and louder." The university's administration either had not permitted the Glee Club to tour or Casasanta had claimed to be too busy with the marching band to take on the task. The alma mater on another spring 1938 broadcast was musically appalling, and Pedtke must have begun plans at that time to take over the choir himself. His copy of the program from Casasanta's final concert in June 1938 is annotated with the names of the young men Pedtke thought worth keeping.

After Pedtke made a report of the needs of the music department—one consistent with the frugalities of the 1930s depression—Fr. O'Hara commissioned Moreau Choir director Fr. James Connerton to review the situation. It is likely Fr. O'Hara, and not Pedtke, insisted on Casasanta's removal, which was announced during the summer of 1938. Paul DeLay ('42) recalls that the mortified Casasanta shunned Pedtke, even in passing in the halls, though the former retained the directorship of the marching band for another three years.

Pedtke took the reins of the Singing Irish in the fall of 1938. A review of his first concert noted that the director's initial offering was "an almost entirely different program from that so well known to concert-goers in the past."[43] The Casasanta programs that favored easy part-songs and rallying school marches were in the rearview mirror. Prefect of Discipline Fr. James Trahey promptly wrote to Pedtke, "I enjoyed every minute of what I heard. . . . There is a finess[e] about this year's Glee Club which bespeaks cultural background and which has been sadly lacking for a number of years. I believe a Glee Club can be, and should be, primarily a cultural influence and not just a 'Rah, Rah Chorus.'"[44] And after the Christmas concert in 1939, the prefect—who, in the days before a department of student affairs was created, had great influence over the Club—was even more effusive. His letter concludes with the words the singers had been longing to hear:

> Please accept my hearty congratulations on a beautiful concert. I don't mind telling you that I was most agreeably surprised with the affair and can honestly say it was the finest glee club concert I have heard in many a year at Notre Dame. Incidentally, it was not Glee Clubbish—if you know what I mean. . . . Kindly convey to the members of the club my appreciation and tell them for me that they have my hearty support for any trip possible.[45]

Within two years, Pedtke could proudly report to President O'Hara that "all of the organizations of the Music Department are now well established and in full rehearsal schedule, and we hope to improve the quality and quantity of programs on and off campus."[46] Dean had delivered, but his work had just begun.

In his thirty-seven years at Notre Dame, Dean Pedtke's contributions to the university and to the community are impossible to measure, extending far beyond his work with the Glee Club. Over the years, he led the orchestra and taught all the music theory courses (composition, keyboard harmony, counterpoint, and formal analysis), plus choral conducting and lessons in piano and organ. He also liked to teach the courses in music appreciation for non-majors. From 1938 through the early 1970s, he served as the organist and choir director at St. Patrick Church in South Bend. Pedtke kept up his performing career as pianist and organist. In 1941, he performed at the dedication of a new electronic organ at St. Joseph Catholic Church in South Bend. He also gave a series of lecture-recitals on Beethoven's violin sonatas in 1949, accompanying his faculty colleague, violinist Charles Biondo, as the latter pursued his doctoral degree.[47] Engagements took Pedtke beyond South Bend as well. In 1969, for example, he gave a post-Vespers organ recital at a prestigious series hosted by Washington National Cathedral. He continued his involvement with the American Guild of Organists, assisting with the examinations and serving as dean of the St. Joseph County chapter in 1958–59.

A glee club is a tradition here and it should be continued. It should develop from within the music department and be offered to students who are seeking something more than trips as their objective. If and when such a club should become good enough to represent the University on a university level it could be sent out to the public. It should aim at doing the best of music and especially should It explore the music treasure of the Church (Harvard Glee Club makes exclusive use of our own 16th-century music on its road trips). A Michigan State faculty group offer[s] to the public (full house present) a performance of Vespers. They have on their faculty several men well educated in Chant. In the second semester their organization Collegium Musicum offered a varied list of nine concerts of music possessing educational and historical importance.

—Fr. James Connerton to Charles O'Hara, 1937

Beyond his impressive display of skill at the keyboard, Pedtke composed and orchestrated as needed for the school, often for celebratory occasions. The director wrote a piece for the Glee Club called *The Arena* for the university's centenary festivities in 1942, and he followed this up the next year with a symphonic choral work with narration titled *The Spirit of Notre Dame*. The text was written by student Kelly Cook, who was serving in the United States Army Air Corps.[48] Pedtke's most enduring musical contribution remains the Glee Club's alma mater "Notre Dame, We Hail Thee," with text by Fr. Eugene Burke, the same lyricist who partnered with Casasanta in the late 1920s. Today, at any formal concert on campus or on tour, "Notre Dame, We Hail Thee" precedes the singing of the university's alma mater "Notre Dame, Our Mother" and the "Victory March" as the final songs in the program. Pedtke recalled that the sentimental "Notre Dame, We Hail Thee" achieved a significant following among students, who lobbied (unsuccessfully) to have this piece replace Casasanta's alma mater in the early 1940s.[49]

Pedtke welcomed opportunities to speak publicly about general issues related to music. In October 1944, the Glee Club director discussed the role of music in the church on a new local radio program *Sign of the Cross*, the theme song of which was sung by an octet of Glee Clubbers. Less than two years later, Pedtke spoke informally on music appreciation in an event sponsored by Catholic Action, which was designed to bring students and faculty closer together. He further gave a talk at the Lions Club called "The Educational Aspects of Music" in a series of lectures in 1949 on the topic of the university's contributions to the South Bend area.[50] One composition on a non-Notre Dame topic was his *Mass in Honor of Saint Jude* for mixed voices choir and organ, written in 1957, though long out of print.[51] The textbook that Pedtke wrote for piano students entitled *Keyboard Harmony* is also out of print, and no known copies are extant.

The Glee Club traveled extensively in Pedtke's tenure, and the seven consecutive annual appearances on Ed Sullivan's *Toast of the Town* were easily a highlight of the thirty-five years. The membership of the Glee Club soared during the early 1950s, reaching 160 men in the combined choirs of 1952–53. The Second World War, on the other hand, took a toll on campus musical life. The viability of the music department itself was in question, and Pedtke, as its head, reflected on the role of music at the university as the nation engaged in battle. Detailed minutes from a 1942 faculty meeting reveal that he spoke "inspiringly of the future responsibility of the music department, with its resources for providing worthy entertainment on the campus of Notre Dame University during the coming months of Her war effort—and of the urgent need of music in the present emergency, and of its power to build and maintain patriotic morale."[52]

Pedtke was a gentle man with a soft voice. His humility and faith were reassuring to more than three decades of Glee Clubbers, and the idea of family was a central concern to this beloved director. Pedtke once remarked

Willis Nutting (left) and Daniel Pedtke

that his daily interaction with the young men meant that he probably knew them as well as anyone did. He was keen on learning about the parents of his singers, or at least their names, which often were kept scrupulously in the file of the group's secretary.[53] When his former students returned to campus, he took as much pleasure hearing about their families as he did about their professional endeavors. Even today, countless former students return to campus for reunions, claiming that the director had a unique influence on their careers, their characters, and their lives. Pedtke's own family, foremost his wife, Helen (a former organ student at the College of St. Teresa), had a close relationship with the group, to be discussed in chapter 12.

Pedtke's retirement came two months earlier than expected after he suffered a disabling stroke in April 1973. From his recovery room, he had to settle for listening to a recording of "his" final Commencement concert, which was capably directed by student assistant Howard Bathon. Able to use only one arm, Pedtke continued to give "three-handed" duet performances on piano with Helen. He was intent on showing retirees that disability can be just a state of mind.

Glee club directors and composers around the country, like Yale's Marshall Bartholomew, had high regard for Dean Pedtke, but the longtime conductor of the Singing Irish never aspired to the national attention that the tours and television appearances brought. He was most concerned for the reputation of Notre Dame and for his singers. On his twenty-fifth anniversary as director in 1963, and as his announced retirement in 1973 approached, throngs of Glee Club alumni gathered to salute him. In the fall of 1974, a special banquet in the Monogram Room of the Athletic and Convocation Center was given to honor Pedtke's career of service. Brought in to the room in a wheelchair, Dean was presented with an extraordinary gift—a brand new 1973 Oldsmobile Cutlass! Although the gift was anonymous at the time, it was later revealed to come from Glee Club alumnus Eugene Fanning ('53), a four-year baritone soloist for Pedtke.[54] The Glee Club also gave Pedtke a trip to the Caribbean.

Other Glee Clubbers who remain anonymous subsequently financed another trip in August 1976 for Dean and Helen to visit their oldest daughter, Dorothy, then living in Turkey with her daughter, Robin. The travel plan included a week for the four of them to visit the Holy Land, where Pedtke could pray for a miraculous cure for his stroke. With determination, Dean walked the Way of the Cross with only his cane and prayed silently at Gethsemane. This trip was preceded by a journey to the Saint Joseph's Oratory of Mount Royal in Montreal with the same goal in mind. Here, Dean and Helen visited the site of a chapel built by Brother André Bessette, C.S.C., known for his miraculous healings. By the fall of 1976, Pedtke understood that alleviating his disability was not the Lord's will and humbly resigned himself to his incapacity.

Longtime Glee Club chaplain Fr. Robert Griffin tried to articulate Pedtke's impact on the young men whom he guided in song: "He is a unique man who could take the boys' singularity and make it into something much bigger than themselves—something of which they could be proud. . . . The group's continuity and ability to pass on to each other more than the tails they wear on stage will keep Dean's name part of the group."[55] Indeed, Pedtke's legacy is ever present.

FIVE

Shaping the Sound II

CONTINUING THE TRADITION

Dean Pedtke died on December 10, 1976, at the age of 70. His funeral Mass at Sacred Heart Church was con-

celebrated by thirty-five priests, with the Glee Club standing on risers behind the altar. Pedtke's successor,

David Clark Isele, led the Club, while the Notre Dame Chapel Choir, under the direction of Sue Seid-Martin,

provided music from the loft. At communion, the Glee Club sang a setting of the "Ave Maria," composed

by the deceased director. This was followed by a moving performance of Pedtke's "Notre Dame, We Hail Thee"

to close the Mass, with help from nearly one hundred Glee Club alumni in attendance. The choirs processed

south from the church to Cedar Grove cemetery ringing out solemn chant and hymns. At Pedtke's burial site,

the men fittingly sang Sir Arthur Sullivan's "The Long Day Closes."[1] A golden age in Glee Club history had

come to an end. And it would be a tough act to follow.

COACHING SUCCESS

The appointment of David Clark Isele as Director of Choral Activities in the Department of Music, signaled in some ways a new direction for the Glee Club but also a stabilization of the group in the aftermath of Pedtke's retirement. Isele arrived with impressive credentials, trained as an organist, singer, and composer. He spent most of his college years at two of the nation's finest music conservatories—Oberlin College (Bachelor of Music, Vocal Education) and the Eastman School of Music (Doctor of Musical Arts, Composition). As an undergraduate at Oberlin, Isele "fell in love" with the organ and then studied with the eminent organist and pedagogue Robert T. Anderson at Southern Methodist University, where he collected two master's degrees. With Pedtke having had a stroke in 1973, the young but qualified twenty-seven-year-old Isele was invited to interview for his position. During the years 1973–79, Isele directed not only the Glee Club but also the Notre Dame Chorale, which he founded, and the Chapel Choir. The latter two were mixed choirs, reflecting the advent of coeducation at Notre Dame beginning in 1972.

David Clark Isele

Pedtke's declining health and Isele's subsequent hiring surprisingly put the Glee Club under great scrutiny. Despite the ensemble's command of the national spotlight, questions regarding the direction of the music program were brewing in the administration not unlike those raised in the Casasanta years. The chair of the Department of Music, William Cerny (Professor of Piano), sought to eliminate the Glee Club and create instead a mixed chorus with loftier repertorial standards. Blindsided by this pressure, Isele fought for the Club's continued existence and instituted two major changes that quelled the department's concerns about the amateur men's chorus. He expanded the repertoire even more than Pedtke had done, reintroducing the Glee Club to madrigals, for instance, a genre of music in which it had only dabbled during its long history. He also pushed the members to memorize their most difficult pieces, for example the male chorus part to Johannes Brahms's *Alto Rhapsody*, which the Glee Club performed in the fall of 1975.[2] Any talk of the group's viability was postponed for several years.

Though the young director was welcomed by Glee Club members, Isele was not warmly received at first by Helen Pedtke, who was concerned about the legacy of her husband now in the hands of a twenty-seven year old. Isele also replaced Pedtke's sacrosanct version of the university's alma mater with his own arrangement of the piece that featured more active counterpoint and richer harmonies. But Isele's relationship with the Pedtkes quickly improved, and he soon became a regular invitee to their family gatherings. The new director of the Glee

Club earned a strong reputation in the Pedtke kitchen for making omelettes, usually served with champagne. Isele earned the nickname "Coach" at his first Glee Club rehearsal. Borrowing a tradition from his former choral director at Oberlin, Robert Fountain, Isele asked his singers to run in place as a physical "warm-up" in preparation for the hour of singing in the early evening. One of the singers, Tom Rooney ('74), yelled out in jest, "Coach!" at the exercise. Students never let go of this nickname, and his former singers still call Isele "Coach" as a matter of course.[3]

Establishing the Notre Dame Chorale in the fall of 1974 was a major achievement of the Isele years. The music department's early attempts at a mixed chorus (University Chorus and Notre Dame Polyphonic Choir) failed, giving the director an opportunity to form a mixed concert choir, one that has survived to the present day. Isele had to petition the administration for a budget and the chance to tour for the Chorale, no small feat given the Glee Club's substantial annual travel schedule. The Club already toured several times per year—a fall weekend, a weeklong fall tour, a spring weekend, and a weeklong spring tour. This left the Chorale with the possibility of journeying over the winter break, which it continues to do, along with regular international tours like the Glee Club. Any perceived threat to the Glee Club by the presence of the Chorale was mitigated by the fact that several members of the Club sang in the mixed chorus. Isele also worked to soothe possible tensions and reduce competition by establishing distinct repertoires for the ensembles.

The conductor's other venture into mixed choral music was his work with the Notre Dame Chapel Choir as its unofficial resident composer. It was in this role that Isele composed the famous "Lamb of God" from his *Holy Cross Mass*, a setting that was written ad hoc for the ensemble when it needed an unaccompanied Agnus Dei for a Mass to be sung at the Grotto, Notre Dame's outdoor shrine to the Virgin Mary. Isele's setting of the "Lamb of God" is still performed in hundreds of American churches today.

Having traveled thousands of miles with the Glee Club across the country and twice to Europe, "Coach" has countless fond memories of the ensemble's many tours. Isele's first was particularly unforgettable—a Thanksgiving tour of the Midwest in 1973, which began with a performance in Milwaukee and an appearance on the local TV program *Kennedy & Company* (later *A.M. Chicago*) on Thanksgiving Day at seven o'clock in the morning. Guests on air that day were comedic actress Jo Anne Worley and cartoonist John Fischetti. After Glee Club members egged him on to draw a caricature of their director, Fischetti whipped up an ingenious sketch of Isele

that soon found its way onto sweatshirts and T-shirts.[4] A West Coast tour in the spring of 1975 featured the premiere of Isele's musical comedy sketch, *Red Hot Riding Hood*, with a small ensemble and chorus. Such "acts," as musical skits were called even in Pedtke's time, were common, but this operetta put a 1970s twist on the old fairy tale, presenting the wolf as Red's love interest.[5] Another indelible memory for Isele was the Glee Club's visit to the Neuschwanstein Castle in southwest Bavaria in 1978. The castle was a retreat for King Ludwig II of Bavaria, designed to honor the operas of Richard Wagner. At this hallowed site, the Glee Club sang a moving rendition of the king's "Prayer" from Wagner's *Lohengrin*, a chorus that is still firmly in the collective musical memory of alumni.[6]

David Clark Isele departed Notre Dame in 1979. He joined the faculty of the University of Tampa in 1980 as professor of music and composer-in-residence, also serving as organist and minister of music at Sacred Heart Church in Tampa. "Coach" continues to be held in high regard by his students and regularly returns for Glee Club reunions. Given the strong threat from the music department to eradicate the Glee Club after the retirement of Dean Pedtke, Isele can be credited with maintaining a distinct profile for the Singing Irish amid the new choral landscape forged at Notre Dame in the mid-1970s.

BELLAND AND THE ARRIVAL OF A CLASSIC

Isele's replacement, Douglas K. Belland, had music training similar to "Coach," earning the Doctor of Musical Arts degree from the University of Cincinnati College-

Conservatory of Music. He specialized foremost in conducting but also brought experience as a composer. Even before he finished his schooling, Belland was more than qualified to take over the Glee Club, having served as composer and arranger for the United States Army Soldiers' Chorus and as conductor of the men's chorus at Wayne State University.[7] According to student director Brian McLinden ('82, '86MA) who studied conducting with Belland, the director had a "child-like enthusiasm" for music and music making.[8]

In his two years with the Glee Club, Belland infused the organization with new repertoire, most of which has disappeared from the Club's canon. Like Isele, he was capable of arranging variety numbers in formal concerts, whether it was a medley from *Guys and Dolls*, excerpts of Motown hits, or Beatles' songs. Belland's published arrangement of the spiritual "Deep River" was particularly memorable in those years. The arrangement, preserved on the Glee Club's 1980 LP *The Gate of Heaven* (the only recording made during his term), was used in concerts by several other men's choruses.

Belland's lasting contribution to the Notre Dame Glee Club was the introduction of the exquisite two-choir setting of the angelic salutation "Ave Maria" by German composer Franz Biebl. The director heard the piece performed by the Harvard Glee Club and quickly obtained a manuscript of the work from the group's director, Jameson Marvin, before the work was published by Hinshaw Music. The piece was written for a vocal trio and a four-part male chorus. Belland rehearsed the trio part (a subgroup of Clubbers) separately from the four-part chorus of the remaining singers. When the parts were sufficiently learned in isolation, the director brought the singers together in a circle around the piano to hear the effect of the seven parts together. Some of the clubbers were brought to tears by the work, which has in turn stirred audiences as a regular part of Glee Club programs to this day. Douglas Belland left the university in 1981 and was the artistic director of the Cincinnati Choral Society from 1995 to 2014.

THE TURN TO STAM

Over its century-long history, the Notre Dame Glee Club has negotiated its role along a spectrum that featured a polished and disciplined representative of the music department on one hand and a fun-loving fraternal organization on the other. Despite Belland's efforts to curb a relative rise in

Carl Stam

Glee Club antics, the behavior of Club members drew the concern of the department and more generally the university administration. The new chair of the Department of Music, Calvin M. Bower, called the Glee Club officers to a meeting, explaining to them that their reputation for cavalier behavior had to change, but that the idea of a men's chorus was still appealing for the university. Bower told them of a recent graduate from the University of North Carolina at Chapel Hill who had sung in a chant ensemble under Bower when the two were there in the 1970s. His name was Carl "Chip" Stam, and Notre Dame hired him at the age of twenty-eight, nearly as young as Isele had been when he began at the university. Originally a trombone player, Stam earned bachelor's and master's degrees in music from North Carolina, finding his calling in choral music during those years. Some Clubbers thought the young new director might be overwhelmed by the culture of veterans in the ensemble, but a group of seniors, facing their third conductor in four years, made a point to welcome the boyish-looking Stam, allowing him to reshape the ensemble. In the course of a decade (1981–91), the infectious energy and optimism of the bright-eyed conductor transformed the group into a more disciplined operation, which it sorely needed.

As the new Director of Choral Music hired at the rank of associate professional specialist, Stam conducted the Glee Club and Chorale during his ten years at Notre Dame and also led the orchestra for two of those years. He taught graduate classes in conducting and even a freshman seminar, "Music, the Arts, and Language." Like his

predecessors, he continued to broaden the repertorial horizons of the group, introducing for instance the musical challenges presented by early twentieth-century composers Darius Milhaud, Francis Poulenc, and Charles Ives. Though raised in the Southern Baptist and Dutch Reformed traditions, Stam infused the Glee Club repertoire with Renaissance polyphony and plainchant from the treasury of Catholic church music.[9] His confidence with plainchant no doubt was gained in Chapel Hill with Professor Bower. Years later, Stam remembered that the Glee Club chanted the sequence "Veni sancte spiritus" ("Come Holy Spirit") at the opening Mass of each academic year at Sacred Heart Church.

Members of the Glee Club under Stam's direction have indelible memories of their director's unconventional comportment in rehearsal. Like Isele's technique of running in place, Stam sought energy from his singers after a long day of classes. The dynamic director kept rehearsals light and humorous, but without compromising his exacting standards. Among Stam's tactics was a flick of his baton up into the air, in an attempt to make it stick to the ceiling tiles. Then he would leap up and grab it, sometimes in time for the next downbeat. The conductor's athleticism in the rehearsal room was exemplified in his signature "turn" in which he jumped

up and spun 360 degrees in the air, landing in his starting position.[10] Stam's "vertical" was well served in basketball, which he played regularly on campus. His "Bookstore Basketball" team, which included future Notre Dame provost Nathan Hatch, was named "The Old and the Injured," and it won more than its fair share of games, including ones against varsity athletes.[11]

Stam had other feats that he called "Stam tricks." For instance in 1988, he drew campus-wide attention for eating live goldfish during rehearsal; he also took bets outside of South Dining Hall on whether he could tear a phone book in half with his hands— he did.[12] Though less of a trick, Glee Clubbers from the Stam era vividly recall that their director taught them how to bow together at the end of concerts. The singers were to receive the signal to bow from their director and then count to three while their heads were down. Counting to three, however, evolved into saying the director's name three times ("Stam, Stam, Stam"). If one listens carefully during concluding applause even today, the director's name—whether Daniel Stowe or a student conductor—will be uttered by the members while bowing.

The Glee Club ventured to Europe three times with Stam and gave more than a hundred performances around the United States. But it was the little things he did on tour that reveal his selfless personality and tireless spirit. On one long bus ride through the Midwest in the spring of 1982, the bus driver announced that he would be stopping at a McDonald's within the hour at the upcoming rest stop. Stam immediately pulled out a sheet of lined music paper and arranged the McDonald's jingle of the time ("You deserve a break today…") for his four-part male chorus. The director moved through the aisles of the bus, teaching his arrangement of the McDonald's song to the singers. The men entered the fast-food restaurant in small groups, so as to not arouse suspicion. Stam then gave the starting pitch, and the choir unleashed the enhanced jingle to the amazement of the employees and customers in the restaurant.[13] The director gave of himself not just in music, but in his relationships with his singers. During the Club's European tour of 1984, Stam purchased Swiss Army penknives for the graduating seniors at a stop in Zürich and had them engraved with "Notre Dame Glee Club" on one side.[14] It was a memento that Stam continued to give to departing members of the group during his term.

Ever the team player, Stam was active as a choral conductor and served in a number of leadership roles at the national level as a service to his discipline. He was the national chair of the American Choral Directors Association's (ACDA) Repertoire and Standards Committee for Men's Choruses, organizing the National Men's Honor Choir in Washington, DC, in 1995.[15] Besides the extensive touring of the Stam years, two appearances at conventions of choral directors further reveal the high bar set by the director and the achievements of the Glee Club during his time. In the spring of 1988, the group was invited to perform in Cleveland at the Central Division meeting of the ACDA, and this event was trumped by a call to sing at the national ACDA convention in Louisville in 1989. Stam supplemented the latter appearance with two ninety-minute interest sessions (also featuring the Glee Club) on the use of plainchant in choral music, again drawing on his experience with the genre from his days in Chapel Hill.

It is impossible to capture Stam's character without recognizing his unwavering Christian faith. He and his family worshipped at the South Bend Christian Reformed Church during his decade at Notre Dame, but he was called on to assist on campus at Sacred Heart Church, too. He served as cantor for the Easter Vigil for three years, certainly the first Protestant to assume that role. Stam admitted to learning much about Catholicism during his tenure and found many parallels with the Protestant traditions that had formed him.

> [T]here are people in all these Christian traditions who are going hard after God, wanting to please Him in every area of life (personal devotion, family, civic service, local church ministry, outreach to the lost, broken, and lonely), and there are those who never connected the dots that a relationship with God through Christ is something that can inform and fuel every aspect of life. There are clueless Catholics and clueless Southern Baptists when it comes to the essentials of the Christian faith and knowledge of our mighty and merciful God. God help us.[16]

Clubbers admired Stam for his exemplary Christian model; his ability to assimilate the faiths around him was a rare gift. Alumnus Fred Scott ('89, '92L) remembered Stam as "a good and decent man who, through his daily work, ministered to young men. Through his example, a diverse group of men selflessly gave of themselves—for their fellow clubbers, for those touched by the Club's music, and for Notre Dame. In essence, he taught Christian service. . . . [H]is Christian example knew no denominational boundary."[17] Stam's values were, in his words, "admired by many, despised by some."[18] His positive example was commended in a letter from football coach Lou Holtz in 1990,[19] and he became the first lay member of the faculty to receive the Father John "Pop" Farley Award for distinguished service in student affairs.[20] Stam returned regularly for Glee Club reunions.

Stam loved his work at Notre Dame and the students he encountered, but the death of his father in 1990 seems to have set in motion thoughts about leaving the university. The life of a Glee Club director is one lived outside of traditional business hours. After-school rehearsals, evening concerts, and frequent tours were taking its toll on Stam's family. His wife, Doris, recalled: "Our nuclear family was not thriving, and we wanted to make steps to improve our marriage and help our [two] boys."[21] Doris and he decided to return to North Carolina, and the former Glee Club director became the pastor of worship and music at the Chapel Hill Bible Church, which would allow him to be close to his mother and to focus on family life. As difficult as it was to leave Notre Dame, Stam showed that family came first. In 2001, the family relocated again to Louisville, as Stam returned to academic life at the Southern Baptist Theological Seminary. He was appointed professor of church music and worship at the seminary and became the founding director of the seminary's Institute for Christian Worship.[22]

In 2007, Stam began a battle with non-Hodgkin lymphoma, which he courageously waged for four years with the same energy, genuine curiosity, and concern for others that characterized his life. Never one to sit on his hands, Stam organized a nationwide stem-cell drive to identify matches for him and patients like him in need of a bone marrow transplant. Moved by his determination, the Glee Club took up their former director's cause, coordinating a bone marrow donor campaign in his name and registering nearly five hundred new donors (in addition to many Glee Club alumni) in 2010 with the "Be The Match" Foundation on the Notre Dame campus. "I can still walk on my hands across the room," Stam wrote in 2010, during a period of remission, but the cancer soon returned.[23] On May 1, 2011, Carl Stam lost his battle with the disease at age fifty-eight. The most animated director the Glee Club had ever known brought back home to his Maker the boundless energy of his 360-degree turns that he shared so freely on Earth.

MARK RING AND EAST COAST CULTURE

The Department of Music continued its trend of hiring young directors with graduate degrees when it appointed Mark Ring to the position of Director of Choral Activities at Notre Dame. Ring, like Isele and Belland, had just earned the Doctor of Musical Arts degree prior to his arrival at Notre Dame, but would only last two years in his first job as Glee Club director. A newly-minted graduate from Yale University in conducting, Ring was a musician with high standards, accustomed to leading serious East Coast musical enterprises with committed students. Having also received an organ performance degree as an undergraduate at Union University (Tennessee), Ring was clearly a well-trained player from a strong Protestant background. The Notre Dame Glee Club—as much a social institution as a musical one—would challenge the young conductor in the relaxed environment of the fraternal singing group. Ring would be the last director to oversee both the Glee Club and the Chorale.

Like all new Glee Club directors, Mark Ring had his own ideas of how to elevate the repertoire of the ensemble. But the Glee Club's typical pool of untrained singers limited the pace of musical progress that the director could make with his vision. Roderick O'Brien ('95), who sang Bass II, remembers Ring investing significant time helping students without extensive musical backgrounds to learn their parts. As a bass voice himself, the director spent considerable energy on the low, foundational range of the choir more generally, contrasting with the tenor-dominated, melodic focus of Stam (a tenor) in the previous decade. One of the musical highlights in the brief Ring term was a visit to Notre Dame from one of his mentors at Yale, Fenno Heath, who was retiring after having conducted the Yale Glee Club since 1953. It was a daunting moment for the young Glee Club director, as he put forward his amateur collegiate male chorus in front of one of the great choral icons of the twentieth century. For all of Ring's anxiety over a coaching clinic followed by a few guest-conducted pieces as part of the campus concert, this brush with choral greatness was viewed as a positive moment by members during the 1992–93 academic year.

The Glee Club's travels during the brief term of Mark Ring highlighted the strict standards of the conductor in the face of a group that had its heart set on conviviality as much as song while on tour. In the spring of 1992, Ring led the Glee Club to its first and only visit to Puerto Rico. Describing a concert performed before mountain villagers, Glee Club chaplain Fr. Robert Griffin was inspired to see "women and young people giving the music their undivided attention," but he also hinted at his distaste for the new director's austere handling of the ensemble on that trip.[24] Future tours bore further witness to an unraveling between the music director and his singers, notably on a tour of the East Coast in the fall of 1992. Poor group conduct on the trip landed the president of the Glee Club in the office of the vice president for student affairs in the spring of 1993, and some organizational privileges were temporarily revoked. Although Ring remembered uplifting experiences from the European tour of 1993 (such as bursting into song before Pope John Paul II), the university had appointed a representative, Fr. Terry Linton, in addition to chaplain Fr. Griffin, to travel with the Glee Club to observe its behavior and interaction with the director. Logistics around the cancellation of a tour stop in En-

niskillen in Northern Ireland—due to political unrest—caused tensions to boil over between the director and the student tour manager and with Glee Club leadership more broadly. Select members met with Ring at the end of the tour to express their lack of confidence in his continued directorship should he return in the fall of 1993, but a search for his successor appeared to be under way already.

There is no single reason to explain the departure of Mark Ring after just two years at Notre Dame. The singers repeatedly cited dissonance between the rigorous, Yale-inspired choral standards of the director and the more easygoing conduct of Glee Clubbers. But when tensions grew, the Glee Club student officers were unable to navigate and negotiate an understanding with Ring about the nature of—and expectations for—the celebrated male chorus at Notre Dame. Alumni from the previous decade recognized parallels to the short stint of Douglas Belland. It was a short but volatile moment in Glee Club history that sullied the group's reputation, at least in the view of campus authorities.

THE JOURNEY WITH DANIEL STOWE

In the spring of 1993, while finishing graduate studies at Cornell University, Daniel Stowe applied for a position at Notre Dame that would combine a directorship of the Chorale with some teaching responsibilities in the music department, whether in music history or music theory. Though the search committee asked him to submit additional materials, Stowe did not get the job. Having no prospects for the coming

Daniel Stowe

year, he and his future wife Faith Fleming embarked on a backpacking trip to Kings Canyon National Park in his native state of California. From a motel in Fresno, Stowe phoned his parents in Los Angeles, who told him that the chair of the music department, Ethan Haimo, was trying to contact him. A position of Glee Club director was also open, and the search for this candidate began with the same stack of applications as the Chorale job. Haimo invited Stowe for a half day of interviews with faculty members and student representatives of the Glee Club, including senior Mark White ('94) who emphasized to the candidate how much the Glee Club loved its "rah-rah" music.[25] Scarcely knowing the Notre Dame culture, Stowe was offered—and took—the job at age thirty-two.

With a master's degree in conducting, Stowe was well qualified to lead an amateur all-male collegiate chorus, but another master's degree in musicology set him apart from his predecessors. Stowe's first year was exceptional in many ways. Due to student code infractions accrued during the Ring tenure, the Glee Club was suspended from touring in the director's first semester, but the ensemble did participate in the 1993 fall Alumni Reunion concert. Stowe had to decline the invitation for the Glee Club to sing at the annual Christmas Mass and brunch sponsored by the Notre Dame Club of Chicago, an unintentional snub that strained relations between the chorus and the largest alumni club in the country.

Stowe's introduction of especially challenging repertoire for his ensemble of young men was also met with some internal pushback, except from freshmen who were just getting to know the musical traditions of the Glee Club. The musical offerings for the spring 1994 concert, held in the newly redesignated Basilica of the Sacred Heart, were entirely sacred and much of it written before 1600, a tough sell for seasoned members. The singers were proud of the accomplishment, though, in the decidedly "down" year. The first of Stowe's seven recordings with the Glee Club, *Music from the Basilica*—easily his most daring and unconventional with the group—grew out of this performance.

According to Stowe, the combination of difficult modern music and a complicated foreign language nearly caused an "open revolt" in the fall of 1994 with his selection of the Hungarian folksongs *Székely népdalok* (1932) by Bela Bartók.[26] When the director took this piece on tour that semester, an unlikely voice supported the increased presence of "heavier" repertoire. After a concert in Amarillo, Texas, Stowe remembered staying at the home of a local high school choir director, who encouraged him to stick with the daring music for the all-male group: "You really established your musical integrity in the first half." Glee Club programs under Stowe continue to wade into audacious territory for male choral music—at least in the first half of programs. Notable challenges have included Igor Stravinsky's opera-oratorio *Oedipus Rex*, Arnold Schoenberg's poignant *A Survivor from Warsaw*, and Krzysztof Penderecki's densely textured "Benedicamus Domino." Lately, Stowe has learned the benefits of eliminating choir folders as much as possible during concerts, and this has forced the director to think about balancing the most demanding and risky repertoire with music that is more easily memorized: "I've since been persuaded that the more we can put the books down, the better; challenging material remains, but not so much of it, to allow us to learn it more thoroughly."

Though there was no change in his responsibilities, Stowe felt the complexion of his work change when Notre Dame opened the DeBartolo Performing Arts Center (DPAC) in the fall of 2004. With the construction of this cultural monument, Notre Dame made an unprecedented commitment to music, in addition to investments in live theater, dance, and cinema. Before the first home football game in 2004, the Glee Club performed a concert in the new nine-hundred-seat Leighton Concert Hall to an electric atmosphere. Stowe remarked, "I'm still amazed anew when I walk into the concert hall that they actually built it. It's a continual motivation to prove ourselves worthy of it." The following spring, the Glee Club was treated to unforgettable master classes at the DPAC by two iconic performing ensembles, Ladysmith Black Mambazo and the King's Singers.

Outside of the repertorial upgrades, Stowe's greatest impact with the Glee Club in his twenty-two years has been in the area of touring. The geographic horizons that the director opened up for the university's musical ambassadors has been nothing short of breathtaking and rivals the itineraries of some of the most well-traveled ensembles in the country. Stowe's recollections of the last two decades—and those of many of his students—principally revolve around experiences away from campus, bringing the spirit of the university to all corners of the globe.

The year after his first European trip with the Glee Club in 1996, which included memorable stops in Galway, Florence, and Munich, the group was invited to Israel to perform major works with the Jerusalem Symphony Orchestra. Among the side trips was one to the hills above the Sea of Galilee, where Fr. Michael Driscoll celebrated Mass. Not to be outdone, Stowe brought the Glee Club on its first tour of Asia in the summer of 2001, with performances at the National Concert Hall in Taipei and Hong Kong.[27] The experiences of the Night Safari in Singapore, golfing in Bangkok, fresh dumplings in Shanghai, and a mass singing session in a Beijing park will not soon be forgotten by the director and members of the Glee Club alike.

After nine international trips with the ensemble, Stowe's most meaningful venture with the Glee Club was his tenth, in 2013, when the group traveled to Spain to experience the Camino de Santiago, the famous pilgrimage route for medieval Christians that winds through Spanish towns and finishes at the magnificent Cathedral of St. James in Santiago de Compostela. While Stowe described his more recent trips to Europe as "familiar, yet euphorically new," the trek on the "Way of Saint James" was unparalleled in Glee Club history and would have life-changing impact for the singers and for Stowe, who called the experience both a "physical test" and a "spiritual journey."[28] The Glee Club journeyed on foot for one of the two weeks, averaging about fifteen miles per day on the walk. By remaining in Spain, the group was afforded the chance to slow down the typical frenetic pace of European tours. The extraordinary journey culminated with the ensemble appearing at the daily noontime Pilgrim's Mass at the historic cathedral, site of the relics of the apostle St. James.

Stowe carefully expanded his musical leadership role at Notre Dame not long after his arrival on campus. In 1994, he began a noncredit early music ensemble, Collegium Musicum, which included some Glee Club members. (Today, the Collegium ensemble carries credit and rarely includes members of the Glee Club.) The next year, Stowe was named director of the university's symphony orchestra, a group that boasts more than ninety members on the current roster. After a Glee Club tour to Central America in 2005, Stowe decided to return there in 2009 with the both the Glee Club and the Notre Dame Symphony Orchestra. The director remembers, "The singers and players were cheered like rock stars when they entered the cathedral in Guatemala City for their concert. Weber's 'Hunter's Chorus' from *Der Freischütz* was our opener." It is believed to be the first collaboration between the Glee Club and the Symphony Orchestra since the early 1940s.[29]

Stowe's character and interaction with the Glee Club has been on its own kind of journey for the past two decades. In his first four years with the ensemble, Stowe was unmistakably an older brother to the group's members (a "pal," to some extent), but he has become more of a father to the singers since the turn of the century, stepping back from his previous social, "after-hours" role with the ensemble. This mature and deliberate withdrawal happened to coincide with the director's decision in 1999 to rent a car or van to trail the tour bus during national travel, a move that further separated him from the juvenile antics that sometimes materialize on extensive trips. Stowe commands authority that the young Isele, Stam, and Casasanta could not muster as relatively young conductors at Notre Dame, yet he is no soft-spoken, well-tempered Pedtke. He radiates an inspiring brand of choral strictness and demands precision in rehearsal and on stage, shunning complacency. Glee Club alumni from the Ring years and earlier instantly recognize the attention to musical details and the warmth in the choral sound, which Stowe has cultivated in his two decades on the podium. The 2013–14 Glee Club president Brian Scully will never forget Stowe reminding the young men that "*Everything* is important, *every* time." During formal concerts, the director has always spoken knowledgeably and eloquently before audiences, illuminating his programming rationale. This is the musicologist in him that cannot be matched by the conductors before him.

At the same time, Stowe has always been quick to admit mistakes and can be highly self-critical away from the concert stage, a quality many find refreshing in Notre Dame's culture of overachievers. Once wary about the highly networked inner-workings of the Notre Dame alumni base, Stowe has embraced and enhanced his personal "rolodex"—beginning with Glee Clubbers—and calls regularly on the worldwide ties of the school to ensure rich experiences for the group on tour. At heart, he is a free spirit, never swayed by fads or gentility, and at peace with the beauty of nature, true to his California roots. Though far from a socialite, he cares deeply about the singers entrusted to him. His patience and self-control, he admits, is a work in progress with his flagship ensemble, even after twenty-two years. Stowe is humbled, in his words, by the "continual flow of ever-more talented, motivated, extraordinary young men who want to be part of this experience, who make it a place where still other such men want to be. Our Glee Club is both a destination and a journey."

SIX

Concerts at Home

These singing lads are good. So good they tour around the country. Alumni flock to hear their angelic voices and remember the good old days at Notre Dame. In order to have this privilege after you graduate, you must attend a Glee Club concert now, so you'll have something to be nostalgic about later.[1]

That was the recommendation from *Scholastic* in advance of a Glee Club concert on campus in the fall of 2002. Today, with dozens of official performing arts clubs on campus, and with hundreds of performances each year by local and visiting artists at the DeBartolo Performing Arts Center and other campus venues, the Glee Club's importance as an arts organization may go unnoticed. For all that has been said—and will be said—about the national and international travels of the ambassadorial chorus, the concert traditions of the Singing Irish arose on the grounds of the university, and there they grew through the decades. The Glee Club's on-campus appearances are at the heart of its organizational being, shared before audiences that know them and the school culture best. This chapter reviews some of the early campus appearances of the Glee Club, the Glee Club orchestra that shared its stage, the cycle of annual performances and venues, and notable collaborations with other ensembles in South Bend.

THE EARLY APPEARANCES: VAUDEVILLE AND ORCHESTRA

At the turn of the twentieth century, collegiate glee clubs were small social groups that gathered informally both to imbibe and to sing light musical material—in that order. Historian Jeremy Jones described a typical glee club of this time as "a drinking society with a singing problem."[2] When glee clubs appeared on stage, they mixed the popular genres of the day within a variety show format. Light entertainment ruled the day, for example in short comedic skits, impersonations, or popular numbers from Tin Pan Alley. Banjo and accordion accompaniment reinforced the "low" style of the material. At Notre Dame and other universities in small towns, students staged their own vaudeville shows because traveling troupes did not usually stop at these colleges. (Professional vaude-villians were also considered too earthy for young Catholic men.)

Before the official arrival of the Notre Dame Glee Club in 1915, the university glee club furnished an annual vaudeville show on campus. Between 1909 and 1911, rich descriptions survive, detailing the Glee Club's involvement in the yearly act. Their vaudeville shows steadily shed the image of the preceding era of blackface minstrelsy, offensive to modern taste though still quite popular a century ago. But remnants of the old stage tradition from the mid-nineteenth century, which saw white men apply burnt cork to their faces to imitate and lampoon black people, surfaced. Under the direction of Professor Carl Petersen, the Glee Club was to perform a vaudeville show in May 1909 in Washington Hall, after deciding against offering a minstrel show. The Club's repertoire featured "choice songs, both comic and sentimental," that had been rehearsed for weeks.[3]

Charles Butterworth

Walter O'Keefe

Concerts at Home

Among the novelties that have been forgotten about the early Glee Club concerts on campus is the presence of a jazz-type orchestra that performed regularly with it. Although the university orchestra was its own enterprise since the nineteenth century, it would become closely associated with the Glee Club on its tours by 1916.[4] By the next year, the *Dome* yearbook noted that the Club was unique among university musical organizations because it "was able to boast of its own orchestra."[5] The contingent of instrumentalists that played in Glee Club concerts varied. In 1919 and 1920, Glee Club's sidekick band—between twelve and twenty pieces—was known as the "Novelty Orchestra" under the direction of Charles Davis ('21).[6] By 1922, the term "Glee Club Orchestra" appeared with regularity.[7] Harry Denny ('20), a talented violinist and future professional bandleader, took charge of the group, whose featured instruments included the violin, trumpet, saxophone, trombone, euphonium, banjo, xylophone, and piano. A 1921 music department report described a fairly peripheral role for Denny's ensemble: the orchestra "furnished an opening overture and kept the audience well entertained during the intermission."[8]

At the same time, the "Glee Club Orchestra" was also known to play outside of Glee Club concerts. Not only could it present entertainment for post-concert dances, as it did in 1922, but the orchestra could also be hired independently of the Club.[9] That it was central to the Glee Club on the whole was unquestionable, however. *Scholastic* judged it to be a "thoroughly first-class orchestra," and the 1922 *Dome* yearbook raved about the orchestra's contribution to Glee Club programs, observing how it "burst forth in melodies, rhapsodies and harmonies characteristic of the world's best jazz artists."[10]

Instrumental groups accompanying Glee Club formal concerts are rarely mentioned after 1927. Besides later collaborations with the South Bend Symphony and a few appearances with the Notre Dame Band around football weekends, the only formal band or orchestra to accompany the Glee Club was a twelve-piece group led by Jack Molloy ('43), sometimes called "The Cavaliers." During World War II, the Club enlisted Molloy's band strictly for accompaniment on the lengthy piece *Song of the Free*, a nationalistic work for chorus and narrator that surveyed the history of American song, written by Glee Clubbers Felix Pogliano ('41) and John White ('41).[11] Glee Club members have also been deployed as solo instrumentalists in concerts on campus and on tour. Though today's Glee Club invariably engages individual instrumentalists only as part of choral works, the complexion of Glee Club programs through the 1950s permitted instrumental soloists to be featured, even in large-scale works. Cecil Alexander was a violinist who won acclaim for his solos in the late 1920s, while William Mooney, James C. Etling, and Richard Casper performed outstandingly as piano soloists, each having played the virtuosic music of Franz Liszt in Glee Club performances.[12]

> The Glee Club owes much of its success to the work of the Orchestra at all concerts, for the organization never failed to impart the old "N. D. pep."
>
> —*Dome* (1920)

Edouard Steinbrück, German, 1802–1882, *Adoration of the Magi* (detail), 1838. Purchased with funds provided by Mr. and Mrs. Robert L. Hamilton, Sr. Reprinted courtesy of the Snite Museum of Art, University of Notre Dame.

"ON CHRISTMAS NIGHT"
THE UNIVERSITY OF NOTRE DAME GLEE CLUB
CHRISTMAS CONCERT

CAMPUS CONCERTS: NUTS AND BOLTS

"Under the leadership of Mr. Ward Perrott, the University Glee Club made its first bow to the public last Saturday night. A select and qualified audience voted this first appearance a triumph."[13] With that description of a concert from December 11, 1915, an uninterrupted tradition of Glee Club performances took root. The event—three months in preparation—featured some fifty voices in the Glee Club, as well as contributions from the university orchestra and the mandolin club. The concert took place at Washington Hall, the center of performing arts activity on campus since the later nineteenth century. The program did not feature music for Advent or Christmas, as one might expect in December, but rather a variety of numbers mixing classical and lighter genres.

Today, the Notre Dame Glee Club presents four major campus concerts each year. These include a fall and spring formal concert at the DeBartolo Performing Arts Center, as well as a Christmas program before the end of the fall semester and a Commencement concert to close the academic year. Preparations for these concert offerings have always been extensive, as the Glee Club rehearsed daily for much of its history. In the early years, Washington Hall was the site of rehearsals held in the midday, yielding in the mid-1950s to practices in the early evening at a second-floor classroom in O'Shaughnessy Hall. The Crowley Hall of Music (formerly Hoynes Hall), the home of the music department, opened in 1976, and the Club rehearsed in that building until the new performing arts center offered a magnificent rehearsal space for the club in 2004—Penote Performer's Hall.

In the first generation of Glee Club activity, concert offerings on campus were far from predictable, but two formal programs seemed to be the norm. The first performance on campus fell between November and March in the academic year, and a Commencement concert followed in June.[14] Rosters took longer to form in those years, and broadcast appearances often occurred

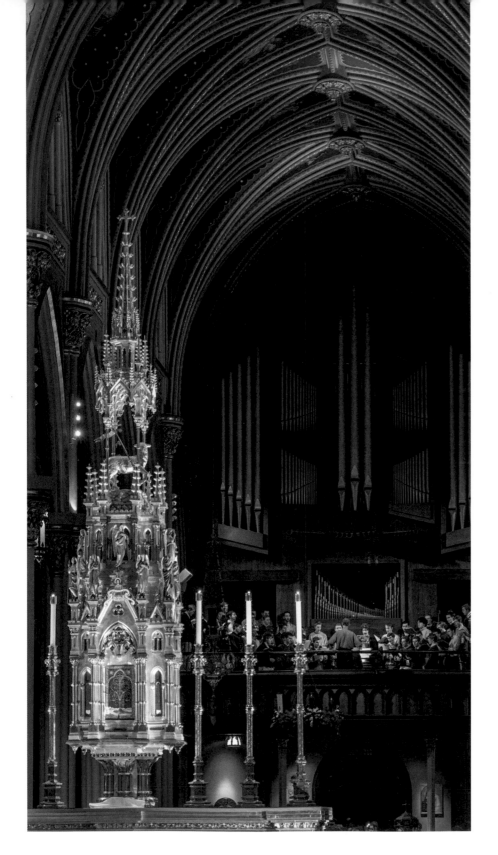

in the fall, pushing campus concerts relatively later in the year. In early 1930, following a fall semester that included radio appearances and other travel, *Scholastic* noted that the Glee Club declined offers to appear in other cities that year so that the ensemble could "spend the winter in preparation for the annual concert given here at the University."[15] An annual fall concert was presented consistently during the Pedtke years, with the date settled in October by the mid-1950s. By that time, the membership had increased to unprecedented numbers, and some concerts were reprised the following day to accommodate the crowds.[16] For all of these formal events, the young men characteristically dressed in tuxedos with white ties.[17]

Although Washington Hall remained the dominant venue, the Glee Club found other locations on campus or in South Bend to stage its formal performances in its century-long history. The group has occasionally offered concerts in the Basilica of the Sacred Heart, for instance, in 1973, 1996, and 2003.[18] "Concerts at the Basilica," Daniel Stowe remarked, "remain a treat, though they're much rarer now."[19] In the 1950s, the Club held some performances in the cavernous Navy Drill Hall, and it commonly appeared in Stepan Center—a multi-purpose, geodesic-domed building that stands on the northeast corner of campus. The giant facility could seat well over a thousand concert-goers, especially at Commencement and (beginning in the 1980s) at Christmastime, but this venue required amplification and elaborate staging. Another large performing space nearby was O'Laughlin Auditorium on the campus of St. Mary's College. Shortly after this 1,300-seat auditorium was built, Dean Pedtke led the Singing Irish in joint performances with the St. Mary's Glee Club in 1958, 1960, and 1961. Other South Bend venues attracted Glee Club programs in the 1920s, namely, St. Patrick Church and the big band dance hall known as the Palais Royale.[20]

Of the annual Glee Club concerts performed on campus, those at Christmas and Commencement have drawn the most at-

The annual Glee Club concert at Commencement was normally a time when the director visited with the parents and families of his singers. Dean Pedtke, in particular, cherished these moments. But in 1947, the director contracted rheumatic fever and was unable to direct the Commencement concert. Because of his absence, parents were invited to the Pedtke house to meet the conductor at his bedside. A large group arrived at the house. Helen Pedtke remembered, "It turned into a huge party." Following that episode, the Pedtkes began a tradition of inviting families to their house for a post-concert celebration. About two hundred people attended the gathering each Commencement weekend.

tention over the past century, both among students and in the press. Singing at the university's Commencement exercises is by far the oldest tradition of the Glee Club. In 1880, the Club performed with the Notre Dame Band in a Commencement concert, and in 1908, one finds the name of two pieces the group sang at the ceremony—Charles Gounod's two-part "Praise Ye the Lord" ("Laudate dominum") and a curious number that has escaped the repertoire of school songs, "Queen of the West, Notre Dame."[21] During the early Casasanta years,

the Glee Club sang with the Moreau Seminary Choir for the Baccalaureate Mass associated with Commencement, and the two groups also performed jointly that week in a send-off concert at Washington Hall.[22] A report of the 1956 Commencement concert revealed some surprising news about the attire of the Glee Club—they changed formal outfits from the first to the second half.

> The mood of the first half of the concert will be of a formal vein, with the Glee Club dressed in tails to present religious and serious numbers. The second half of the program will be more informal, with the members of the Glee Club dressed in blazers, presenting a humorous sketch of life here at Notre Dame.[23]

The large Commencement concerts were moved to Stepan Center in the 1960s and were still nearly filled to capacity, as many Notre Dame students and their parents flocked to hear the Glee Club one last time on campus.

Christmas concerts—though now a perennial event on the Glee Club calendar—were not held regularly until the late 1940s. In 1942, director Pedtke announced a special concert by the Club with seasonal favorites that was to be sung in Washington Hall, but this was not the start of an annual tradition.[24] The following year, the Club seems to have opted against a formal concert, instead electing to sing carols on Christmas Eve at individual dorms under Pedtke's supervision.[25] (Some students remained on campus for the Christmas holiday during the war.) In the succeeding years, a day of caroling inched earlier in the month of December. On December 14, 1945, for instance, *Scholastic* reported: "In accordance with a long-established custom, the entire Glee Club will tour the campus one night this coming week and sing familiar Christmas carols so much loved by everyone." Similarly in 1947, there is no mention of a formal Christmas concert, rather "the entire organization of 130 members [will] rove the campus, singing Christmas carols."[26] However, by the next year, a single campus concert by the Glee Club in December was described as "annual."[27] Demand was high for these Christmas concerts in Washington Hall, and by 1952 Pedtke offered two concerts instead of one to reduce what he called the "frustrated music-lovers" wishing to see the Glee Club for free.[28]

As with Commencement concerts, Glee Club Christmas programs outgrew Washington Hall. By the late 1980s, Carl Stam had to move the concerts to Stepan Center.[29] Two or three thousand could be expected in attendance at Stepan Center by 1990, and admission to the Christmas concert was no longer free. Many were still being turned away from Stepan Center, prompting a temporary move in 1992 to the Joyce Athletic and Convocation Center, the hockey arena in particular, a space that could hold up to five thousand people. This was also the same year that proceeds from ticket revenue were directed to South Bend's Center for the Homeless.[30] Glee Club Christmas concerts continue to benefit the Center for the Homeless, but earnings are also shared today with the Food Bank of Northern Indiana. The annual holiday concerts returned to Stepan Center from 1995 until 2003, and the Glee Club began to offer two performances of the program to accommodate the thousands of concert-goers, as Pedtke had done. Leighton Concert Hall at the DeBartolo Performing Arts Center now provides the Glee Club a world-class performing space for its Christmas concerts. With Leighton's nine hundred seats and no dip in interest from Notre Dame students and South Bend residents, the Club has presented *three* performances each year since 2010 to please the throngs.

CONCERTS IN MINIATURE

Formal or "mandatory" concerts on campus represent the fruit of the Glee Club rehearsals during the academic year. But they account for a small fraction of the total number of concerts offered during a given year. Concerts on national and international tours begin to fill in the picture of the Glee Club's concert life, but, in truth, it is the less ceremonial performances of the ensemble—whether for organized groups or for the public at large—that consume the Club week to week. Mini-concerts (or "minis") are naturally shorter than formal concerts, lasting from fifteen minutes to a half hour.[31] The group will almost always present lighter repertoire, including the alma mater and the "Victory March." One would never see a tuxedo-clad Clubber in a mini-concert; attire ranges from a blazer and tie to khakis and polo shirts, depending on the request. Mini-concerts encompass a wide range of presentations, from official university gatherings (for example, Junior Parents Weekend or freshman orientation) and pre-game football concerts to private alumni gatherings, Christmas caroling at dorms, and late-night serenades near the hallowed dome of the university's main building. Depending on the venue, the Glee Club may charge for its services, and the director will usually be present to lead a mini-concert when the stakes are high. A student director conducts in his absence. The full membership of the Glee Club is not expected to attend every "mini" accepted by the director or the officers, but neither will the group agree to perform in a private setting if a critical mass of singers cannot be assembled.

It is impossible to summarize the smaller events that have drawn Glee Club members into informal concerts in the past century. A few notable examples will have to suffice. An unusually formal instance of an informal concert occurred in the Casasanta years, when a forty-minute outdoor program was offered to the student body on the main quadrangle in May 1933. The music was uncharacteristically heavy, consisting of Latin motets, a "Gloria" by Charles Gounod, part-songs, and the "Victory March."[32] Of course,

not all of Casasanta's mini-concerts were so elaborate; in 1930, for example, his Singing Irish sang a short concert for the sisters and nurses of St. Joseph Hospital in South Bend, following the group's East Coast tour in the spring.[33] Goodwill concerts of this sort were quite common. The Club also sang for numerous events sponsored by the local chapter of the Knights of Columbus.

Ceremonies of any sort on campus could be enhanced with music from the Glee Club. They sang at the dedication of several campus buildings, such as O'Shaughnessy Hall (1953) and the Notre Dame Post Office (1967).[34] In 1975, President Gerald Ford received an honorary doctorate from Notre Dame, a ceremony that was accompanied by the Glee Club singing Jan Pieterszoon Sweelinck's "Arise, O Ye Servants of God."[35] Since the turn of the century, the Club has sung small concerts in the presence of major figures, often with music tailored to their interests. In February of 2000, the group performed a "mini" at the Union League of Chicago, attended by former president George H. W. Bush, who proudly stood when the group sang the fight song of the U.S. Naval Academy, "Anchors Aweigh." In July of that same year, a quartet of Glee Clubbers and director Daniel Stowe traveled to Washington, DC, to sing for a Congressional Medal ceremony honoring Fr. Theodore Hesburgh.[36] The Club at large was also invited to sing concerts on campus honoring Supreme Court Chief Justices William Rehnquist and John Roberts in 2002 and 2008, respectively.

Evening serenades are about as informal as small concerts can get. In the fall of 1991, a small group of Glee Club freshman would meet on Thursday nights, calling female students from the freshman directory. Joe Dziedzic, Sean O'Brien, Roderick O'Brien, and Joey Coleman (all class of 1995) hosted these sessions, phoning select individuals to sing the classic "Good Night Sweetheart" with the hopes of positive reactions. After a few weeks of making these "secret admirer" calls with singing, the group decided to invite these women to the Golden Dome to hear more singing at midnight. Rarely would the group be alone. Usually, a small crowd from five to twenty-five students would assemble in anticipation of the promised concert. After some love songs and school rah-rah songs, those gathered would disperse back to their dorms, though there was often conversation between the Clubbers and those invited by phone. This tradition carries the name "Troubadours" and is still very much alive today.

Among the Glee Club's smaller concert events, fundraisers were a specialty. In the late 1880s, more than one Glee Club concert was performed to benefit the "Football Association." A generation later, the group performed several benefit concerts under director John J. Becker in honor of various causes related to World War I. One particular Glee Club concert sung for the fallen heroes of the war garnered special attention because of the severe lack of student attendance at the event (and therefore lack of funds raised). A *Scholastic* reporter lamented:

> The University Glee Club gave a concert Sunday evening, but where was the University? . . . The point is that nobody was asked to support the Glee Club: they had volunteered for a purpose which any American worth his standing-room will eagerly support. It did not seem too much to demand that Johnny go marching off two years ago, but it does seem excessive to ask of certain Notre Dame men a few cents in memory of the lads who did not come back. . . . To the Glee Club we can merely extend our thanks for the valiant attempt to break the regrettable reserve which exists in these parts.[37]

Other fundraisers staged with Glee Club entertainment were more successful. In September 1953, Notre Dame football coach Frank Leahy requested that the Club perform at his home parish in Michigan City, with all proceeds directed to the church's benefit fund.[38] Mini-concerts have occasionally taken small groups of Glee Clubbers to more distant places for raising funds. In August 1977, thirteen singers flew to Greenville, South Carolina, to perform at the Rose Ball benefiting St. Francis Hospital. And in October 1989, the Archbishop of New York, John Cardinal O'Connor, invited twenty members of the Glee Club to the Big Apple to sing for a charity event that raised several million dollars for abused and battered women. The young men were thrilled to be staying at the luxurious Waldorf Astoria hotel as part of the trip.[39] A more recent and less formal fundraiser enriched by the strains of the Glee Club was the lighting of the Christmas tree at Carroll Hall, typically blessed by a priest on campus. At the fifth annual "Carroll Christmas" in 2002, attendees of the Glee Club–aided event were encouraged to donate books or toys for the charity Toys for Tots.[40]

JOINT VENTURES

It has already been mentioned that the Notre Dame Glee Club combined forces with choirs at St. Mary's College in the Pedtke years and with the Moreau Seminary Choir for some of the early Commencement concert offerings. The Club has, in fact, collaborated with many individuals and groups in its history. The St. Mary's Glee Club in particular was a frequent partner in Notre Dame Glee Club concerts from the middle of the twentieth century until the dawn of coeducation at the university, which coincided with the hiring of director David Clark Isele and the founding of the Notre Dame Chorale. The all-women's chorus at St. Mary's was a natural choice for the Glee Club to pursue traditional four-part music during Pedtke's term. The two ensembles teamed up to perform such classics as Bach's *Mass in B minor* (1950) and *Magnificat* (1958), Handel's *Messiah* (1957), and lesser-known works like Alan Hovhaness's *Magnificat* and Giuseppe Verdi's *Te Deum* (both in 1960). Members of the

two glee clubs also led a special community-based activity in the 1950s. The student councils of both Notre Dame and St. Mary's allocated funds for buses to drive singers and students from each campus around South Bend to carol together in December for the city's residents. In 1956, the buses shuttled student carolers, led by "clubbers" from both schools, to more than fifteen locations in the city to share musical good will with their fellow neighbors.[41] Recent collaborations have occurred between the Glee Club, Chorale, and the Women's Choir at St. Mary's, notably in a 2010 performance of *A German Requiem* by Johannes Brahms, dedicated to the memory of the longtime director of music at the Basilica of the Sacred Heart, Gail Walton.

In 1917, the glee club of the University of Chicago was scheduled to come to South Bend for a joint concert with the Notre Dame Glee Club, but plans were thwarted when members of the Chicago club were forced to cancel the event "on account of a quarantine."[42] The Notre Dame Glee Club has, however, participated in many successful joint concerts with choirs both on and away from campus. The University of Michigan Men's Glee Club—the second oldest glee club in the United States after that of Harvard University—has been a frequent partner for concerts, first visiting Notre Dame to perform jointly with Carl Stam's group in 1982, after which the Notre Dame Glee Club performed in Ann Arbor in 1987 and 1991.[43] In 2001, just days before the birth of Daniel Stowe's daughter, the Glee Club again traveled to the University of Michigan for a joint program, and the rival glee club again returned the favor with concerts in 2007 and 2012 at the DeBartolo Performing Arts Center.[44] Stowe remarked, "They've always brought out the best in us." Jerry Blackstone, who conducted the Michigan Men's Glee Club from 1988 to 2002, remembers the Notre Dame Glee Club as having "high musical standards, beautiful singing, and warm camaraderie" in his several encounters with the group. The military academies have also combined with the Notre Dame Glee Club in well-received concert appearances. The Men's Glee Club of the United States Naval Academy collaborated with the Notre Dame Glee Club in 2000, 2005, and 2010, while the West Point Glee Club, a choir of mixed voices, visited campus in 2006, an event attended by the Secretary of the United States Army.[45]

In the spring of 1960, the combined glee clubs of Notre Dame and St. Mary's College sang a pair of concerts—one on each campus—featuring Gabriel Fauré's *Requiem*.[46] The group numbered 180 voices and was accompanied by an orchestra, principally members of the South Bend Symphony. The Glee Club has shared the stage with the South Bend Symphony on several occasions. One early appearance was the symphony's final performance of the 1945–46 season, as the Glee Club sang Randall Thompson's *The Testament of Freedom* in Notre Dame's Navy Drill Hall. A faculty member at the University of Virginia, Thompson set this work for male chorus and orchestra to honor the bicentennial of the birth of that university's founder, Thomas Jefferson.[47] Thompson's work was not conducted by Dean Pedtke but rather by Edwyn Hames, who led the South Bend Symphony for forty years. The Club sang with the South Bend Symphony Orchestra again in the spring of 1954, this time at the auditorium of John Adams High School in South Bend.[48] Later works that the chorus performed with the South Bend Symphony Orchestra (sometimes joined by local choirs) under maestro Tsung Yeh include Beethoven's *Symphony No. 9* (1988), Schoenberg's *A Survivor from Warsaw* (1996, with Daniel Stowe as narrator), and Benjamin Britten's *War Requiem* (2013). Various patriotic pieces were billed in a 2006 Veteran's Day program, in which the Club and orchestra were joined by the St. Mary's College Women's Choir and the Notre Dame marching band's brass section.[49]

POSTSCRIPT: CONCERTS WITH SPECIAL MEANING

One of the most poignant "concerts at home" benefitted one of the Glee Club's own members. Senior Club member Cole Barker was diagnosed with a malignant brain tumor and withdrew from the university in the fall of 2004. The officers of the Glee Club took action for their friend in the only way they knew how—through song. On April 10, 2005, the ensemble honored Barker through a special concert entitled "Brothers in Song: A Benefit Concert." Glee Club president Paul Sifuentes captured the Club's sentiment: "We have a gift in our music and our song, and we wanted to use these gifts to show Cole how much we appreciate him and that we will always support him. A benefit concert in his name seemed like the perfect idea."[50] Barker, his parents, and his brother attended the event at the De-Bartolo Performing Arts Center, which included a set of the senior's favorite songs and spoken words by cancer survivors. More than five hundred people attended the concert, and more than $10,000 was raised to support Barker's treatment and to donate to the American Cancer Society. The senior made remarks at the conclusion of the concert and proudly conducted the ensemble in the university's alma mater. The Glee Club members ended the production by giving their friend a bag of hair that they had shaved from their own heads to show solidarity with their colleague. Barker was told he had no more than six months to live in 2004, but he courageously returned to Notre Dame to graduate in 2006. He battled cancer valiantly for six years, succumbing to the disease in 2010.

Cole Barker

For more than a hundred years, the Glee Club has remained an organization constantly in motion around campus and in South Bend more generally. The group continues to be invited to perform at both momentous and casual celebratory events and has been a frequent collaborator with choruses and ensembles throughout its history. One final example—another collaborative venture with the South Bend Symphony Orchestra—shows the ensemble's commitment to community engagement. Nearly ten years after the terror attacks in the United States on September 11, 2001, the Glee Club sang in the world premiere of *Requiem for the Innocent*, a memorial for victims of terrorism around the world and an affirmation of a unified humanity more broadly. The composer, Jorge Muñiz, a professor at Indiana University at South Bend, was a direct witness to events of September 11, 2001, when he was a student at the Manhattan School of Music; as a Spaniard, he also experienced terrorism in his native land. The unique experience for the Glee Clubbers brought them in contact not only with a monumental modern work with political force, but also with four other local choirs (including the Shout for Joy Children's Chorus) that were required to execute the hour-long piece of seven movements.[51] In this civic display of unity, in this moment of shared humanity through music, the Glee Club was not the featured performer, but part of something bigger, a refreshing position no doubt for Notre Dame's prized musical ambassadors.

SEVEN

Touring Life

BEYOND THE DOME

One of the reasons that the Glee Club origins have been marked in 1915 is because that academic year (1915–16) featured the first coordinated arrangements for appearances away from campus. George Shanahan and Richard Daley were elected assistant business managers of the group in that year and were charged with helping Glee Club vice president Harold McConnell with plans for out-of-town engagements.[1] Predictably, the Club did not venture far from South Bend in the early years, making run-out concerts to nearby Michigan City, Indiana, and St. Joseph, Michigan.[2] But audiences were eager to hear this traveling ensemble. A concert in Indianapolis in the spring of 1916 boasted an audience of two thousand, including the local bishop, the city mayor, and the state governor.[3]

Over time, the Singing Irish brought their music regularly to the Chicago area while also reaching toward the East Coast in the 1930s. Today, the Glee Club enjoys global touring opportunities that are rare among collegiate or even professional music ensembles. This chapter explores the nuts and bolts of Glee Club touring before fixing the spotlight on several tours—both domestic and international—that either shaped the group's identity or became legendary in the history of the ensemble.

ANATOMY OF A TOUR

Small scale, local gigs were the norm for the Glee Club before 1920, but brief weekend trips were soon supplemented in the mid-1920s by more extended tours around the Easter holiday and during the winter break following exams in the later part of January. In 1924 during the term of director J. Lewis Browne, *Scholastic* noted, "It is the intention of Dr. Browne and the officers of the Club to book concerts in some of the large cities of the middle West, as separate week-end trips, independent of the long tour to be taken during the Easter vacation."[4] The winter tour between semesters and the Easter tour were still common in the 1950s.

A Thanksgiving tour of less than a week was added to the Glee Club tour schedule in the 1960s and early '70s. By this time, the break around the Easter holiday was distinct from a full-fledged spring break. The university's fall hiatus also became an opportunity for touring in the years under director David Isele, though weekend gigs, even around Thanksgiving, were not uncommon. For fall and spring tours at that time, the administration could allow the Glee Club extra days off to complete its travels; hence, one witnesses tours of eleven or twelve days in the itineraries. As the winter break between semesters moved earlier in January, the Notre Dame Chorale, established during Isele's time, traveled during this interval and therefore did not intersect with the Glee Club's touring schedules.

Once a travel window was known, the business manager—in consultation with the Glee Club president and director—worked closely with prospective cities to develop a list of stops. Not only Notre Dame alumni clubs but also Knights of Columbus chapters ("councils") were the primary sponsors of tour concerts. The business manager then partnered with host cities to generate hype for the event and to ensure that the group's accommodations were under control. The university did not set aside funding for the Club's tours, so it was imperative that these trips at least broke even.[5] That the Glee Club financed its own tours did not diminish its standing among similar groups around the country. A 1955 meeting of the National Intercollegiate Choral Association found that, of the nation's forty-five collegiate glee clubs, only two—Purdue and Notre Dame—operated with a budget of over $10,000 per year.[6] Still, no chances could be taken with the sponsors of planned tours, and no stone was left unturned to guarantee financial success at each venue. A brochure given to host cities in 1950 shows the unusual detail that the Glee Club shared with its presenters, from anticipated cash flow to a series of press releases that publicized the event in the month leading up to the concert.

Host cities often used Glee Club concerts as fundraisers. Once the choir's concert fee was met, remaining funds were profit for the sponsoring organization. A letter from a 1954 tour program in Springfield, Illinois, explains the financial rewards of hosting the Singing Irish on its travels:

> Just in case somebody wonders why we brought the University of Notre Dame Glee Club back to Springfield for the third time, I'll give you the reasons. First, we consider them to be the best college Glee Club in the nation. This should surprise no one—they have the habit of producing champions at N.D.! Secondly, let's face it—we sponsor this concert to make money for the growing program of our parish! We know that the Glee Club can be sold and that those who buy will be more than satisfied. And yet—and here is the point—we do not have to give Notre Dame 90% of the gate [concert revenue]! We are able to make a modest and satisfactory profit.[7]

Not unlike any collegiate touring ensemble, the Glee Club worked with sponsoring towns to arrange smooth accommodations upon its arrival. Dinner was often provided by the hosting organization, and lodging with host families was typically assigned for the evening. Nights in hotels are rare on domestic tours. Group activities before an evening concert can range from school appearances to free time to explore local points of interest.[8] Particularly enthusiastic host cities have bestowed special proclamations on the Glee Club or provided it "keys to the city" as a gesture of welcome.[9] The group's token of gratitude to host cities in the last half century has been a framed picture of the "Glee Club caricature," a whimsical black-and-white drawing of a few men in tuxedos made by member Ivan Osorio ('60), autographed by the current members of the ensemble.

A major consideration in Glee Club touring is the traveling roster of singers. Club tours through the end of Dean Pedtke's term averaged just under forty singers, with higher numbers in the 1930s and '40s. Touring members were selected from the general roster, which swelled to more than one hundred singers in the years after World War II. Freshmen rarely made the tour roster, though if one were a first tenor, there was a chance of being selected to travel. Baritones, always heavier in supply, could expect to journey

only once in their sophomore year. The mid-semester tour in January 1948 was exceptional, with sixty singers making the trip in what were described as "nice, big, shower-less buses."[10] The 1960s and '70s witnessed tour rosters between thirty-four and thirty-seven, but the size of the buses increased in the 1980s, allowing for rosters of over forty singers in director Stam's tenure, still a number whittled down from a larger group. Daniel Stowe, however, has extended tour privileges to nearly all singers at the outset, and the traveling roster routinely exceeds sixty members.

The preferred mode of transportation has naturally shifted over a century of Club history. Trains were the primary means of hauling the Glee Club around the Midwest and East Coast in the early years through director

NOTRE DAME GLEE CLUB

Southwestern Tour ----- Itinerary

January 26 to February 6

January 26: Board the bus at the Music Hall at 2:00 P.M. Remember your toothbrush and snake bite medicine. (Somebody make sure Al Gavan is aboard -- He's got the money.)

January 27: Arrive in Leavenworth, Kansas about 8:00 A.M. Concert at 10:00 at Xavier College. No Tails. Another concert in the evening (In tails) in Kansas City. Overnite accomodations at Pedtke's Pool Emporium (35¢ a nite)

January 28: Mosey around Kansas City--You should find everything up-to-date there. (Good dinners at the Paul Owens Memorial Bar & Grill, 134 So. Skid Row) Get to bed early.

January 29: Sunday. Get to mass early and leave at 9:00 A.M. A mere 408 mile drive to Little Rock, Arkansas. We'll stay overnite someplace in Little Rock (At the Rock?)

January 30: Monday. Enjoy your breakfast in bed while you can. Board the bus at 10:00 and drive to Greenville, Mississis-issippippi. Overnite stay at the Hotel Greenville (Down the road apiece from GAVAN'S Bar & Grille.)

January 31: Tuesday evening is the Greenville concert. Get to bed early; we leave for Houston at 6:00 A.N.

February 1: Concert in Houston. Stay overnite at the Rice Hotel and leave about 10:00 A.M. Enjoy your sleep; it may be your last.

February 2: Concert in Corpus Christi. Either get to bed early, or don't bother going to bed at all. (Who do you know in town?) We leave at 5:00 A.M. sharp. That's A.M., son; Morning!

February 3: Arrive in San Antonio, Texas in time for a morning concert. Another concert in the evening; a few short ones; and off early in the morning. (Someboyd remember to wake Al Gavan)

February 4: Drive, drive, drive, and drive, to St. Louis. 1043 miles!

February 5: Arrive in St. Louis in time for mass Sunday morning and a little sleep in the afternoon. (Stop in at Pedtke's Bar & Grill before the concert.) We leave right after the concert. Carry your own snake bite medicine--no time for partying! Long overnite drive to South Bend, Indiana (A few blocks from Paul Owens Memorial Bar & Grill.)

February 6: As soon as we arrive at school, pick up your class cards & pencil boxes and rush off to class, kiddies, ---- you're late!!!!

NOTE: Texas is half-dry. That means they don't serve mixed drinks in the bars. You bring your own bottle and they sell you a "set-up".

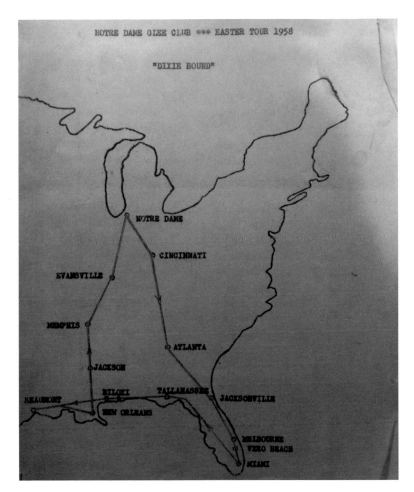

NOTRE DAME GLEE CLUB *** EASTER TOUR 1958

"DIXIE BOUND"

Casasanta's term. The Glee Club still toured by rail in the early 1950s, for instance in a journey to California during the winter break of 1952. On that trip, the accompanying tour chaplain, Rev. Charles Carey, C.S.C, set up a portable altar for the celebration of Mass in the coach car as the train made a stop in Denver.[11]

Chartered buses entered the picture in the Pedtke era, and Indiana Motor Bus remained a preferred carrier of the Glee Club for more than two decades. Letter writing and diary entries were popular diversions for those on the bus in the earlier days. Idle chatter, singing, and horseplay have never gone out of style. Special folding "jumpseats" were noted in a bus from 1950 that made playing card games (like Bridge, Whist, Hearts, Euchre, and Spades) quite easy. Walkmans (personal cassette players with headphones) were popular on the bus in the late 1970s, along with simple electronic games and cell phones in later decades. Activities in the back of the bus ("BOB") were notoriously questionable, and the restroom in the rear was known as "The Animal." It was best to not approach it unless absolutely

Dick Aust

necessary. On the other hand, Club members on tour viewed the front of the bus as a more pristine haven for quiet activities and conversation. Glee Club chaplains touring with the group, such as Fr. Daniel O'Neil (1960s) and Fr. Robert Griffin (1970s through the early 1990s) often occupied a seat in the front of the bus and were visited by members with more serious things on their minds. The director also would be seated near the front, though since 1999 Daniel Stowe has opted to trail the tour bus in a rental car.

The drivers from Indiana Motor Bus vied for the chance to travel with the Glee Club on its tours. For nearly a decade (1957–66), a driver by the name of Dick Aust—described as "legendary" by Glee Clubber John E. Fisher ('65)—transported the Club thousands of miles in a vehicle that was sometimes branded with the group's name on the side. Aust not only shuttled the young men around the country but also faithfully attended its concerts. He typically stood in the back of the performing space during Glee Club tour programs and would sometimes make mocking gestures that provided levity for the group on stage. That Aust returned for a reunion of the Glee Club in the early 1970s speaks to the high esteem with which members held their loyal bus driver.

Beneath the bus were the risers on which Glee Clubbers stood for concerts. In the days when upperclassmen represented the majority of touring members, a group of eight (then called the "stand detail") was appointed to move the heavy risers from the bus to the concert space at each stop. When underclassmen began to travel more regularly in the 1980s and onward, service on the so-called "stand crew" was a rite of passage for the young singers and "rookies," symbolically reminding them of their status in the organization. Within the last few years, Daniel Stowe eliminated the use of risers on tour, not only because the size of the traveling group had ballooned but also because many venues (often churches) had a set of stairs that served the same purpose.

The group has visited the forty-eight contiguous states and countries in both hemispheres.[12] In the Casasanta and early Pedtke years, domestic tours were concentrated in the Midwest and on the East Coast, but the later Pedtke years, and those under Isele, Stam, and Stowe, featured more balanced coverage of the United States. Since the Glee Club draws its membership from a wide geographic area, it is not uncommon to plan a tour stop in a singer's hometown. In the winter tour of 1925, for example, the group performed in Escanaba in Michigan's Upper Peninsula, the hometown of its business manager, Victor Lemmer ('26). According to a post-tour roundup in *Scholastic*, the city was "practically turned over to the Glee Club," as they had a toboggan party, several side trips, and a lavish banquet, in addition to the concert they were to perform.[13] Since the term of director Douglas Belland (1979–81), members whose towns are visited by the Glee Club are offered the chance to conduct the ensemble in the singing of the university's alma mater "Notre Dame, Our Mother."

Of all the listeners away from campus touched by the power of the Glee Club's music, none were more central at the outset than those found in Chicago. The Windy City and its suburbs hosted dozens of Glee Club appearances and deserve pride of place in this touring review. Select domestic tours and international trips that brought the group new fame will also be highlighted. By no means is this an attempt to capture the full extent and meaning of the Glee Club's travels; rather, it is a modest effort to focus on some key excursions that exemplify the spirit of the ensemble when it left the confines of Notre Dame and spread the good name of the university to the world in song.

JAUNTS TO THE WINDY CITY

The Glee Club has made near-annual trips to Chicago throughout its history. In the 1920s and early '30s, the Windy City was a destination for nationwide radio broadcasts and appearances in studios for recording phonograph albums. However, the Club's first journey to Chicago—expected to be a triumph—was almost a tragedy. On the day after Easter in 1917, a fifty-voice Glee Club and its eponymous orchestra, under the direction of

One never knows what kind of audience the Glee Club will encounter in its tour concerts. At a performance for the annual Universal Notre Dame night at Chicago's Palmer House in the spring of 1941, the Glee Club sang *Song of the Free*, a survey of American history and song with narration, written by two senior English majors in the group, Jack White and Felix Pogliano. White narrated the work that evening, and his delivery was evidently so crisp that it caught the attention of the staff of Chicago's WLS radio, who were in attendance. On the spot after the performance, White was offered a position to work at the station.

Samuel Ward Perrott, performed at Chicago's Orchestra Hall, which was followed by a highly touted dance at the Congress Hotel, sponsored by alumnae of St. Mary's College. After a stop in suburban Elgin on the same trip, the Glee Club avoided a potentially deadly disaster. Traveling at a high speed aboard a train on the Chicago and Elgin Electric line, the car carrying the Club collided with a loaded coal car at a switch. Members were shaken up from the impact, and one student suffered an eye injury from flying glass, but no other major injuries were reported.[14]

Since director J. Lewis Browne lived in Chicago and commuted to Notre Dame, it comes as no surprise that the Glee Club made more than a few appearances in Chicago during his tenure at some of the city's historic arts institutions. In May 1925, the Club performed a concert under Browne's direction in connection with the Commencement exercises of Chicago's De La Salle Institute. The program was given at the Auditorium Theater in the city's Loop, and the Club was joined by soprano Sara McCabe, who had been featured in performances with the Glee Club in Chicago and in South Bend.[15] A year later, the group returned to Orchestra Hall in a concert jointly conducted by Browne and his protégé Joseph Casasanta. Sara McCabe again appeared in the concert, along with violinist Wally Heymar.[16]

In the time of Casasanta, the Glee Club made annual appearances in Chicago between 1927 and 1930, often in local radio studios for national broadcast on major networks. The director was able to arrange large groups to travel to the city, including as many as seventy students in 1936 for a radio broadcast on the network of the Mutual Broadcasting Company.[17] In the Pedtke era (and mainly after World War II), the Club sang more "occasional" concerts for a wide variety of sponsoring organizations in Chicago, both charitable and corporate types. Among the hosts who invited the Club to perform were the National Council of Catholic Women (1938), the Illinois Athletic Club (1951), the National Conference of Christians and Jews (1950, 1951), Independent Telephone Convention (1954), and the Inter-Racial Council of Chicago (1956).

The Glee Club saturated the city of Chicago with appearances in the 1950s, including one of the largest attended events in the group's history on February 20, 1950, at the Chicago Stadium. On that night, forty singers under Pedtke's direction sang in a concert sponsored by the Dominican Fathers. The event featured an all-star cast of American entertainers, including Ann Blyth, Jimmy Durante, Claude Kirschner, Phil Reagan, and Pat O'Brien, who had played the title character in the Notre Dame–inspired film *Knute Rockne All American* (1940). It was reported that twenty thousand people attended this event in Chicago, easily the largest audience to hear the Glee Club live in a single concert to that point.[18]

Following the performance at Chicago Stadium, the Glee Club was whisked to a dinner at the all-female Rosary College (now Dominican University) in the western suburb of River Forest. The Club's interactions with Rosary College in general represent the most important partnership with a Chicago institution in the ensemble's history. Between 1942 and 1957, Rosary College hosted the Glee Club for concerts and for joint

Concert with the Rosary College Glee Club

performances on multiple occasions. The women's college was the first tour stop, for instance, on the Glee Club's itinerary after the end of World War II. According to a post-concert review, "The audience was most enthusiastic, applauding ceaselessly and demanding several encores. Before the concert, the guests were entertained by the young ladies of the college." In 1947 and 1948, the Notre Dame Glee Club combined with the Rosary Glee Club for performances at the luxurious Grand Ballroom of Chicago's Hotel Stevens (now Hilton Chicago) before crowds of at least a thousand people.[19] Other times, the two choirs met to perform on the Rosary campus in River Forest. In December 1949, the Glee Club met the Rosary club at WMAQ studios in Chicago's Merchandise Mart to record a program of Christmas music to be broadcast nationwide on Christmas Eve.[20]

Since the arrival of director David Isele in 1973, Chicago has continued to play host to the Glee Club for media appearances, tour concerts, or short run-out events. In 1973 and 1975, the Club sang on the variety show *Kennedy & Company*. In 1976, they performed at a convention of the fraternal organization known as the Sons of the Wabash. Isele completed an arrangement of "On the Banks of the Wabash" at the request of the event organizers. In the 1980s, the country's biggest alumni club—the Notre Dame Club of Chicago—invited the Glee Club to sing for its annual Christmas Mass and brunch in December. Given the time of year, this appearance would sometimes involve a subset of singers; nevertheless, the gig became a welcome run-out tradition. For the 1993–94 academic year, the Glee Club had its touring privileges suspended because of a violation of student conduct. This caused Daniel Stowe to decline the annual invitation from the alumni club of Chicago. Though it has not been asked back to the yearly Chicago Christmas event, the Glee Club has still found ways to penetrate the Chicago area with its music in the last two decades, often exploring suburban venues through connections with its own members.[21]

DOMESTIC TOUR HIGHLIGHTS

The Notre Dame Glee Club has made its mark with alumni and general audiences well beyond the Chicago area, visiting all sections of the country with equity, particularly in the last three decades. Like any choir on tour, the Club returns from its trips with vivid memories, strengthened friendships, and new audiences. While it is a daunting task to select certain tours to accent in this survey of touring life, several domestic ventures stand out in Glee Club history that deserve mention.

The two-week winter excursion at the turn of the 1927 calendar year was no ordinary tour of the East. After leaving on a train bound for Erie, Pennsylvania, the forty-person Club gave concerts in western Pennsylvania and western New York before heading to Boston for the weekend. On New Year's Day, the group gathered in the studios of WEEI, New England's widest-reaching radio station, to perform a program of forty-five minutes preceding the Rose Bowl game between Stanford and Alabama. The Club's radio airtime was not finished for the day. That evening, the group's performance was rebroadcast with a nationwide hookup, fol-

UNIVERSITY OF NOTRE DAME GLEE CLUB AFTER VISITING PRESIDENT COOLIDGE JAN 7th 1927 WASH, D.C.

lowing a concert by famous Irish tenor John McCormack. Director Casasanta had already organized several radio appearances in Chicago for national broadcast, so this exposure was not groundbreaking in itself. Nor were the concerts to follow in the New York metropolitan area and in Philadelphia. What made the tour "the greatest trip any Notre Dame musical organization has ever taken" was the chance to visit the White House in the company of sitting President Calvin Coolidge.

At noon on January 7, the young men from Notre Dame were each able to shake the hand of Coolidge in a quiet ceremony that evidently did not include singing. The meeting was arranged by the president's private secretary Everett Sanders. Senator James E. Watson, who had received an honorary Doctor of Laws from Notre Dame, introduced the Glee Club to Coolidge. That evening, the Club performed in the auditorium of the opulent Mayflower Hotel in Washington, DC. In attendance were three U.S. senators, Supreme Court Justice Pierce Butler; Charles Lyons, the president of Georgetown University; and Delia Field, wife of American retailing icon Marshall Field.[22] Credit for this opportunity was due not only to Casasanta but also to business manager Andrew Mulreany. Mulreany's business acumen was also on display for the following year's breathtaking six-thousand-mile tour to the American West and South in which the Club appeared before more than

twenty thousand people, but never again would the Club perform before as many dignitaries as it did that day in 1927.[23]

The Glee Club benefited from the increased radio exposure and a twelve-minute film made during the 1928 tour. Travels in 1930 and 1933 exemplified the advancing commercial profile for the ensemble, one that set it apart from peer glee clubs. The Easter tour of 1930 was not remarkable for its stops in New Jersey, Pennsylvania, and western New York (including Niagara Falls): singing in small cities in these states was the norm on tours of the East Coast. What was extraordinary was how the group triumphed on the Broadway stage in New York City's theater district. The thirty-four traveling members of the Glee Club appeared in *twelve* concerts during the four-day Easter holiday at the massive Hippodrome Theatre, one of the world's largest metropolitan theaters of the time. A prospect like this could only have succeeded with the help of an agent, and indeed the Club collaborated with a partner from the Radio-Keith-Orpheum circuit to manage the run of shows and to take care of the group's expenses. The result of the four-day stop in New York was awe-inspiring in the context of Glee Club history. Packed houses three times per day at the Hippodrome Theater meant that well over sixty thousand people encountered Casasanta's Singing Irish in these concerts.[24]

The director's dreams for the group did not stop there, as Casasanta set his sights on the most ambitious travel itinerary in the Club's annals: an exceptional twelve-week tour of the East in the summer of 1933. Forgoing traditional sponsors such as the Knights of Columbus and again seizing the power of stage production syndicates, the Notre Dame Glee Club sustained its touring activities that summer by attracting thousands not to churches but to theaters. A select group of thirty Glee Club members left campus on June 3 and headed to Washington, DC, for the group's opening concerts. They planned no fewer than three weeks of performances in New York City, before circling back to the Midwest and then venturing on to the West Coast. These extensive travels, arranged by a professional touring agent from Chicago, took Casasanta's Club to city opera and play houses on two chartered Pullman cars, each branded with "The University of Notre Dame Glee Club."[25] No domestic tour, before or since, has run even half as long as this one.

On the dizzying summer tour of 1933, Radio-Keith-Orpheum, Loews, and Lyceum were among the syndicates that picked up the Glee Club, often for a week at a time. The group performed on a double or triple bill with other variety show performers of the day, and the marketing machines of the companies ensured strong advertising and concert reviews of these events. Amid the shuttling around the Eastern seaboard, the group was able to appear on several radio broadcasts and to film another short for Vitaphone entitled "Hot Pepper Novelties." For all of the hype of this summer odyssey, expenses outpaced revenues, and the Club was forced to release more than a dozen members at the tour's midpoint.[26] As the theater circuits that they performed on were considered low entertainment, being regarded as stage performers—and unprofitable stage performers to boot—probably caused some lowering of the Glee Club's stature with the university's academic vice president Fr. John O'Hara, a strict moralist who would become president the following year. O'Hara would rein in the Glee Club tour schedules for

With the Eastern approbations still ringing in their ears, the songsters invaded the South and took Nashville faster than Grant took Richmond. It was the same story everywhere the men went: "…a distinctly superior group of singers, welded together by the skill of a director who knows and loves his music, the Notre Dame men gave a program that will be remembered for some time …"

—*Scholastic* (1947)

the next five years until Daniel Pedtke took over the direction of the Club and former Clubber Fr. Hugh O'Donnell became university president. In 1940, prefect of discipline Fr. James Trahey wrote to Pedtke that he was impressed by the higher tone and quality of performances and that touring outside the Midwest would once more be permitted.[27]

Domestic touring was limited for the years spanning World War II. An entry for the Glee Club in the *Dome* yearbook of 1943 explained the lid on Glee Club travel: "War demands didn't permit frequent or long trips, and the major portion of the Glee Club's activities were confined to South Bend, except for one trip to Elkhart."[28] The travel radius expanded east and south by the late 1940s after the war's end. The year 1949 marked the Glee Club's first trip to the Deep South and on to South Florida, as well as its return to New York City for the first of seven consecutive Easter Sunday appearances on Ed Sullivan's *Toast of the Town* television program.

Stories of two trips in the 1950s have been told and retold in Glee Club history. The first occurred on an excursion to Philadelphia where the Club had the honor of being the first university chorus to appear in the city's annual music festival. On June 12, 1953, the young men appeared in Municipal Stadium (later John F. Kennedy Stadium) in a charity performance before more than eighty thousand people. Ed Sullivan personally recommended the Glee Club to the organizers of this star-studded musical event. Pedtke's Club was featured along with singer-actress Jeanette McDonald, singer Eddie Fisher, actor José Ferrer, and conductor Arthur Fiedler, who directed Philadelphia's Robin Hood Dell Orchestra.[29] It is safe to say that the Glee Club performed for its largest live audience that day.

The second epic journey of the 1950s was a five-thousand-mile Easter tour of the West and Southwest in 1957, planned as a result of losing their commitment from Ed Sullivan's show. However, the Glee Club continued to rub elbows with Hollywood stars. A special concert at the Los Angeles Philharmonic Hall featured the group with actress Erin O'Brien and singer-actress Ann Blyth, with whom the Club had performed in Chicago Stadium in 1950. They made a guest appearance on the CBS daytime series *The Bob Crosby Show* during this tour, and the trip included a diversion to the newly built Disneyland.[30] Stops in Denver, Las Vegas, Phoenix, Gallup, Amarillo, Tulsa, and St. Louis rounded off this extensive spring trek, in some ways reminiscent of the long journey made in 1928 by Casasanta's Club.[31]

It is hard to imagine a tour like that of 1957 could take place on a school break and without recourse to air travel. Besides an ad hoc trip to California for a spot on the *Andy Williams Show* in 1966, the Glee Club did not travel by plane domestically until 1975 when it flew from Chicago to Denver to begin a West Coast tour. Air transportation was essential by 1985, for the longest domestic tour since 1933. Carl Stam's Glee Club began its spring break by flying from Chicago to Jackson, Mississippi, for a one-time program with that city's orchestra.[32] From Jackson they flew to Dallas and then to Phoenix for a performance. The group then drove to Riverside, California, for the first of eight days in the Golden State. Within a day, the bus transported the group to San Francisco for a concert at one of the largest performance venues in the United States, the San Francisco War Memorial and Performing Arts Center. The group returned south to the Los Angeles metropolitan area with concerts in Burbank and Anaheim, as well as a run-out to San Diego between these stops. After a choral master-class at Loyola Marymount University, the Glee Club sang a concert in Las Vegas, rode the bus the next day to Phoenix, and flew to Chicago via Cincinnati. This particular escapade represents an exhilarating (or exhausting) two weeks in Glee Club tour history.

Whirlwind tours and brimming audiences aside, perhaps the most meaningful and poignant Glee Club journey was to New York City just five weeks after the September 11, 2001, terror attacks on the World Trade Center towers. The Club's fall break tour of that year had many stops that were little changed from tours of the past: a visit to the Liberty Bell in Philadelphia, a concert at the all-women's Immaculata College, a day at Niagara Falls, and a walk on Broadway. But nothing would compare to the concert they gave at the Church of St. Peter in Staten Island, New York, on October 25 to raise money for the Twin Towers Fund, a charity to benefit the families of first responders who died on September 11. The Club's pre-concert visit, with hard hats, to a viewing area of Ground Zero reopened the emotional wounds of 9/11 and reminded the young men of the rawness felt by the victims' families who would be in attendance that night.[33] The concert venue was just down the street from the stadium of the Staten Island Yankees, which was transformed into a morgue to receive bodies from Lower Manhattan. The adjacent Staten Island Ferry shuttled rescue workers in and out of the World Trade Center site.

The Church of St. Peter was set up with broadcast equipment to air the Glee Club's performance on public radio. At the beginning of the concert, the ensemble was escorted to the front of the church by New York Police Department bagpipes. Glee Club business manager Chris Clement ('02) distinctly remembers that "cheers from the crowd, even before the concert really began, showed their relief at being able to do something 'normal.'"[34] The crowd that evening was so large that the back doors of the church had to be opened for overflow. The first half of the program concluded with Franz Biebl's stirring "Ave Maria" for two choirs, followed by a special presentation of Big Apple lapel pins for the Glee Club members, which they donned for every concert in the year 2001–02.[35] During the performance, several firefighters in the audience were called away for an emergency, but a fire truck—a potent symbol of September 11—pulled up to the church at the end of the evening with those who were forced to leave the concert. The firefighters returned to thank the Glee Club for its charity.[36]

Rudy Reyes ('03), wrote in a 2002 Glee Club Alumni newsletter about his experience in a New York concert after September 11: "We had work to do: this was our own tribute—all that we could do as musicians—our hymn of praise, our song of thanksgiving for the brave of New York's police and fire department.... It was the group's finest hour, sharing in the sorrow of those who most closely felt the tragedy of that horrible day in September by bringing our treasure of joy in music. That would, though, seem to be what the group does best. What a privilege; what a humbling honor."

The Glee Club returned to Ground Zero in the fall of 2004, singing "America the Beautiful" and "The Star-Spangled Banner" at a firehouse in Lower Manhattan that lost its crew on September 11. The group also revisited the Church of St. Peter before a crowd that remembered the group well for the moving performance it gave three years previously. Even a third visit to Ground Zero in 2010, to see the progress in reconstruction, was an emotional experience for the sixty young men, though none of them were the same as those who first came in 2001 when air was filled with dust and debris.

INTERNATIONAL ESCAPADES

In 1928, the Yale Glee Club was the first American university chorus to travel overseas. Others would follow after World War II, such as the University of Michigan Men's Glee Club in 1955. Despite its high-profile domestic

Daniel and Helen Pedtke meet Pope Paul VI

travels, the Notre Dame Glee Club was a comparative latecomer to international tours. Detailed plans for a fifty-two-day European tour in the summer of 1960 survive from March of that year. On the itinerary were to be stops in Dublin, Paris, Rome, Zurich, Amsterdam, Bonn, Cologne, Frankfurt, and West Berlin. The trip was on track by all accounts, and significant projected revenues would ease the burden of the travel expenses.[37] *Scholastic* reported, "All that remains now is the official go-ahead signal from the University, and this permission is merely a formality, as the trip will be entirely financed by the tour service out of concert receipts. Not only this, but the club will also be paid for each individual concert, of which they are guaranteed five a week."[38] By May of that year, even more details were secured. With help from university president Fr. Theodore Hesburgh, the Club would have "an audience with Pope John XXIII while they are performing in Rome."[39] Permission from the university was never granted, however; the travel plans were scrapped at the last minute, presumably due to the U-2 incident that brought further unrest in the Cold War.

In 1963 and 1965, there were more plans for an inaugural jaunt to Europe that did not materialize, likewise attributable to rising political conflicts. In the former year, a full itinerary was developed with the option of an "extension" tour for Glee Club members who wanted to stay beyond the group's official travels. In the surviving documents, however, there are no concert venues listed; this was a hypothetical tour—a geographic wish list.[40] In 1965, the Club attempted to arrange a tour of the European continent with assistance from the Department of Defense Overseas Touring Program, which many universities exploited at the time.[41] Yet again, the trip plans were dropped.

Finally, in 1971, a breakthrough. The Glee Club fundraised heavily and creatively for a planned venture to Europe, but the trip became a reality with a gift from Glee Club alumnus and university trustee Alfred C. Stepan Jr. ('31).[42] With each Glee Club member paying a discounted rate, Dean Pedtke's group would finally journey overseas, organized by tour managers

Alfred C. Stepan Jr. presents a check for the inaugural European Tour

Mike Leonard ('72) and Dave Zabor ('72). The inaugural European tour brought the Glee Club to Munich, Vienna, Rome, Milan, Zurich, Paris, and Brussels, the last performance including a half-hour appearance on Belgian national television. In Rome, the Club was able to join an audience with Pope Paul VI. Also noteworthy was the university's willingness to provide funding for Pedtke's wife, Helen, to travel with the Glee Club. Having some of her seven children at home always, Helen rarely traveled with the group. With the tour of 1971 in the Club annals, travel every three or four years to Europe became the norm through the present day.

The Club's second tour to Europe, in 1975 under the direction of David Isele, touched many of the same countries that the first one did: Belgium, Germany, Austria, Switzerland, Italy, and France. Special performances were given at the Mozartsaal of the Wiener Konzerthaus (Vienna) and the Teatro Quartiere in Milan, part of the Italian Summer Arts Program. But tour manager John Moe ('72, '75L) sent the choir on to Ireland as well, a logical addition for a group of Singing Irish. The choir sang not only in the magnificent rounded atrium of the U.S. Embassy in Dublin and in the coastal community of Avoca, but also at Ireland's leading cabaret venue in Limerick. European tours to the present day have had similar complexions, with several European countries

on the itinerary. Some are linked to Notre Dame study-abroad programs, and time in Ireland is always an easy sell to Clubbers.

The international reach of the Glee Club expanded in the summer of 1997, as Daniel Stowe's Glee Club was invited to perform with the Jerusalem Symphony Orchestra in Israel with conductor David Shallon. This rare opportunity opened the floodgates to travel options outside of Europe. The Club prepared the male chorus part to three major works—one in Latin, one in Russian, and one in Hebrew. The highlight was a semi-staged opera, Igor Stravinsky's *Oedipus Rex*, in which Club members were cast as a savage-looking Greek chorus, dressed in all black with their faces painted white. On a separate billing, the group stood on a set of bleachers behind the orchestra to sing Dmitri Shostakovich's Symphony no. 13 (*Babi Yar*), based on gripping poetry by Yevgeny Yev-tushenko that starkly highlights the massacre of thousands of Russian Jews in Kiev in 1941. On this same program was yet another depiction of World War II atrocities, Arnold Schoenberg's *A Survivor from Warsaw*, with Stowe narrating the text and the Glee Club finishing the work with a powerful atonal declaration of the Hebrew prayer Shema Yisrael. Outside of its concert responsibilities, the Club was able to visit venerated sites such as the Church of the Holy Sepulchre, and tour chaplain Fr. Michael Driscoll said a memorable Mass for the group on the hills above the Sea of Galilee.

A new rhythm of Glee Club touring emerged after the concerts in Israel. Stowe has now established an arrangement that features international travel every two years. Every other trip would be to Europe beginning in 1999 and the other "odd" years were slated for travel to other continents. The Club ventured for three weeks through East and Southeast Asia in the summer of 2001. They started the trip in Singapore and then stayed for a few days each in Bangkok, Beijing, Shanghai, Hong Kong, and Taipei, air travel being the principal mode of transport between the cities. At least two familiar faces greeted the Glee Club on its journey. Glee Club member Thana Taerattanachai ('98B) welcomed the group to his family's palatial residence in Bangkok, while Tsung Yeh, music director of the South Bend Symphony, led the Glee Club in concert with his other orchestra, the Hong Kong Sinfonietta. The Club had the full weight of the university behind it on this tour of Asia. A delegation of Notre Dame

officials was deployed with the young men to advance broader institutional initiatives, such as establishing alumni clubs and building study-abroad programs in the cities visited. Besides the expected fascination Clubbers had with Asian cuisine, a walk along the Great Wall of China, and the urban bustle of Hong Kong, the highlight of the tour occurred at its end, when the group had the opportunity to perform a concert at the National Concert Hall in Taipei, a stage that had featured internationally acclaimed tenor Plácido Domingo and American soprano Kallen Esperian in a program of opera arias and Broadway numbers the previous night.

Latin America was the next frontier for Notre Dame Glee Club travel in its ever-expanding tour horizons under Stowe. In 2005, the choir made stops in Nicaragua, Panama, Mexico, Guatemala, and Honduras, greeted by Notre Dame alumni groups with stunning homes along the way. The members of the Club notably began the trip with their heads shaved in honor of Cole Barker (chapter 6), which produced identical sunburns for the first few days spent on the beach. Concerts to full houses in city centers were balanced with peaceful nature reserve settings for post-concert gatherings. Dennis "DJ" DiDonna ('05) recalled not only witnessing a volcanic eruption in Mexico, but also experiencing the unusual bus conditions on this trip, which resulted in the "first and last" reversal of seating hierarchy in transit. Because the bus had four air conditioning vents in the front, the upperclassmen fled their normal position in search of the cool air and left the younger cohorts to swelter in the back of the vehicle.[43]

The Club returned to Central America in 2009, but now with twenty-five members of the Notre Dame Symphony Orchestra, an ensemble that Daniel Stowe has conducted since 1995. This was the first joint trip (international or domestic) for the two organizations. Hosted by the alumni club of Guatemala, the Symphony Orchestra and Glee Club had major performances in Guatemala at the Iglesia San Francisco El Grande in La Antigua and the Cathedral of Guatemala City. These concerts featured choruses from an array of operas including Wagner's *Tannhäuser*, Mozart's *The Magic Flute*, and Beethoven's *Fidelio*.

Following a 2011 European tour, the Club broke the string of appearances on other continents by returning to Europe in 2013 for an extraordinary experience that will be long be remembered in the group's history. The young men spent three weeks in Spain, visiting Madrid, Toledo, and Burgos. Audiences spilled into side chapels of major cathedrals to hear the Club, as has always been typical in Spain. But on this special trip, the choir seized the chance to journey on the Camino de Santiago, the storied medieval pilgrimage route that Christians for centuries traversed across northern Spain, concluding at the Cathedral of St. James in Santiago de Compostela. Walking an average of fifteen miles per day for one of the two weeks en route to their destination, Glee Club members found a new way to bond through the physical test of the "Way of Saint James." Glee Club president Brian Scully ('13) remembers the Spanish trek as a time when friendships were enriched, "talking philosophy, telling stories, playing games to pass the time, or complaining how much our legs hurt."[44] Most of the concerts on the trip were performed in Galicia, a region in northwest Spain uniquely infused with Celtic cultural heritage. The group learned two Galician folk songs in preparation for those venues ("O voso galo" and "Catro vellos mariñeiros"); these songs were met consistently with standing ovations, even in the middle of concerts.

OFF THE RECORD

It is impossible to sum up life on tour for the Glee Club over its history. The astounding number of cities visited in the past hundred years prevents an easy analysis, and key personal moments shared by the Singing Irish do not survive in official itineraries, though they can be pieced together from newsletters and from individual memories. In 1949, when the Club returned with photos of idle time spent in Miami between concerts, *Scholastic* noted that the Glee Club was much better treated on its tours than the band: "Stand the itineraries of the recent band and glee club tours side by side and you get a shocking picture. Why must the hard-working band have to do so much more for their meals on these trips?"[45] For all of the triumphs of Glee Club experiences on tour, there has been no shortage of missteps and mishaps, as well as traditions around journeying that have been kept relatively private. Among the more innocent, but common, tour accidents is the loss of tour essentials on a trip such as clothing or music. In 1956 for example, a second tenor left his tuxedo pants at a stop in Houston, but was unexpectedly called by director Pedtke to do a solo the next evening in Tulsa. The young singer stepped out in gray flannel pants, noticeably adrift in his attire.[46]

It is one thing to lose materials, and quite another to lose people. Oftentimes Clubbers have been left behind at tour stops by business managers who insisted on keeping to the bus schedule to meet the host at the next town. The problem has virtually been eliminated in this day of cell phones and an auxiliary vehicle that follows the bus, but there was a time when a boy with little money could find himself in a big jam. On a tour of southern Indiana in the spring of 1922, Glee Club members were to catch a train at 5:00 a.m., departing West Baden, Indiana, bound for Washington, Indiana. Young Rubio missed that call, and the Club left without him. Rubio miraculously reappeared at one of the subsequent stops on the tour, in Henderson, Kentucky, just south of Evansville, Indiana. Rubio "told of an exciting chase all over the southern part of Indiana in search of his fellow singers."[47] Illness also affects and sometimes displaces singers on tour. On the Easter tour of 1949, for instance, baritone Jerry Boyle fainted in his room in Pittsburgh due to a severe boil on his neck. He was hospitalized for four days, and the Glee Club chaplain for that trip, Fr. Joseph Barry, remained with Boyle during his recovery.[48]

Tours prompted members to produce closely guarded documentation that showed the group in a less than flattering light, not unthinkable for college students together on the road on a temporary release from academic life. Beginning in the 1950s, a mimeograph tour magazine prepared by the Glee Club's business manager was sometimes circulated before the group departed South Bend. The casual prose of these throw-away handouts stood in contrast to the official itineraries that parents received by mail. By the end of the decade, the tour magazines had titles such as "Tour City Tabloid," but the titles and topics eventually devolved into ribald double entendres. The material included satires, spoofs, limericks, and caricatures, where singers' physical differences and perceived shortcomings were on full display.[49]

The Notre Dame Club of Boston
and Notre Dame Academy
Presents

No. _____

the singing irish

Notre Dame Academy
1073 Main Street
Hingham, Mass.

Donation:
Adult - $5.00
Student - $3.00
ADMIT ONE

Tuesday Evening
October 19, 1976
8:00 p.m.
Reception following

One way that the Glee Club recapped its travel experiences was through a mock conferral of awards. Not surprisingly, these honors were given to members who had engaged in the most inappropriate or unfortunate conduct. The "Rag Man" Award celebrated the touring member who complained ("ragged") the most on the trip, while the "Wee Willie Upchuck" badge honored the singer who lost his lunch on tour, usually on the bus. Other awards were "memorials" bearing the names of past Glee Club members, and several honors have been developed around the courting of women, often based more on perception than reality. A more generic "Tour Rookie" award is reserved for the young man who understood his place on tour and fit in well with the group, perhaps entertaining the upperclassmen in an unexpected way without overstepping as a fledgling member of the choir. Since the mid-1990s, other shared stories and foibles of tour life in the Glee Club have been chronicled in the form of "Top Ten" lists (in the style of former late-night television personality David Letterman) and in "bus quizzes," all announced over the bus's loudspeaker.

Glee Club tour life has thus had its share of highs and lows, successes and struggles. No one understood the contradictions of travel with the Club better than its longtime chaplain Fr. Robert Griffin, who, in his regular column in the campus daily the *Observer*, compared travel with these young men and the sometimes harsh conditions to "an evening in Animal House" or, worse, "a foretaste of damnation." Though well attuned to the severity of tour life for the uninitiated, Griffin always saw the good in these travels and was in awe of the effect the singing had on audiences.

> Exposed to the smell of unwashed clothes and day-old orange peels, with other fragrances that remind me of the unburied dead, I'm apt to be in a state of mind like Cardinal Newman's when he prayed that the time he spent in Holy Ireland might be subtracted from his purgatory. Imagine being on a bus in need of flushing for ten or twelve hours and then arriving for a concert in a shabby grade-school gym where the audience sits on bleachers. The promised free meal turns out to be Sloppy Joes with a cup of bug juice served by the Mothers' Club on paper plates. Still, the noblesse oblige of the Clubbers would break your heart.[50]

A *Scholastic* article from 1916 about Samuel Ward Perrott's glee club cheered the establishment of the group not only as "an organization of which we may be proud" but also as "a source of unequalled entertainment to the cities which it favors with engagements and a credit to the University."[51] The Glee Club was hardly a traveling organization at that time; indeed, it had only visited a few nearby cities in its first year of operation under Perrott. A century later, this statement still rings true. Glee Club tour stops rarely leave audiences feeling empty; rather, the group showcases the promise of the next generation in song and remains a "credit to the University" with its spirited school songs known to millions, Catholic and non-Catholic alike.

EIGHT

Songs of the Singing Irish

A CENTURY OF GLEE CLUB REPERTOIRE

The Notre Dame Glee Club's concert on December 11, 1915, was hailed as "a present gratification as well as an assurance for the future." It was by no means the first performance in the Club's history, but it was the first under director Perrott, who brought Harvard's Glee Club culture of serious repertoire to Notre Dame. *Scholastic* sensed the shift in programming, calling it "fresh and well advised" and noting further, "There was a welcome absence of the time-worn merrily-we-roll-along thing."[1] The evening's entertainment began with an unnamed selection from the university orchestra, and the Glee Club sang just four numbers, sharing the program with the Mandolin Club, a vocal quartet, and a solo by Perrott himself. The group performed an arrangement of the Irish melody "Bendemeer's Stream," a texted setting of Joseph Haydn's "Serenade" (a string quartet), "On the Road to Mandalay" by Oley Speaks (with text by Rudyard Kipling), and an unidentified "Notre Dame Song, [sung] to the melody of a Netherland folk song, written about 1600." Of these four songs, only Speaks's "On the Road to Mandalay" would have any longevity with the Glee Club, appearing on programs as late as 1952.[2]

Full program listings in the campus press (in the early years), catalogues of repertoire (after 1975), and nearly a thousand printed concert programs permit a wide view of Glee Club musical offerings over the century.[3] This chapter will not attempt a comprehensive reconstruction of works sung by the ensemble but rather will highlight both the shape of programs over the last century and the peculiarities in music selection that set it apart from typical choral repertoire for men's choruses in the United States. In general, one senses an "all of the above," variety-type approach to Glee Club programming, as the group was versatile enough to tap classical favorites and arrangements of folk melodies in the span of a single program. At the same time, a prevailing theme is that each successive Glee Club director was righting the perceived shortcomings of the previous director's programming, usually injecting more serious repertoire into the Glee Club's musical arsenal.

MUSICAL GENRES AND PROGRAMMING

Scanning the Glee Club programs across the last century, one might find it more appropriate to ask what the group did *not* sing than what kinds of music it did sing. In some respects, there is a survey course in music history built in to the programs of the past hundred years, almost exclusively centered on sacred music. The earliest musical genre found on Glee Club programs is Gregorian chant, the church's musical treasury of Latin melodies for all feasts of the year. In the 1980s, director Carl Stam introduced chant to Glee Club programs, a gesture that not only must have pleased the music department and the university administration, but also grew out of the conductor's personal experience with the style from his education at the University of North Carolina at Chapel Hill. Daniel Stowe has continued to include bits of chant in his programs of the last generation, sometimes as lead-ins to larger works inspired by select chant melodies.

Choral music from the Renaissance has been a part of the Glee Club's repertoire from the early days. A 1924 program "entirely of classics" conducted by J. Lewis Browne reveals that the first four pieces in the concert were all Renaissance works. Michael Praetorius's "Lo, How a Rose E'er Blooming" and Orlande de Lassus's "Matona, Lovely Maiden" were performed in translation, followed by two Latin pieces ("motets") by Giovanni Pierluigi da Palestrina ("Adoramus te" and "O bone Jesu").[4] Although the Baroque period of music history hardly calls to mind male choral repertoire, the years under Dean Pedtke saw engagement with Johann Sebastian Bach's cantatas and the famous "Hallelujah Chorus" from Handel's oratorio *Messiah*, in an arrangement for men's chorus.[5] The Singing Irish twice performed an abbreviated version of the "Hallelujah Chorus" on Ed Sullivan's *Toast of the Town*, fitting for their appearances on Easter Sunday in the early 1950s.[6]

It has already been noted that an arrangement of Haydn's "Serenade" could be found on the first Glee Club program under director Perrott, but other works from the Classical period surfaced in performances. During a concert at the University of Michigan in 2001, the ensemble sang the chorus "O Isis und Osiris" from Mozart's *The Magic Flute*, while talented bass soloist Michael Holderer performed the wise sorcerer Sarastro's arias from the same opera, backed by an ad hoc string quartet of Clubbers. Music from the nineteenth century has been somewhat sparse. Franz Schubert wrote at least one hundred choral works for male voices, but only in the era under Daniel Stowe has Schubert's music appeared on Glee Club programs with any consistency.[7] Performances in 1954 marked the Club's first foray with Johannes Brahms's "How Lovely is Thy Dwelling Place" (arranged for men's chorus) and the "Prayer" from Richard Wagner's *Lohengrin*, the latter work now firmly a classic in the Glee Club repertoire. Opera numbers popped up on programs in the heart of the Pedtke era, but particularly noteworthy was a set of excerpts from Gilbert and Sullivan's *Trial by Jury*, which parodies the English justice system.[8]

Predictably, twentieth-century works have dominated the Glee Club repertoire presented in concert. Arrangements of folksongs have been common, and the concert spiritual—sometimes called the African American spiritual—has played a significant role, but these genres do not necessarily set the Glee Club apart from those at other universities. The group seems to have gotten an early start on concert spirituals, though. After a performance of H. T. Burleigh's "Deep River" in 1939, a *Scholastic* review praised "the keen sense of rhythm coupled with the deep religious feeling so characteristic of the negro spiritual."[9] Despite the popularity of barbershop quartet singing in the United States in the twentieth century, this repertoire was avoided until the Stowe era. "Top 40"–type popular music is probably one of the few genres held out of Glee Club performances for most of its history, though it has emerged in the last generation via small groups of Club members who perform them in concert while the large ensemble takes a vocal rest.

Glee Club audiences across the decades have witnessed a pendulum swinging when it comes to programming. Directors Perrott, Becker, and Browne were cut from a cloth of serious or "high" musical culture rooted in classics perceived at that time. Joseph Casasanta's programs did not entirely abandon the elite repertoire, but were heavily slanted toward secular songs, folk arrangements, and collegiate "rah-rah" music, consistent with

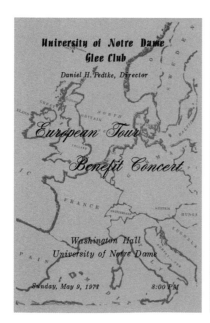

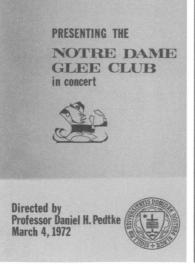

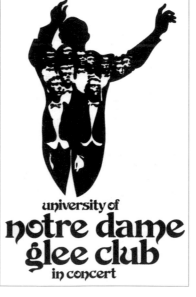

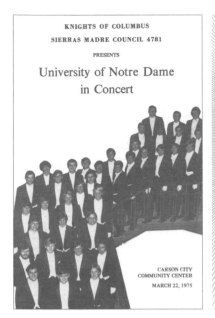

KNIGHTS OF COLUMBUS
SIERRAS MADRE COUNCIL 4781

PRESENTS

University of Notre Dame
in Concert

CARSON CITY
COMMUNITY CENTER

MARCH 22, 1975

university of
notre dame
glee club
in concert

MERCY HIGH AUDITORIUM
11 MILE AT MIDDLEBELT

SUNDAY, NOVEMBER 16, 1975 • 7:30 P.M.

St. Francis Community Hospital
and
The Guild of the Greenville Symphony
present
THE NOTRE DAME GLEE CLUB
with
The Greenville Symphony Orchestra
in

an
all american
evening
of
music

Greenville Memorial Auditorium
Sunday, March 21, 1976
8:15 P.M.

university of
notre dame
glee club
in concert

dans le
grand amphi de l'u.c.o.
lundi 5 juin à 20 h. 30
au profit de la lutte contre la myopathie

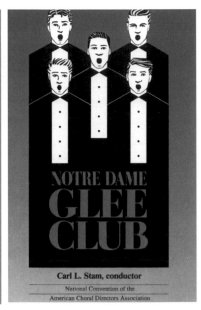

NOTRE DAME
GLEE
CLUB

Carl L. Stam, conductor

National Convention of the
American Choral Directors Association

CARDINAL'S CHRISTMAS PARTY JOURNAL—1989

NOTRE DAME
GleeClub
75
1915
1990

SEVENTY-FIFTH

ANNIVERSARY

REUNION

CONCERT

NOVEMBER 16, 1990

NOTRE
DAME
GLEE
CLUB

COMMENCEMENT
CONCERT

MAY 15, 1993 ∽ 9 PM

MUSIC
FROM THE
BASILICA
NOTRE DAME
GLEE CLUB

DANIEL STOWE, CONDUCTOR

SUNDAY
MARCH
27 · 1994
8 PM

BASILICA
OF THE
SACRED
HEART

Morales   Missa Ave Maria
Poulenc   Laudes for
               St. Anthony of Padua
Motets by Josquin, Rore and Binchois

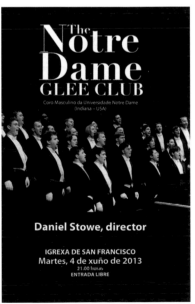

The
Notre
Dame
GLEE CLUB
Coro Masculino da Universidade Notre Dame
(Indiana – USA)

Daniel Stowe, director

IGREXA DE SAN FRANCISCO
Martes, 4 de xuño de 2013
21.00 horas
ENTRADA LIBRE

the director's contribution of marches to the university's musical corpus and his attraction to the national spotlight. The first concert conducted by Dean Pedtke in 1938 was recognized in the press for its freshness and seriousness of programming. The arrangement of Bach's "Jesu, Joy of Man's Desiring" in particular was called a "most startling innovation on the program."[10] The director's daughter Dorothy Pedtke remembers that songs the family heard on the weekly national broadcast of *Music and the Spoken Word* (featuring the Mormon Tabernacle Choir) would often find their way onto Glee Club programs.[11] The venerable classics henceforth in the Pedtke era occupied the first full section of formal programs, which were organized into four or five subsets (often separated by solo performances), inevitably moving from heavier to lighter repertoire. Program eclecticism has been the lifeblood of Glee Club music. A fall concert in 1964, for example, showed great variety "from an exciting Brazilian hymn to hauntingly beautiful English ballads," in addition to excerpts from Leonard Bernstein's *West Side Story* (not even a decade old) and works by Bach and Norwegian composer Edvard Grieg.[12]

Under scrutiny from the Department of Music to lift the Glee Club's musical standards even further, Pedtke's successor, David Clark Isele, instituted programming changes. In 1975, the director commented on his vision for Glee Club programs in general: "One of our chief concerns is to devise a package which will sell to all. We have quite a cross section to please, and one cannot be too esoteric or the audience will lose interest."[13] Isele eased out some of the more gimmicky staples of the Pedtke years, for instance the Gilbert and Sullivan numbers and Aaron Copland's "I Bought Me a Cat." He then proceeded to arrange some thirty works for the Glee Club, of which his "Danny Boy," "Let Us Break Bread Together on Our Knees," and "Blow Ye Winds" have persisted well beyond his years at Notre Dame. Isele also reintroduced the Glee Club to the Renaissance madrigal (for example, Thomas Morley's effervescent "Fire! Fire! My Heart"), a genre that could appeal both to the administration because of its historical significance and to the Club members for its light-hearted nature.[14]

As mentioned earlier, the Glee Club became acquainted with Gregorian chant in the years under Carl Stam, a practical move given the director's familiarity with the genre and its resonance at a Catholic institution, to say nothing of its historical importance. But other songs that endured after Pedtke's retirement Stam let wither away—what Isele called some of the "golden oldies" of the Glee Club (such as James Lynam Molloy's "The Kerry Dance" and Jerome Kern's "All the Things You Are").[15] Programs under Daniel Stowe have in general featured repertoire at a considerably higher level of difficulty than previous ensembles and with greater experimentation with global musics. Exposure to multiple languages has become the norm rather than the exception among the last generation of Glee Club members.

SCHOOL SONGS, "AVE"s, AND OTHER HITS

If there was one mainstay of Glee Club programs for nearly all of its history, it has been songs about Notre Dame. Credit of course goes to director Joseph Casasanta for penning all but the "Victory March." When he graduated Notre Dame in 1924, Casasanta realized that some universities had a small collection of pep songs; he was further concerned that the "Victory March" was being overplayed.[16] From these circumstances, four songs for Notre Dame that have never left the Glee Club (or band) repertoire were born: "Hike, Notre Dame"; "(On) Down the Line"; "When Irish Backs Go Marching By"; and "Notre Dame, Our Mother," the university's alma mater. The campus at large eagerly awaited what hit might come next from the director of the Glee Club and the band: "Professor Casasanta has the gift of producing melodies from an odd note here, a bar there, and at intervals there comes from his little office in [the] Music Hall the announcement of a 'new campus song.'"[17] The savvy conductor programmed his songs with regularity in concerts, which secured their acceptance into the school's musical canon.

In 1940, director Dean Pedtke contributed the other instant classic to the Glee Club musical corpus—the sentimental "Notre Dame, We Hail Thee," known as the Glee Club alma mater. Pedtke set a simple rhymed text in praise of Our Lady and the university written by Fr. Eugene Burke, whom director Casasanta had tapped for the text to "When Irish Backs Go Marching By." Legend has it that the director wrote the song on the back of an envelope on a bus, at a time when Casasanta was unsure if he would give the copyright of his alma mater to the university.[18] The only Glee Club school song without the band's joint custody, "Notre Dame, We Hail Thee," is framed by a chorus of wordless "oo"s that creates an aura of serenity around the sung creed. In this short hymn of just ninety seconds, Pedtke seems to emphasize harmony throughout the piece by employing a melody that is less discernible than that of "Notre Dame, Our Mother." During his long tenure, the director often used to single out members of the Club to sing his piece as a solo, for instance a Clubber whose hometown the group was visiting. Pedtke's "Notre Dame, We Hail Thee" is scarcely known by the Notre Dame fan base today, but it is a song that three generations of Glee Clubbers hold dear.

> Notre Dame, we hail thee,
> Mother fond and true.
> Heaven's beauties veil thee,
> With thy gold and blue.
> Through life's deepening shadows
> or in glory's fame,
> Grateful sons shall love and
> praise thee, Notre Dame,
> Grateful sons shall love and
> praise thee, Notre Dame.

For at least two decades following this composition, the final two numbers that the Glee Club performed in formal concerts were Pedtke's "Notre Dame We Hail Thee" and the "Victory March." The university alma

When four rows of Glee Club singers chant a Notre Dame song; when columns of blue-uniformed bandmen play and march to Notre Dame music—then we forget the ubiquitous campus grinds and gripers, and we hike along, down the line, cheering her name, glad that Irish Backs are marching.

—*Scholastic* (1930)

mater—Casasanta's "Notre Dame, Our Mother"—was conspicuously absent, and some students at one time petitioned the administration to have Pedtke's hymn become the university's alma mater. "Notre Dame, Our Mother" appeared with more consistency on Glee Club programs in the 1970s when director Isele reharmonized it for the group's use. The Glee Club's formal concerts now reliably conclude with all three school songs.

As ubiquitous as school songs on Glee Club programs has been the presence of an "Ave Maria." One of the central prayers of Catholic tradition, the text of the Ave Maria, addressed to Mary, is well suited to be sung in concert by the principal choral ambassador of the nation's preeminent Catholic university dedicated to Our Lady. What is crucial to note is that the chosen settings of the "Ave Maria" have varied across the history of the organization. The first mentions of an "Ave Maria" in Glee Club programs emerge at the end of J. Lewis Browne's term with a setting composed by Tomás Luis de Victoria, a piece still recognized today in choral music circles as a staple of Renaissance polyphonic style in the "golden age" of church music.

Recorded and mass-distributed during the Casasanta years, Victoria's "Ave Maria" was replaced in the Pedtke era by that of German composer Franz Xaver Witt. Witt himself was influenced by Renaissance music and was involved with the nineteenth-century "Cecilian movement" to restore dignity and authority in church music with comprehensible settings of text. Though it engages a rich harmonic palette that explores the lower range of the male voice, Witt's "Ave Maria" delivers the text slowly and deliberately in an effort to focus the listener on the familiar words of the prayer. Around 1963, Dean Pedtke himself penned an "Ave Maria" for the Glee Club, and this piece notably was sung at his funeral in 1976.[19]

As described in chapter 5, director Douglas Belland receives credit for introducing the most memorable version of the "Ave Maria" to the Glee Club repertoire in 1980, written by German composer Franz Biebl. This piece has remained in the Club canon to the present day. Composed for a four-part male chorus and a solo trio, the prayer's short phrases unfold in a series of echoes between the groups building to a climactic "Amen." During a tour through the state of California in the spring of 1995, director Stowe had placed Biebl's "Ave" early in the program but skipped it by mistake one night, discovering the omission in time to present it as the last piece of the first half. The glorious double-choir motet has stayed in that position ever since. Although choirs around the world (notably, the professional men's ensemble Chanticleer) program this piece regularly, the work has become a signature of the Notre Dame Glee Club repertoire. And rightly so: it is a luxurious expression of the most significant of the traditional Catholic prayers, given voice by a choir firmly connected to an institution that remains a bastion of Catholic culture in the United States.

Other pieces achieved considerable longevity in the Glee Club's musical canon. The Irish-infused "Clancy Lowered the Boom" has been noted on concert programs since 1954 and regularly appears in the Glee Club's informal "mini-concerts." As stated earlier, the same year also saw the incorporation of the "Prayer" from Wagner's *Lohengrin*, which likewise has not departed the chorus's repertoire. The rousing spiritual "Ride the Chariot" has remained since the early 1960s, though it is a favorite of many men's choruses. Other songs have

dominated various eras but did not extend to the present like the pieces just mentioned. Audiences consistently heard the poignant Russian folk tune "Song of the Volga Boatmen" on programs of directors Becker, Browne, and Casasanta; the Renaissance madrigal "Matona, Lovely Maiden" (by Orlande de Lassus) also found a place in concerts during this same period. Dean Pedtke programmed the "Crucifixus" by Italian Baroque composer Antonio Lotti with some regularity on Glee Club programs, in an arrangement by Archibald T. Davison, who inspired director Samuel Ward Perrott a generation earlier. The last twenty years of concert programs under Daniel Stowe have shown a marked preference for arrangements by Ralph Vaughan Williams (notably "Loch Lomond") and any number of spirituals and shanties arranged by Alice Parker (with Robert Shaw).

The 1940s was an exhilarating period for Notre Dame football, as coach Frank Leahy's teams earned four championships in that decade. During that time, director Dean Pedtke arranged a medley of the fight songs of the nine schools on Notre Dame's 1946 and 1947 schedules that represented all parts of the country.[20] Known as the "College Medley" (and later as the "Cavalcade"), this series of rollicking school songs was a perfect offering for informal events, particularly on football game days.[21] Small changes were made to the medley over the years, but in the later 1970s, director Isele's version of the "Cavalcade" was locked in place, while Carl Stam began a new tradition of singing the fight songs of the annual slate of opponents to keep things current.[22] Fans of opposing teams have always delighted in the Glee Club's renditions of their team's music; depending on the venue, however, Clubbers have also been known to undermine their opponents' official songs either by performing alternate lyrics or by facing the opposite direction while singing the rivals' fight songs.

Musical comedy was a fixture on Glee Club programs for a little more than half of the Glee Club's history (from directors Becker through Isele). In 1939, Dean Pedtke introduced the Club to a clever version of the nursery rhyme "Old Mother Hubbard" set in the musical language of George Frideric Handel in an arrangement by Victor Hely-Hutchinson.[23] "Let Us Gather at the Goal-Line" was another musical spoof heard in the late 1940s, excerpted from the campus musical *Toplitzky of Notre Dame*.[24] Isele dabbled with the ingenious "The Art of the Ground Round" by P. D. Q. Bach (the invention of satirist Peter Schickele) and, in 1975, the director wrote the slightly risqué mini-operetta *Red Hot Riding Hood* for soloists and choir. George Hammer ('52) vividly recalled the Glee Club quartet "bringing down the house" in the early 1950s with a spoof of Giuseppe Verdi's *Rigoletto* performed at the intermission of Club concerts, a number that continued to be performed in the early 1970s, according to concert programs. But the most comedy relief in Glee Club concerts of the past century came from another parody of Italian opera called "Italian Salad" ("Insalata Italiana") by nineteenth-century Austrian composer Richard Genée. Introduced to the ensemble by director J. Lewis Browne, "Italian Salad" was performed in concerts for about five decades. The song for choir and melodramatic soloists nonsensically traverses through a list of musical dynamic markings, conventional terms from Italian opera, expressive indications, and instrument names—all in Italian. A reviewer for *Scholastic* quipped that "Italian Salad" sounded "like the chorus of Accademia di Santa Cecilia vocalizing to Webster's Dictionary of Musical Phrases."[25] In 1950, "Mr. Television," Milton Berle, commandeered the Club's performance of "Italian Salad" to steal the spotlight on *The Ed Sullivan Show*.[26] Encores of this sidesplitting caricature of Italian opera were not uncommon in Glee Club concerts.[27] An excerpt from the song demonstrates its comedic stylings:

Tra ta ta . . . ! Suona la tromba,	Tra ta ta! Sound the trumpet!
Tra ta ta . . . ! A la vendetta!	Tra ta ta! Revenge!
Tromboni, Timpani, Fagotti,	Trombones, timpani, bassoons,
Contrabassi, Violini, Clarinetti!	Basses, violins, clarinets!
Venite tutti! Si! A la vendetta! Si! Tra ta ta!	Come everyone! Yes! Revenge! Tra ta ta!
Con fuoco, con fuoco!	With fire, with fire!
Staccato, furioso, calmato!	Detached, furious, with calm!
Assai scandaloso, non più lamentoso!	Very scandalous, weep no more!

PREMIERES

The Glee Club has been fortunate to premiere a number of works in programs of the past century, typically "one-hit wonder" pieces. In the spring of 1941, as the clouds of World War II thickened, two senior English majors from the Glee Club, Jack White and Felix Pogliano, wrote *Song of the Free*—a short, narrated history of the United States, with songs underneath the spoken text to be performed by the chorus (see chapter 6). Beginning with "Yankee Doodle," *Song of the Free* highlights music of different eras of American history, including works popular during World War I and the Great Depression. The work was accompanied by a twelve-piece

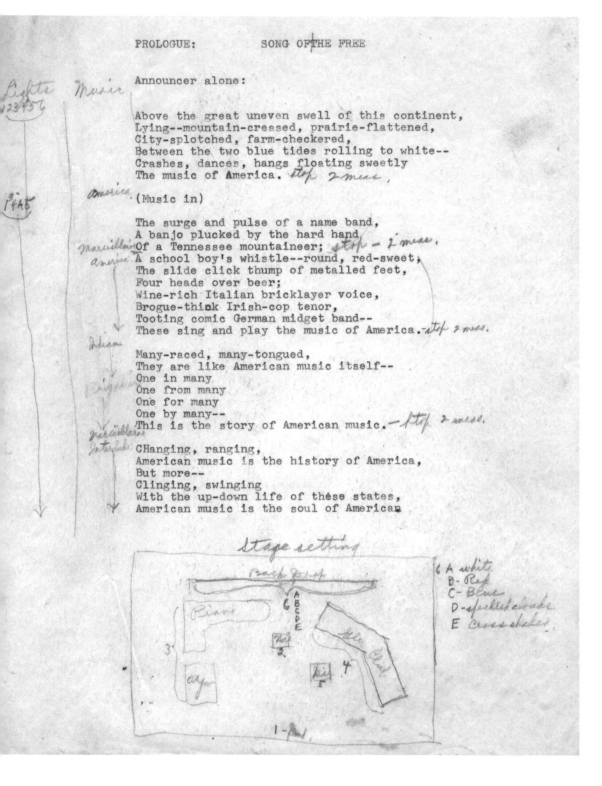

PROLOGUE: SONG OF THE FREE

Announcer alone:

Above the great uneven swell of this continent,
Lying--mountain-creased, prairie-flattened,
City-splotched, farm-checkered,
Between the two blue tides rolling to white--
Crashes, dances, hangs floating sweetly
The music of America. *stop 2 meas.*

(Music in)

The surge and pulse of a name band,
A banjo plucked by the hard hand
Of a Tennessee mountaineer; *stop - 2 meas.*
A school boy's whistle--round, red-sweet,
The slide click thump of metalled feet,
Four heads over beer;
Wine-rich Italian bricklayer voice,
Brogue-think Irish-cop tenor,
Tooting comic German midget band--
These sing and play the music of America. *stop 2 meas.*

Many-raced, many-tongued,
They are like American music itself--
One in many
One from many
One for many
One by many--
This is the story of American music. *— stop 2 meas.*

CHanging, ranging,
American music is the history of America,
But more--
Clinging, swinging
With the up-down life of these states,
American music is the soul of American

Stage setting

6 A white
  B- Red
  C- Blue
  D- speckled clouds
  E cross shades.

orchestra led by Jack Molloy, which traveled with the Club on its spring tour that year.[28] The piece was so popular that it was programmed regularly the following year and then was revived in the mid-1950s, when the script was updated to account for the end of World War II.[29]

In 1943, *Scholastic* raved about another remarkable work that "will be one of the greatest attractions any Notre Dame Glee Club has ever had, and surpasses even the well-known *Song of the Free* of two years ago."[30] The writer was speaking of an occasional work in celebration of the university's centennial entitled *The Spirit of Notre Dame*, the same title as the film Universal Pictures had made a decade previously in the wake of Knute Rockne's death. Described as

a "choral symphony" recounting Notre Dame's history in poetry, *The Spirit of Notre Dame* was written by the editor of the *Dome* yearbook, Kelly Cook. Dean Pedtke arranged the background music and interludes, amounting to ten pieces for the Glee Club and three solos approaching fifteen minutes in total length. In performance, the singers formed a large "V"-shape around a table draped with an "ND"-monogram blanket. *The Spirit of Notre Dame* was premiered at St. Mary's College before an audience of delegates from the National Federation of Catholic College Students; it was subsequently presented in the local WSBT studios for a live radio broadcast.[31]

Yet another work written expressly for the Glee Club emerged in 1948 from the pen of Ed Cashman, a graduate student in the music department who had written two musicals for performances at Washington Hall. Entitled *The Archangel Mike*, this piece was not another script with background music and interpolations (nor was it a musical), but rather was billed as a "cantata." As *Scholastic* rightly pointed out, the piece did not have the shape of a traditional cantata, which mixes solos, duets, and choruses without a specific narrative. *The Archangel Mike* instead tells the story of a little boy who goes to heaven with his toy trumpet, but he is not

Kelly Cook

permitted to play it until he recites the "Ave Maria" prayer, which he cannot remember.[32] The Club performed Cashman's cantata on campus in Washington Hall and also in Chicago in a joint concert with Rosary College.[33]

Some of the works written by directors of the Glee Club have been mentioned, but other members of Notre Dame's Department of Music have composed works for the group. In 1962, the chair of the department, Fr. Carl Hager, composed "Duo Seraphim" for Pedtke's ensemble.[34] Music department professors Paul Johnson, Ethan Haimo, and Calvin M. Bower have also written works for the Glee Club. Bower, who recruited Carl Stam to be Glee Club director in 1981, composed a setting of Psalm 34, "Taste and See," that the Glee Club has used when called to sing Mass, whether on campus or on tour. More recently, the Club has reached out to major composers from outside Notre Dame for commissioned works. Composer and arranger Alice Parker wrote "Gloria/Herzliebster Jesu" for the Glee Club's seventy-fifth anniversary in 1990, and the Club also premiered a men's chorus arrangement of Libby Larsen's "Everyone Sang" for the Year of Women celebration at Notre Dame in 1990–91.[35] More than two decades later, the DeBartolo Performing Arts Center commissioned Timothy C. Takach to compose a work for the Glee Club, envisioned as a companion piece to Biebl's "Ave Maria," a staple of the Club's formal programs. Takach's "Salve regina" for double chorus received its premiere in 2013 in a special collaboration with the professional all-male vocal ensemble Cantus. Commissions in the Glee Club's centennial year are expected from Takach, as well as Augusta Read Thomas, one of the most accomplished composers alive today.

PROGRAM ECLECTICISM AND THE ART OF COMPETITION

As mentioned at the outset of this chapter, the first Glee Club campus concert under director Perrott was held in December 1915. Despite the time of year, this concert did not feature any music for the season of Advent or Christmas, as Glee Club audiences of the present have come to expect. An annual spring concert was the norm in the first two decades of the Glee Club's history. By the time Dean Pedtke took the podium, the group expanded its campus offerings to include a fall concert. A December concert was in place by the mid-1940s; however, like Perrott's inaugural concert, this performance had a curiously significant amount of music that was not geared for the season. Pedtke's 1949 December program began as a Christmas-oriented event with an "Ave Maria" and Sweelinck's "Angelus ad pastores," both appropriate for the season; yet, these pieces were followed by Lotti's "Crucifixus" and Handel's "Hallelujah Chorus," suitable for Holy Week and Easter, respectively.[36]

By the end of the 1950s, Pedtke's December concerts reliably ended with a set of Christmas tunes, but were still peppered with pieces that had little to do with the season, such as excerpts from Gilbert and Sullivan operettas, concert spirituals like "De Animals A-Comin'," and the notorious "Italian Salad."[37] The patriotic *Song of the Free* was even programmed for the 1956 Christmas concert in Washington Hall, accompanied by a seven-piece band.[38] What one learns from these peculiarities of the December concert offerings is that the greatest hits of the Notre Dame Glee Club seemed to trump any seasonal considerations. Audiences expected a diverse set of numbers no matter the time of year, and director Pedtke, for one, obliged.

The eclectic nature of Glee Club programs was also on display at various music competitions and choral festivals, where repertoire and quality of singing were carefully scripted. In 1927, director J. Lewis Browne and Joseph Casasanta—Browne's assistant at the time—prepared the Club for an intercollegiate competition at Orchestra Hall in Chicago. The Glee Club performed three songs, one of which (Robert Schumann's "The Lotus Flower") was sung by all twelve of the groups in the competition as a point of comparison.[39] The other two songs sung by the Singing Irish were written by the director and his assistant (Browne's "June Time" and Casasanta's "Hike, Notre Dame").

Although Notre Dame did not place in this competition, the ensemble did capture the $200 grand prize in another competition in 1931, which convened six glee clubs from the state of Indiana. Each choir was required to perform a concert four times in a single day. Director Casasanta developed a program that featured "an element of classic, Latin hymn [*sic*], humor, college songs." In truth, of the eight songs slated by the director, half of them were the principal "rah-rah" songs of the university.[40] But a win is a win.

A contest of a different sort took place in 1942, in which the Glee Club recorded works to be judged by American entertainer and choral pioneer Fred Waring. Waring opened up the competition to American glee clubs at large

Fred Waring (*left*) and John Noland ('53)

and asked them each to submit a recording of three songs. One of the songs, known as the "Prize Song," was Waring's own arrangement of the Welsh traditional song "All through the Night" (*Ar Hyd y Nos*). Each glee club would then have to sing its school song in unison, plus another piece of its choosing. While it is not known which additional songs the Notre Dame Glee Club submitted, *Scholastic* did note that an agent of Waring's was sent to Notre Dame to assist with the recording and to give Pedtke and his boys some hints about Waring's expectations for the singing. At least one hundred groups participated in the contest, but the Notre Dame Glee Club did not appear to make it out of its "bracket."[41]

Finally, performances at annual meetings of the American Choral Directors Association (ACDA) constituted a kind of competition, as choirs strove for an invitation to perform in front of hundreds of choral conductors from around the country. Glee Club director Carl Stam, himself a lifetime member of the association, garnered invitations for the Notre Dame Glee Club both at a regional meeting of the ACDA in 1988 (Cleveland) and at the national convention in 1989 (Louisville). The program presented to the national convention—consisting of approximately twenty minutes of music—began with Biebl's "Ave Maria," by then a signature piece of the Glee Club. The concert continued with two avant-garde works by French composers Darius Milhaud ("Psaume 121") and Francis Poulenc (*Laudes de Saint Antoine de Padoue*), who were colleagues in the compositional coterie known as "Les Six." The set concluded with Gail Kubik's choral profile of "Oliver De Lancey" and a nod to long-time Yale Glee Club director Fenno Heath, in his arrangement of "Sometimes I Feel Like a Motherless Child." This concert on the national stage in front of an audience of choral professionals was a high point for Stam and for the male chorus he had cultivated over the course of a decade. In the Stowe era, the Glee Club appeared at the national convention of the ACDA in 2001 in San Antonio, Texas. In addition to singing a short program, the group was invited to do workshop sessions with Jerry Blackstone (director of the University of Michigan Men's Glee Club) and Jameson Marvin (director of the Harvard Glee Club).

A set of expectations accompany any program performed by an all-male glee club. One would not be surprised to see the academic hymn "Gaudeamus igitur," Arthur Sullivan's "The Lost Chord," or a concert spiritual like "Ride the Chariot" in concert by glee clubs across the United States. From the outset, the Notre Dame Glee Club has met and exceeded the repertorial expectations of a university male chorus. The group's propensity for variety and unpredictable juxtapositions in programs reflected both the wide-ranging tastes of Glee Club directors and the freedom of college life in general. While "Italian Salad" and settings of the "Ave Maria" held sway on programs through a good part of the chorus's history, school songs have been a calling card of Notre Dame Glee Club concerts, and recent engagement with global musics will not soon be duplicated by collegiate ensembles. This is music that reveals the distinct character of the group and reflects the excellence of the university on the whole when shared in performance.

NINE

Recordings, Airwaves, and the Silver Screen

The Notre Dame Glee Club's frequent and substantial interaction with emerging media platforms helped define the group's success in the years under Joseph Casasanta and secured its place as one of the leading college choruses in the United States by the mid-1950s. Copious recordings of various lengths and formats, appearances on national radio and television broadcasts, and brushes with the movie industry raised the public profile of the ensemble well beyond the campus, in turn helping elevate the status of what was already recognized as America's foremost Catholic university—and football powerhouse.

A Glee Club quartet, accompanied by Harry Denny's dance orchestra, had recorded the "Victory March" and Casasanta's newly released "Hike, Notre Dame" in 1924 for Autograph Records. However, the stream of studio recordings featuring the Glee Club began in earnest on December 16, 1925, when a group of twelve singers journeyed to Chicago to record the same two songs for the Victor Talking Machine Company, as part of a larger project by the company to capture the sound of collegiate organizations around the country. In an intense three-hour session on the seventh floor of the Webster Hotel, the Glee Clubbers were joined by forty members of the Notre Dame Band to perform the two pieces for Victor's new "Orthophonic Victrola," the world's first phonograph to play sound disks recorded electrically, invented that same year. The household penetration of this recording cannot be overestimated, as sales exceeded even the highest expectations set by Victor.

The "Victory March" in particular swept the nation. Not even two years from the issue of the recording, Notre Dame English professor Charlie Phillips attended the fiftieth anniversary dinner of the Chicago Society (an organization of Polish American professionals and businessmen), where a University of Michigan cheerleader, John Polaski, roused the crowd of six hundred with an impromptu singing of Notre Dame's "Victory March" backed by an orchestra. "The curious part about it all," observed Phillips to the *Scholastic* editor, "is that they knew our N.D. song perfectly. But perhaps that is not so strange after all. The Glee Club, with its popular gramophone records, has made the song known from one end of the country to the other."[1]

Some two dozen commercial recordings would follow, more than half of them issued during the tenures of Dean Pedtke and Daniel Stowe. But the fact that the recordings stretched over the twentieth century means that one can trace the evolution of recording technology with the release of each album. In April 1926, just weeks after the issue of the first record, the Singing Irish were asked to record again for Victor, this time in the company's New York studio while the group was on tour. The ensemble recorded two sacred works, but nothing was ever released.[2] Sacred music and campus fight songs were then combined in a 1928 four-song release by Brunswick Records in Chicago, on which the Club recorded Victoria's "Ave Maria," paired with a modest setting of "O salutaris hostia" by Charles Gounod. These devotional pieces—by no means "classics" of the choral repertoire at that time—were counterbalanced by Casasanta's "(On) Down the Line" and "Hike, Notre Dame." Because the university's orchestra recorded on the Columbia label in 1928, Notre Dame could boast, in fact, that it was the only university in the United States to have its glee club, band, and orchestra record music on three major labels (Victor, Brunswick, and Columbia).[3]

Notre Dame's band and Glee Club would partner again in 1932 under Casasanta for a special all-steel disc known as a "Voice-O-Gram," issued by the Sound and Television Company of Chicago. The compilation was uniquely flexible: customers could choose one or two school songs ("Notre Dame, Our Mother" and "When Irish Backs Go Marching By"), each one recorded once by the Glee Club alone and again with Glee Club and band, for a total of four possible tracks. The reverse side of the album was left blank, so that purchasers could record their own personal messages. Notre Dame's Music Hall was furnished with the apparatus to record the messages at the point of sale.[4] The 1932 "Voice-O-Gram" recording was

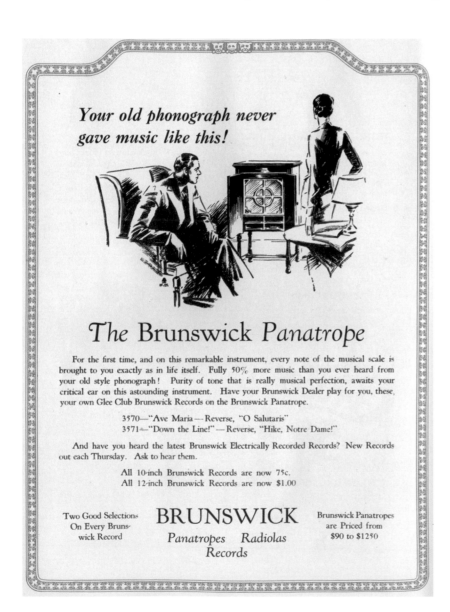

the last recording documented in the Casasanta years, and another Glee Club album would not appear until after World War II.

In 1949, the 78 rpm record was the format of choice when the Capitol Record Company released a collaborative effort between the glee clubs of Notre Dame and UCLA, which included director Dean Pedtke's own "Notre Dame, We Hail Thee" coupled with the "Victory March." Pedtke led the Glee Club in no fewer than six commercial recordings during his term, which ended in 1973. In 1953, another collaboration between the band and the Glee Club, mainly featuring school songs, appeared in the new 33 rpm format from RCA Victor. The chorus asserted its independence and breadth of repertoire in 1956, as MGM Records released the group's LP (long-playing) album titled *The Notre Dame Glee Club*, a record that included works by George Frideric Handel and Johannes Brahms.[5]

In addition to an LP issued in collaboration with the Notre Dame Band in 1964 (*Music of the University of Notre Dame*), the 1960s saw the continued expansion of mass-marketed music for the university's esteemed male choir under Pedtke. The 1965 album *Notre Dame, We Hail Thee* showcased not only the Glee Club's own alma mater of the same name but also arrangements of two songs from the 1957 musical *West Side Story* ("Maria" and "Somewhere"). The Glee Club's first Christmas album, *Here We Come A-Caroling*, was released on LP in 1969.

Conductor David Isele continued to channel the holiday spirit by recording two Christmas-themed LPs with the Glee Club: *Christmas with the ND Glee Club* (1974) and *A-Caroling* (1977). The latter album was recorded in Chicago on December 11, 1976, the day after the group received the sad news of Dean Pedtke's passing. The other LP supplied in Isele's tenure was *Wake Up the Echoes* (1975), a collection that included many school songs and two of the director's own arrangements ("Away Rio" and "Blow Ye Winds").[6] The ensemble's last LP, *The Gate of Heaven* (1980), was released during the brief directorship of Douglas Belland. Recorded at Sacred Heart Church, the album consisted of all sacred music. While Victoria's "Ave Maria" was a fortuitous point of continuity with the early Glee Club repertoire, Belland demonstrated a commitment to accessible, contemporary composition by including works by Flor Peeters, Vincent Persichetti, and Randall Thompson. The increasing role of the concert spiritual in Glee Club programming may also be noted on the 1980 record.

The ensemble made two signature recordings in the time of director Carl Stam. *From the Heart*, which by no means was an album of all love songs, was issued on cassette in 1986, but *Shake Down the Thunder* (1989), originally on cassette and later issued on CD, has continued as the top-selling Glee Club album to this day. It features the "Victory March," the alma mater, and other school songs. The traditional Notre Dame songs are also found on *Vive la Compagnie* (2005) and *On the Rocky Road to Dublin* (2012), recorded in the Stowe era.

While the Glee Club appeared on two recordings in the short tenure of Mark Ring, Daniel Stowe has released seven albums to date in his twenty-two years at Notre Dame, all in compact disc format.[7] This does not count the Glee Club's cameo appearance on a 2005 album of Christmas classics sung by the television star and unabashed Notre Dame alumnus Regis Philbin ('53). On the album *From the Heart: Then and Now* (1996), Stowe sought to remaster some of the music from Stam's album of the same name and contribute a few tracks from the

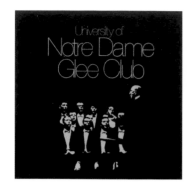

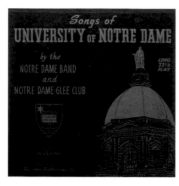

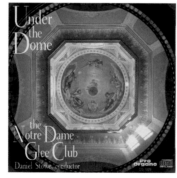

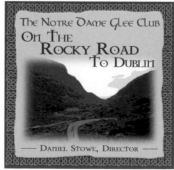

present group, including a poignant setting of the traditional Irish Blessing set by Charles Callahan. Perhaps the boldest of the seven recordings in the Stowe years was his first, *Music from the Basilica* (1994), currently out of print. With the exception of Francis Poulenc's dynamic *Laudes de Saint Antoine de Padoue* (1959), the disc centered on chant and polyphonic music of the fifteenth and sixteenth centuries. Sections of the Mass Ordinary by Cristóbal de Morales and shorter choral works by Gilles de Binchois, Josquin des Prez, and Cipriano de Rore heard on this recording were sailing uncharted waters in collegiate programming across the United States.

Four of the last five albums to date, beginning with *Under the Dome* (2000), have been released on the Pro Organo label, which has been a steady distributor of organ and sacred choral music since the mid-1980s. Those of recent years (*Vive La Compagnie, Beautiful Rain,* and *On the Rocky Road to Dublin*) are reflective of the musical diversity typical of live Glee Club concerts, and it can be said that Stowe's eclectic taste—in particular, his partiality toward Renaissance sacred music, folk songs of the British Isles, and barbershop arrangements—have not only shaped records and programs of the past two decades but also armed the ensemble and its individual members with music for virtually any occasion.

RADIO REVOLUTION

By the 1920s, radio was a viable electronic mass medium increasingly present in American households. Together with its early recordings, the Notre Dame Glee Club appeared on many broadcasts around the country, particularly in the Casasanta years, and stood at the vanguard of this powerful means of audio transmission. The ensemble first took to the airwaves in 1923, on the Tribune Radio Station (today's WGN) in Chicago.[8] The Windy City would remain the Club's base for radio broadcasts, and the group tapped its lighter musical fare as its strains reached the living rooms of Americans around the country. In 1927, the ensemble was twice invited by the Brunswick-Balke-Collender Company on Chicago's Municipal Pier (now Navy Pier) to perform nationally on "The Brunswick Hour of Music" from the studios of station WCLF. The programs highlighted not just the forty-member group but also the Glee Club quartet, a soloist, banjo players, and even violinists. The standard school songs were only part of these programs: spirituals, shanties, and playful variety-show material could also be heard on the broadcasts.[9]

Between 1929 and 1932, the Glee Club was invited to Chicago no fewer than three times by NBC to broadcast nationwide on the *Armour Hour*, a radio program that mixed music with football pre-game chatter. The appearance of the group on November 15, 1929, the eve of a football game against the University of Southern California, was remarkable for linking Notre Dame's glee club in Chicago with that of USC and their band located at a studio in Los Angeles. Each university held court for a half of the hour-long show, and the Singing Irish seem to have performed not only their own school's songs but also two from the USC repertoire—"Fight

On" and "The Cardinal and Gold."[10] In separate occasions on the *Armour Hour*, the Glee Club also rang out the rallying songs of West Point and Northwestern University, preceding the gridiron matches against the respective schools.[11] As described in chapter 8, the Club's tradition of performing Notre Dame competitors' fight songs publicly has continued to the present day.

Glee Club appearances on nationwide radio continued through the 1930s (mainly in the Casasanta years) in connection with the university's contagious football culture, and the group sometimes took to the local or national airwaves using the custom-built studios on campus for WSBT in South Bend.[12] Jaunts to Chicago for features on stations such as WENR, WMAQ, or WGN were still common,[13] and even New York City was the site of at least two radio broadcasts that featured the Glee Club during its annual Easter tour, including a spot on the NBC radio program *Paul Whiteman's Musical Varieties*, hosted by the popular American bandleader and self-proclaimed "King of Jazz."[14] In 1941 and 1942, Glee Clubbers were heard on NBC's radio show *Sports Network of the Air*, also called the "Colgate Sports Newsreel" because of its corporate sponsor.[15] The fifteen-minute weekly program was hosted by sports announcer Bill Stern. Still broadcasting in an age of limited media outlets, Stern's show reached 22 million listeners (15 percent of the population at the time), further augmenting the profile of Notre Dame's musical ambassadors.

The Glee Club's sound was transmitted internationally by radio as part of a university-sponsored program known as Universal Notre Dame Night, produced by NBC in partnership with the Studebaker Corporation of South Bend. Begun in 1924, the annual show was a kind of "audio alumni reunion," with a state-of-the-university address by the president for the Notre Dame diaspora unable to return to campus during Commencement week. The Glee Club's contribution of fight songs to the alumni broadcast was evident in the mid–1930s and continued until the early 1940s. In 1935, Universal Notre Dame Night had alumni listeners on 132 stations extending from the United States to Mexico, Cuba, and Rome. In the 1942 program, which aired on stations in a dozen Central and South American countries, the Glee Club incorporated a wider range of works into its segment, including Michael East's madrigal "How Merrily We Live" and the Naval Academy fight song "Anchors Aweigh," the latter notably in the immediate aftermath of the attack on Pearl Harbor.[16] Into the Pedtke years, the Glee Club's presence on radio seems to have softened, and only local broadcasts were noted in the press.[17] But the group's nationwide reach would grow even stronger in the 1950s, as the mass media landscape shifted with the roll-out of television.

SINGING FOR ED SULLIVAN

There was never a more public image in the history of the Notre Dame Glee Club than the one forged by the group's annual appearances on *The Ed Sullivan Show* (originally launched as *Toast of the Town*) from 1949 to 1955.[18] The top-rated prime-time variety show, airing Sunday evenings on CBS, was much imitated during its twenty-three-year run, but had no peer. Sullivan was a devout Catholic, but it was the show's producer, Marlo Lewis, who established communication with Notre Dame. In a quest to fill an empty slot during the show's first season, Lewis asked director Dean Pedtke to send a quartet of Glee Clubbers to perform on the show, when the group was on its annual East Coast tour during the Easter break. The four members selected for the first show from the forty-two-person traveling contingent were Jack Powell ('51), George Bariscillo ('44, '49L), Michael Kelly ('52), and Joseph Harrison ('53). Pedtke recalled their appearance:

> They sang two numbers, then the *Victory March*. And they had trouble because they had to wear blue. They couldn't take white—in the early days of television, you could never wear white because it would blur. So they had to get blue shirts for their tails, and they had to have tails, you know. Well they did, and then the next year Ed Sullivan wrote to us and asked if we were coming east again, and he said he would like to have us on his show.[19]

For the next six years on Easter Sunday, the Notre Dame Glee Club was welcomed back by Sullivan to the Maxine Elliott Theater on West 39th Street in midtown Manhattan, where the full choir would be on stage for nine or ten minutes of music making, which invariably included the "Victory March."[20] On each occasion, Marlo Lewis arranged lavish accommodations for the group at the famous Biltmore Hotel at Grand Central Terminal, predictably the best lodging the group received on tour. The ensemble was also paid between $500 and $1,000 for its performances.[21] With each appearance, Sullivan generously plugged both the Glee Club's concert tours and the university. Many singers remember well the 1951 performance, after which Pedtke wished his daughter Theresa a happy third birthday on camera.

Ed Sullivan (*center*)

The music that the Glee Club sang on *The Ed Sullivan Show* was always diverse. They performed anthems appropriate for Easter from Handel's oratorios, including the "Hallelujah Chorus" (*Messiah*), "Let Their Celestial Concerts All Unite" (*Samson*), and "Hallelujah, Amen" (*Judas Maccabeus*). But they also presented lighter fare, such as a medley of Jerome Kern songs and a version of "Old Man River."[22] Sullivan, a former newspaper columnist who was famously uncomfortable on stage, favored gimmicky acts, and the Glee Club happily obliged. In 1950, guest host Ken Howard asked to conduct the opera parody "Italian Salad," only to be interrupted by "Mr. Television," Milton Berle, who emerged from the back of the risers to sabotage the number with his own faux-operatic singing. The next year, the group notably joined forces with bandleader Phil Spitalny's all-female orchestra and chorus for "The Battle Hymn of the Republic" and Handel's "Hallelujah Chorus."[23]

Recordings, Airwaves, and the Silver Screen

It is not clear what caused the string of appearances on *The Ed Sullivan Show* to be broken in 1956. This is probably known only to Pedtke, with whom Sullivan and his producer communicated regarding the Club's appearances. Glee Club president Jerry Pottebaum ('56) remembers not only the disappointment that Club members felt to be discontinuing the tradition of singing on the show but also Sullivan's notice to Pedtke that "his hands were tied."[24] Indeed, union musicians were forcing strict priorities on talent for variety shows, and professional singers and choruses were to be first in line for the spots on the show, the military academy glee clubs being the only exception.[25]

Students from Pedtke's later classes recall other reasons for the snub in 1956. John F. Fisher ('65) remembers Pedtke telling him that Sullivan felt the invitations to perform on national television in some ways correlated with the success of the Notre Dame football program. (Notre Dame's dominance on the gridiron indeed began to slip in the mid-1950s.) Others, like Joseph Mulligan ('59), heard that the Glee Club's national television appearance on the prime-time variety show *Coke Time with Eddie Fisher* in 1955 was to blame. The program was taped in South Bend to celebrate the dedication on campus of WNDU-TV.[26] Since WNDU was an NBC affiliate, this might have caused the executives at CBS (Ed Sullivan's network) to withdraw future invitations to the Glee Club. The Club's connection to Ed Sullivan's show was lost, but its image as one of the leading choruses in the United States was assured, having entered the homes of millions of viewers as the program set ratings records in the 1950s.

The *Toast of the Town* spotlight was by no means the only attention the Glee Club drew from television. In the early 1950s, the group was heard in association with football promotional events, the team reaching a high-water mark after winning four national championships under Frank Leahy. The Club sang the "Victory March" and other favorites on film

Eddie Fisher

shorts that were inserted before or during the halftime of nationally broadcast football games, sometimes being replayed after the games if the network ran short of its allotted time.[27]

In its national television appearances without a football connection, the Singing Irish maintained its ties to big-name celebrities, beyond the spot on *Coke Time with Eddie Fisher* in 1955. In 1966, crooner Andy Williams enlisted the Glee Club not only to sing two patriotic songs and the "Victory March" on his show but also to provide the choral background for "The Village of St. Bernadette," which the singer said he had held back from performing on his show until he found the right group to back him up. Accompanied by a harpist and the Glee Club, Williams echoed the song's "Ave Maria," a borrowed refrain from the hymn *Immaculate Mary* (Lourdes Hymn).[28] The next year, the singer–actor John Davidson

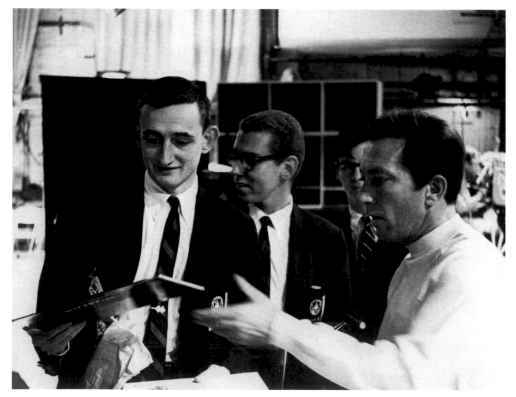

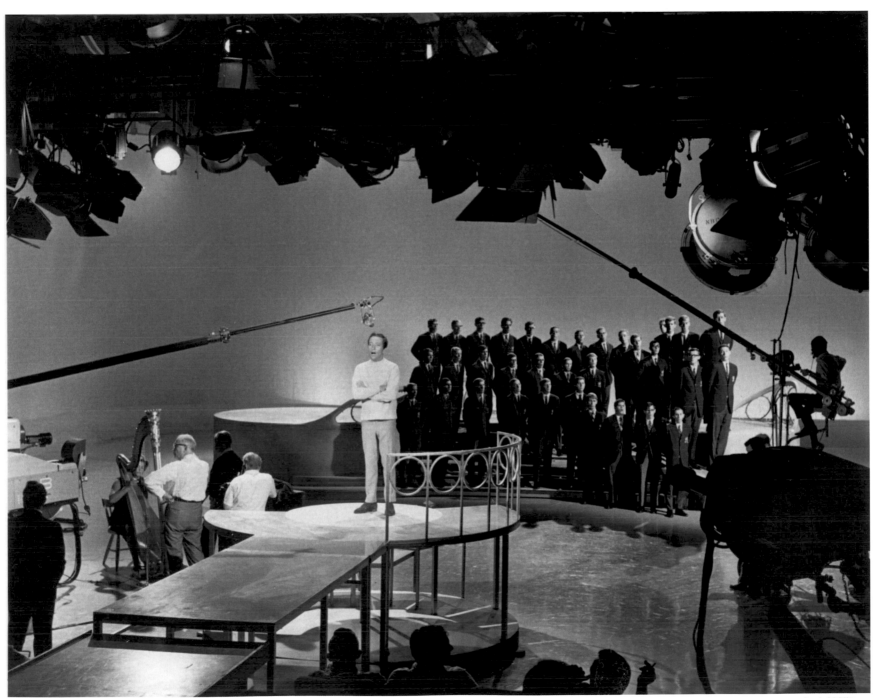

Andy Williams

starred in the ABC television special *John Davidson at Notre Dame*, which was filmed at the university's Stepan Center. The Club sang several songs, including "I'll Always Be Irish," and appeared with guests George Carlin, Judy Collins, and the folk-rock band Spanky and Our Gang.[29] As mentioned in chapters 5 and 7, the Glee Club appeared two times on *Kennedy & Company* during the 1970s, a Chicago variety program that later—as *A.M. Chicago*—would launch the career of Oprah Winfrey as host.

By this time, the era of the variety show was over, and no TV producer would book a college chorus of any kind on a national program. But the nascent cable television industry presented opportunities for distribution of independently produced programming. In 1981, comedian Bob Newhart took a serious turn as host of a TV special, *The Visitation Mystery*, released through religious networks. Notre Dame football coach Gerry Faust

Recordings, Airwaves, and the Silver Screen

brought along the Glee Club (directed by Douglas Belland) to provide the musical background for the show, though the real star power of that program came from a humble nun, Mother Teresa of Calcutta. At the end of the Stam era, the group released a thirty-minute video, *Christmas with the Notre Dame Glee Club*, which aired on PBS stations across the country and on cable television.[30] Daniel Stowe's Club likewise recorded Christmas music for public television in 2003, but this aired only on the local level (station WNIT). Television spots have been rare in more recent years other than local segments, though the Club did receive brief national cameos both in 1989 and 1995 on the syndicated morning show *Live with Regis and Kathie Lee*, again reflecting the host's tireless promotion of his alma mater.[31]

AT THE MOVIES

In the winter break bridging the years 1927 and 1928, the Glee Club embarked on a tour of the southern and western United States, covering some six thousand miles by train. In his second full year as director, Joseph Casasanta brought the group in touch with yet another medium of mass entertainment—motion pictures, a business itself in the midst of a significant period of transition. Warner Brothers Pictures had just revolutionized the industry with the release of the feature film *The Jazz Singer*, the world's first "talkie" that showcased the new technology of synchronized sound. The end of the silent film was in sight. Warner Brothers also produced "shorts" to accompany both silent and talking films under the "Vitaphone" name; the Glee Club would be among the earliest acts to star in these ten- to twelve-minute spotlights.

Recordings, Airwaves, and the Silver Screen

Despite packed concerts that drew some twenty-thousand viewers in total, the Glee Club's winter tour missed its financial marks, and the group was in search of $300 to help them return by rail to South Bend. Fr. Hugh O'Donnell, a former Glee Clubber and future president at Notre Dame, traveled with the group, and he looked to Hollywood to resolve the dilemma. He approached Bryan Foy, a former child vaudeville performer with the family act "Eddie Foy and the Seven Little Foys," for help. Foy was a young Hollywood director, who produced some of Warner Brothers' shorts, and he suggested to O'Donnell that he could use the Glee Club in a Vitaphone short to be called "The Notre Dame Glee Club, Premier Collegiate Glee Club." The next morning, the ensemble recorded a one-reeler and was paid the handsome sum of $1,500, five times the amount needed to return by train car.[32]

Despite the unexpected profit from the 1928 trip, the group would have to wait twenty-five years to tour the Pacific Coast again. However, that didn't stop Hollywood from coming to Notre Dame. When Coach Knute Rockne died in a plane crash in 1931, Universal Pictures rushed out a football story, *The Spirit of Notre Dame*, set on the campus and featuring many of Rockne's greatest players as themselves, with Lew Ayres as the self-centered quarterback who finds redemption in Rockne's spirit. The Glee Club sang at the film's premiere, wearing the flashy white sweaters that Casasanta ordered for the occasion. The Glee Club would film another "short" for Warner Brothers on its first and only summer tour of the East Coast. This second Vitaphone miniature, called "Hot Pepper Novelties," was shot in New York City in July 1933.[33] On Notre Dame's campus in that same year, it premiered in November as a lead-in to the feature film *Topaze,* starring John Barrymore and Myrna Loy.[34]

For all of the exposure that the Glee Club garnered on the big screen in the first half of the past century, it should be noted that the group was neither heard nor seen in the classic *Knute Rockne All American* (1940), starring Pat O'Brien and Ronald Reagan. The Moreau Seminary Choir, directed by Glee Club alumnus Fr. James Connerton, sang in the memorable funeral scene, though many of Pedtke's young men filled the church pews as extras. The Club did, however, perform in the week-long festivities heralding the world premiere of the film in South Bend. On October 4, 1940, singer and radio sensation Kate Smith and a host of Hollywood stars came to South Bend to help promote the premiere of *Knute Rockne All American*. Her hour-long variety show featuring celebrity guests was broadcast coast-to-coast on the CBS radio airwaves from the auditorium of John Adams High School. Forty members of the Glee Club and the Notre Dame Band were invited to sing as part of Smith's program.[35] The Clubbers sang several school songs, and the band played the "Victory March." To close the program, Pedtke's chorus backed up the incomparable "First Lady of Radio" in a special arrangement of her signature song, "God Bless America," no doubt one of the most thrilling moments in the history of the group.[36]

Two short documentaries on the university were completed in the 1950s and included the sound of the Notre Dame Glee Club. In 1953, the group recorded background music for a movie short produced by Professor Ed Fischer's film class. Called *Shake Down the Thunder*, it told the history of the "Victory March."[37] Four years later, the Club—along with the band and the Moreau Seminary Choir—laid down music for Owen Murphy Productions, which produced a twenty-nine-minute film titled simply *Notre Dame*. The promotional piece, filmed on 16 mm

color stock, was first shown at the 1957 Universal Notre Dame Night and later released for general use by local television stations. Joe Boland, who was the play-by-play voice of Notre Dame football on radio, narrated the film, which balanced attention to the tradition of Notre Dame on the gridiron with a closer look at life on campus, from classrooms and chapels to residence halls and libraries.[38]

Two modern films have featured the Notre Dame Glee Club on their soundtracks. The ensemble's recording of the Advent hymn "Lo, How a Rose E'er Blooming" appeared (rather inexplicably) in the romantic thriller *Two Moon Junction* (1988). More recently, the Glee Club can be heard singing "Hike, Notre Dame" and the "Victory March" in the Notre Dame football story *Rudy* (1993). The latter song notably played during the scene in which the teammates of the main character, Rudy Ruettiger, humiliate the undersized player on the practice squad, hitting him hard repeatedly in their drills. When *Rudy* premiered in South Bend, members of the Glee Club performed at a number of events and attended the movie's gala premiere.

In a world of countless media outlets, it is difficult for any entertainer today to break through the clutter that comes from a splintered broadcast environment. Not so in the first half of the twentieth century, a time of limited networks with mass reach. During this period, the Notre Dame Glee Club made splashes on the national stage not only with recordings on major labels but also with many radio and television appearances. Seven years of features on *Toast of the Town* signaled the height of the Glee Club's national fame, but the group's musical strains would not disappear into the ether. Recordings, as well as domestic and international tours, have played a much stronger role in maintaining a hold up to the present, generating an international reach for the group's music and developing new audiences that could not have known that the Notre Dame Glee Club approached the status of a household name in the 1950s.

TEN

The Glee Club and the Gridiron

The shadow of the football program at Notre Dame is unavoidable. Glee Club members have always been well versed in the game, and several of them played on the team in the early years. Hugh J. "Pepper" O'Donnell was an exceptional case: he played starting center on the varsity football team, *directed* the Glee Club in the fall of 1916, and later became president of the university (1940–46).[1] Another extraordinary example of a singer–football player was Harry Baujan, a first tenor in the Glee Club from 1915 to 1917.[2] After playing two years of professional football with the Cleveland Tigers/Indians following a military stint, Baujan coached football at the University of Dayton, achieving a record of 124 wins and 64 losses in his 22 years at the helm. Known as the "Blond Beast" for his strictness on and off the field, Baujan was inducted posthumously into the National Football Foundation's College Football Hall of Fame in 1990. Glee Club performances—formal and informal— have taken place before, during, and after football games, rallying fans' emotions on game day. While the football team has long been known to "barnstorm" across the country to attract the attention of fans in scores of cities, the Singing Irish have also been ambassadors for Notre Dame, with extensive tours to hundreds of towns, big and small, showcasing the best of the university away from the gridiron.

When the football program was in its infancy in the late nineteenth century, the university evidently relied upon the Glee Club to generate revenue for those on the gridiron. In 1888, the singers billed one of their on-campus concerts as a fundraiser to buy uniforms for the still-winless football team:

J. Hugh O'Donnell (*above*), 1940s; in uniform (*right*), 1915

An entertainment which had been gotten up by the College Glee Club for the purpose of raising funds to provide a suitable outfit for our Rugby football association was given last Thursday evening in Washington Hall. It proved a big success, both financially and in every other wise.[3]

Seven years later, *Scholastic* also noted how the members of the Glee Club would "go on tour when the football glow is waning, and they collect large sums of money from elite alumni audiences. And they have receptions and hops along the way."[4] As the football program claimed the spotlight for a good part of the twentieth century, it would no longer need the Glee Club to help the bottom line of the university, but the all-male chorus maintained links to the university's powerful football culture in many ways.

For starters, the nickname of the football team—the "Fighting Irish"—was made popular by a former member of the Glee Club at a time when other nicknames were applied to the team. Francis Wallace ('23) was the Club's business manager in his time at Notre Dame; he later became one of the nation's top sportswriters, working for the *New York News* and the Associated Press. In Wallace's first job at the *New York Post*, he regularly referred to the team as the "Fighting Irish," a name used among some students during that time when the team

The miles logged by the Glee Club in the interwar years were comparable to those traveled by the football team. *Scholastic* reported in 1946 an old campus adage: "If you want to see the world, don't join the Navy but the Notre Dame football team. If you can't make the team, try the Glee Club."

Football team in formation, 1915 (*front row, far left*) Harry Baujan and (*front row, center*) Hugh O'Donnell

was more commonly known as the "Ramblers." The new catchphrase, secured by Wallace and others in the press, signaled the determination that characterized the football teams of Knute Rockne's era and is surely rooted in the campus demographics of the time.[5] Whatever the naming origin, none other than a Glee Clubber helped bring it to national attention.

Rockne's death in the spring of 1931 shocked not just the Notre Dame public but the nation at large. In the extensive memorialization of the legendary football coach, the Glee Club was much in demand. In a "varsity show" just four weeks after Rockne's death, two students—Frank Carideo (a football player) and Charles Andres—paid tribute to the late coach on stage. The two knelt before an "illuminated white monument" on which the names of deceased football players and coaches were inscribed. Members of the Glee Club meanwhile stood behind a curtain humming the "Victory March."[6] Music was also composed in Rockne's honor in the aftermath of the plane accident that took his life. Student W. Franz Philipp wrote the march "Carry on for Rockne" with words by Austin Boyle. The song was quickly picked up by Universal Pictures for use in a 1931 sport series filmed on campus. Joseph Casasanta, who directed both the Glee Club and the band, arranged the chorus for his ensembles.[7]

Already mentioned in chapter 9, the Glee Club members did not play a role in the 1940 film *Knute Rockne All American*, but many of the boys sat as extras in the congregation of the funeral scene filmed in Sacred Heart Church. The group further participated in the "Rockne Week" activities surrounding the premiere of the movie in South Bend, singing a set of school songs in a special radio broadcast with the "First Lady of Radio," Kate Smith, in her hour-long program on the CBS network.[8] To this day, the family of Knute Rockne continues to commemorate the great coach on campus. Each year during the spring semester around the birthday of Knute Rockne (March 4), the Glee Club is asked to sing at the chapel of Dillon Hall for a Mass attended by the family.

Three unremarkable football seasons under head coach Hunk Anderson followed Rockne's untimely death. During the brief Anderson era and a little beyond it, the Glee Club was recognized in the campus press for playing a significant role during football games. When Notre Dame trounced the University of Pennsylvania 49–0 in November 1931, about 120 members of the Glee Club sat together to lead the student body in singing the school's pep songs, emulating a similar musical practice of the military academies at football games.[9] In 1933 and 1934, the section of Glee Clubbers was expressly located behind the band around the 30-yard line, a move orchestrated by Casasanta for "the purpose of stimulating organized singing and cheering among the students."[10] It is not clear precisely when this tradition faded.

Glee Club singing during football games has been relatively rare since the 1930s. In the 1950s, national broadcasts of Notre Dame football sometimes featured film shorts of the Glee Club singing the "Victory March" and other fight songs during halftime, and occasionally these bits would be replayed if the game finished ahead of the network's allotted time.[11] During several Glee Club reunions, the group has been given the honor to assemble in the northeast corner of Notre Dame Stadium to sing "The Star-Spangled Banner."[12] For the group's reunion

in 2009, however, NBC ran a pre-game show that was to feature the band playing the national anthem instead of the hundreds of gathered Glee Club alumni and current club members who were prepared to sing it. The snub drew national attention, and the Glee Club has not sung the anthem at a home game since.[13] The ensemble has made on-field appearances away from the campus, singing the national anthem with the University of Illinois Varsity Men's Glee Club at the Illinois-Michigan game in Champaign-Urbana in 1961, and in Philadelphia's Veterans Stadium for the 1974 Notre Dame–Navy game. Similarly on a fall 1995 tour, the group was invited to sing "The Star-Spangled Banner" jointly with the Army Glee Club before the 1995 Notre Dame–Army game in Giants Stadium in East Rutherford, New Jersey.[14]

In 1980, the Glee Club's fall tour included the singing of the anthem at Lambeau Field for a Packers-Vikings game. Technically this had nothing to do with the Notre Dame football culture *per se*. Though it was only the last Sunday in October, winter had come early that year. By game time, the temperature at the "frozen tundra" had dipped below freezing when a busload of parka-clad Clubbers huddled for warmth at the corner of the end zone. Perhaps inspired by the Packer diehards who sport nothing more above the waist on game day than green and gold body paint, Glee Club director Douglas Belland spontaneously threw off his hat, gloves, and overcoat just before the group was introduced. He stepped in front to direct the stunned ensemble in nothing warmer than the traditional blue blazer and gray slacks. If Belland was affected by the cold, he didn't show it and neither did the majority of the Clubbers who followed suit and belted out one of the most vigorous renditions of "The Star-Spangled Banner" in memory.[15] It was the first time the Glee Club performed at an NFL football game.

Vikings fans also witnessed the second and last time the Glee Club sang the national anthem at a professional football game—at the Metrodome in November 1991 on Monday Night Football against the Chicago Bears. After singing "The Star-Spangled Banner" with its unpredictable echo in the indoor facility, a few senior Glee Clubbers tracked down a former classmate on the Bears' sideline, Notre Dame All-American nose tackle Chris Zorich ('91). Unlike the trip to Green Bay, the Glee Club's invitation to sing at the Metrodome was a true run-out performance, not part of a tour—all the more euphoric for those missing class to be singing on national TV.

PRE- AND POST-GAME SINGING

In Notre Dame's own charged football environment, the Glee Club has made its biggest musical impact outside the stadium, both before and after the games. The rallying songs of the group continue to be welcome around game day festivities in South Bend. Casasanta's marches incite throngs gathered for football games, and even the university's alma mater, "Notre Dame, Our Mother," has the power to unite fans with both its solemnity and heroic ending. In October 1942, rallies were hosted after football games in the courtyard space between Dillon and Alumni halls, and these would include a Glee Club concert in the same area.[16] By mid-November of the same year, *Scholastic* reported that "the Glee Club concerts in the Alumni-Dillon court are fast becoming a tradition," and that all gathered would join in the singing.[17] It is not known whether Dean Pedtke conducted at these events, but it is not likely. The post-game rallies, in any event, were a short-lived phenomenon, called into question in the same year they began.

By the mid-1950s a new event had replaced the post-game rally of the previous decade—the victory dance. Again, members of the Glee Club played a role. A few mentions of the group at victory dances refer to performances by the Glee Club quartet or octet, the subset of singers dispatched by Pedtke to meet the numerous requests for smaller, informal concerts that emerged with regularity.[18] The victory dance that followed the 1957 Purdue game, called the "Purdue Prance," featured Gene Bertoncini and his Lettermen as the main entertainment, but the intermission included the performance of a medley by the Glee Club octet.[19] A few years

later, the entire Glee Club seems to have appeared at these victory dances. Following a loss to Navy on November 4, 1961, the Singing Irish performed at LaFortune Student Center during the event. "Dancing stopped for twenty minutes while the Glee Club, led by student director Philip Jones ('63), sang seven of its most popular numbers to an enthusiastic group of students and their dates." Among these songs was the concert spiritual "Ride the Chariot," still popular today.[20]

Appearances of the Notre Dame Glee Club before football games have been better documented and have taken on many forms. During the tenure of Joseph Casasanta, the Glee Club sometimes performed on national radio on the Friday before a game. Each year between 1929 and 1932, the ensemble sang live music for NBC's *Armour Hour*, a broadcast from studios in Chicago that reached thirty-seven states from coast to coast. The 1929 radio program in particular produced widespread praise. As explained in chapter 9, on the Friday night preceding the Notre Dame–Southern California game at Chicago's Soldier Field, members of the Notre Dame Glee Club prepared musical material for the first half of the *Armour Hour*, while the USC glee club and band furnished

music from a Los Angeles studio for the second part of the program.[21] The broadcast excited two illustrious fan bases; the official attendance of the game the next day was 112,912, which stood as the record for a Notre Dame football game for more than eighty years.[22]

Evidence of Glee Club entertainment before games on home football weekends can be found as early as 1940, when the group was reported to have sung "serenades" on the Friday before the big game.[23] More consistently, the Club appeared at school pep rallies at the Notre Dame Fieldhouse, beginning in 1946 and continuing through the end of the era of football coach Frank Leahy (1953).[24] Before the capacity crowds of four thousand, the ensemble would share the stage with galvanizing speakers, ending with Leahy. New Friday evening traditions emerged in the last thirty years. Glee Club directors have opened up Friday afternoon rehearsals to the public, as the group polishes up numbers to be sung on game day. The young men then proceed *en masse* to South Dining Hall, where they sing fight songs for the gathered fans in a unique way—standing on chairs at the long head table known as the "altar." The Glee Club has partnered with the band a few times in joint concerts on Football Fridays at the DeBartolo Performing Arts Center to perform school songs and sometimes Broadway-type material.

For some thirty years beginning in the early 1980s, brief Glee Club performances took place in the Athletic and Convocation Center (today's Joyce Center) before Saturday kickoffs. The group has lately experimented with performances outdoors both near the Hesburgh Library reflecting pool and at the "Irish Green" south of the DeBartolo Performing Arts Center. The pre-game performances draw hundreds—sometimes thousands—of fans. Called "ND in Revue," these concerts survey the lighter repertoire of the Glee Club and never last more than thirty minutes. Alumni of the chorus are invited up to sing the last three songs—Pedtke's "Notre Dame, We Hail Thee," Casasanta's "Notre Dame, Our Mother," and the "Victory March." While the early 1930s showcased the Glee Club as a kind of "twelfth man" in the stadium, the group has always played a role in stirring up fans' spirits around the intense football Saturday atmosphere.

PEDTKE BOWL

The Notre Dame Glee Club has been recognized for its musical contributions in and around the football culture of the university, but, like so many Notre Dame students, the members of the Glee Club *played* the game of football, too, a tradition that complemented the more cerebral and sedentary activities of the rehearsal room. On October 16, 1948, more than one hundred Glee Clubbers gathered at the home of director Dean Pedtke for a picnic. Pedtke's "farm" north of the campus had spacious grounds for the event, and the picnic was an ideal opportunity for members of the varsity Glee Club to fraternize with underclassmen on the "B team" chorus that Pedtke had organized a decade earlier. Despite the threat of rain, the event was a success. There were hot dogs and potato chips for all, and several portable radios broadcast an away game. (The Fighting Irish pummeled the

University of Nebraska Cornhuskers 44–13.) The main activity of the day, however, was a game of touch football that pitted members of the Glee Club against each other. It was reported in *Scholastic* that an ankle injury to freshman Bud Johnston ('52) marred the otherwise enjoyable day of football at Pedtke's rural estate. The group ended the day singing four-part harmony around a fire.[25] This event spawned a tradition—now spanning three generations—of spending a fall afternoon at the Pedtke house. By the 1980s, the annual football game would be called "Pedtke Bowl," sometimes preceded by an outdoor mass.

It is clear from the early years that this event was billed principally as an opportunity to give freshman a taste of Glee Club culture outside the rehearsal room. There were chances to sit and talk, or to display athletic prowess. In 1949, the activities expanded to include a game of softball in addition to the touch football game, but from 1950, it seems that football was the chief business of the afternoon on Pedtke's makeshift gridiron.[26] The tradition continued into the 1960s, but the event no longer featured a touch football game. By the end of that decade, the game had turned to tackle football without pads. A team of underclassmen was matched against the varsity Clubbers, and freshmen who excelled on the field sometimes became targets "to be put in their place" in the course of the afternoon. Injuries were the norm at these rowdy games. After a couple of hours of rough play, one would be lucky to come away from the contest with a deep bruise or a twisted ankle. Concussions, dislocated shoulders, and broken bones were not uncommon.

The annual Pedtke Bowl continues to this day, hosted by the former director's daughter, Dorothy, who lives in her parents' home. In thanksgiving for letting the Glee Club use the large backyard for the game, members report a few hours before kickoff to do yardwork for Dorothy, clearing the woods and fields surrounding her house. Pedtke Bowl still pits upperclassmen against underclassmen, the former usually pronounced the victors, no matter the exact final score. Not unlike the first gathering at

Pedtke's sixty-seven years ago, food and fraternity complement the afternoon of football, advancing the brotherly bonds so central to the Glee Club experience.[27]

That the activities of the Glee Club were not completely separable from the spirited football environment of the university is made clear in a campus report from 1925. Describing the state of music at the university, the author compared the Glee Club and the Varsity quartet with the profile and actions of the current football team: "The Glee Club emulates the football team of Notre Dame in certain particulars. It has teamwork down to a nicety. In its ensemble numbers, it has true harmony. It has its 'four horsemen' too. The Stuhldreher-Layden-Crowley-Miller backfield of the gridiron has its counterpart in the [Varsity] quartet composed of Butler, Haley, Koch and Meyers."[28] In promoting its own touring appearances in cities around the country, the Glee Club sent out press releases for many years highlighting its similarities to the football team.[29]

The football atmosphere of the University of Notre Dame continues to inspire millions around the world, but the Glee Club has not been far behind in its ability to embody the ideals of the school and to reach those captivated by the spirit of Our Lady's university. The group's role in football game day culture has been extensive since the proto–glee clubs of the nineteenth century. The Glee Club brings the march of Notre Dame football alive in the closing numbers of each concert on its national and international tours, sustaining the devotion of legions of Notre Dame followers in areas of the country that the football team will never reach.

ELEVEN

Traditions Public and Private

Many traditions in the Notre Dame Glee Club have been mentioned to this point, whether on the concert stage, on campus, or on the tour bus. This chapter is a catch-all for various aspects of Glee Club life that have been missed, recounting more of the activities, personalities, and rituals that have formed the Singing Irish over the last century. The "miscellaneous" nature of this endeavor prevents the presentation of a clear narrative. What follows below begins with a review of Glee Club chaplains who have served the organization and continues with fraternal traditions of the group, some publicly visible and others closely guarded by its members.

FAITH AND SERVICE

Associated with the nation's foremost Catholic university, the Notre Dame Glee Club has never shied away from its religious heritage. Audiences especially recognize the unique spirit of the church that is channeled through the voices of the young men, most visibly in the sacred music that infuses concert offerings. In 1925, the business manager of the Glee Club, Victor Lemmer, received a letter from a priest whose parish had recently hosted the group in Barnesboro, Pennsylvania. The Club's connection to the Catholic faith was clear.

I was anxious to have the students from a representative Catholic University visit in our midst, and when the opportunity presented itself from Notre Dame, so well known, I was delighted; for I thought it would mean much for the people here not only for the chance of hearing excellent music but for the good of the cause of religion. I take pleasure in whatever reflects credit on the Church and its institutions.[1]

Another visible sign of the Glee Club's religious character is the chaplain who attends to the group, particularly in its travels. The constitution of the organization describes the role of the chaplain:

> In keeping with the Catholic nature of the University, the Glee Club shall have a Chaplain who shall be a priest of the Congregation of the Holy Cross. . . . The Chaplain shall be the Spiritual Director of the Club. He shall be asked to preside at celebrations of the Eucharist and to lead the other spiritual exercises of the group. The Chaplain shall tour with the Club.[2]

Father Robert Griffin, C.S.C., and Darby O'Gill

Well over a dozen Glee Club chaplains have served the group in some capacity across its hundred-year history. Most of these priests are mentioned in connection with Glee Club tours, though rarely at any length. The most ambitious chaplain on record was former Glee Club member J. Hugh "Pepper" O'Donnell, later president of the university. On the 1928 tour of the West, O'Donnell talked Warner Brothers into putting the Glee Club in a twelve-minute "talkie," a story told in chapter 9. Andrew Mulreany ('28), who had been the business manager of the trip, wrote fifty years later that O'Donnell had hopped off the train west of Salt Lake City when they came upon a fatal car accident and administered last rites to the dying motorist.[3]

Several names of Glee Club chaplains appear after World War II during the Pedtke era: Frs. Joseph Barry, Joseph Kehoe, Charles Carey, James Norton, James Thornton, William McAuliffe, Daniel O'Neil, Hubert Schwan, James Riehle, and Michael Heppen. As mandated by the Club's constitution, all were priests of the Congregation of the Holy Cross. Some of these priests were reluctant conscripts assigned by the office of student affairs to monitor the behavior of the boys away from campus. But one chaplain had a record stint with the Glee Club beginning in the 1968–69 academic year—Fr. Robert Griffin ('49, '58 MA). For more than a generation, "Griff" (as he was affectionately called by the young men) shepherded hundreds of Clubbers in their faith lives and vouched for the work and integrity of the ensemble as directors came and went.

Griff first toured with the Club as a replacement for Fr. Daniel O'Neil, who had traveled for several years with the group in the 1960s. Griff resided in Stanford Hall at Notre Dame and had a cocker spaniel named Darby O'Gill ("D.O.G."), after a fictional Irishman from a 1959 Disney movie. He also wrote a column for the *Observer* entitled "Letters to a Lonely God," in which he discussed moral issues but never failed to stamp his essays with his sharp wit and humor. His articles were nationally syndicated by various Catholic publications, and many of

Is the Glee Club damned from here to eternity?

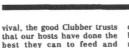

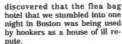

Father Robert Griffin
Letters to a Lonely God

I have heard them singing in the great cathedrals of Europe; and the beauty of their "Ave" at Notre Dame in Paris left the members of the congregation transfixed, as though they were being introduced to the Catholic soul of the city.

I have heard them singing hymns of Christ's passion in the Catholic chapel at Dachau; the effect was like seeing for the first time Marc Chagall's great painting called "The White Crucifixion," which shows Christ as a brother to the Jewish victims who have died in pogroms and holocausts.

I've spent 100,000 miles, more or less, riding with the Glee Club on buses, examining each new season's crop of campus extroverts; and I think I have a clear picture of the traditions and discipline which have turned them into the brotherhood of Johnny-one-notes whom America hears singing.

Like the Whiffenpoofs at Yale, most glee clubs appropriate Kipling's barrack-room ballad as their personal anthem.

"We're poor little lambs who've lost our way, Baa! Baa! Baa!/We're little black sheep who've gone astray, Baa-aa-

vival, the good Clubber trusts that our hosts have done the best they can to feed and shelter the travelers.

The good Clubber's duty is to show, by his graciousness, how grateful he is for small favors, and how unspoiled he is, as he faces a famine and pretends it's

discovered that the flea bag hotel that we stumbled into one night in Boston was being used by hookers as a house of ill repute.

In Vienna, our hotel rooms were haunted by the ghosts of old Nazis. In a youth hostel in Brussels, we were chewed up

communicate. Now Notre Dame is making a place for other singing groups who will follow in their footsteps.

Each group will develop its own wonderful traditions, but not one of them can claim that they owe the Holy Father in Rome a concert. Pope Paul VI was waiting to greet the Glee Club in their first visit to Rome in 1971.

Those students had to miss meeting the Pontiff because on Wednesday when their audience was scheduled, they had promises to keep up the road in Milan, and many miles

---

them were collected in his book *In the Kingdom of the Lonely God*, issued in 1973.[4] Griff also founded "Darby's Place" in the basement of LaFortune Student Center, where he counseled students—not just Glee Clubbers—on all matters at all hours of the night. His Saturdays were dedicated to nurturing children; in the morning, he hosted a radio show in which he read comic strips to kids. And on Saturday evenings, he celebrated an "Urchins Mass" in the Stanford Hall chapel for young children.

Having traveled tens of thousands of miles with the Glee Club as its chaplain, Griff had an unmatched perspective on the organization's culture. He recognized, for one thing, how Glee Club members positively channeled the image of the university around the world. In an interview with *Scholastic*, he took note of the group's efficacy as a university ambassador.

> The Glee Club is one of the least expensive and most effective P.R. gestures operating for the University. Other clubs do not have the vehicle which the Glee Club has and few are so articulate in their message. To many of the people they sing for, the boys are a glossy image of what they would like their own children to be. They are somewhat embarrassed by the clean-cut image they project of a "better hope," and Notre Dame's answer to a pot smoking, grungy, hippy-type world, yet another side of them shows that they share much with their generation.[5]

Griff was never shy about pointing out the ironies of Glee Club tour life and was constantly aware of his place in it. Though he and the director usually constituted the extent of the mature adults traveling on tour, Griff did not police behavior, but was nevertheless quick to aid when students came to him. The anniversary date of his ordination often coincided with European tours, and he would preside at a Mass honoring that occasion, notably at St. Mark's Basilica in Venice at the tomb of the titular saint (1971), at the Cathedral of Notre Dame of Paris (1975, 1978, 1981), and at the Dachau concentration camp (1984). On the other hand, Griff

A 1966 Glee Glub tour magazine included the following: "Perhaps the presence of a chaplain, on even as brief a trip as this, would serve to hasten the aging process of some of our upperclassmen. Perhaps this trip has taught us the most important—but at the same time, hidden—function of the chaplain. His presence keeps us constantly aware of our Christian responsibility.... Being stable himself, our chaplain by association may lend some stability to our own actions which reflect our characters. Perhaps he will remind us of who and what we are—this will result in some stability, and an important stop in the maturation process."

more than once remarked on the sense of loneliness that a chaplain may endure on the road with the young singers. Describing the European tour of 1990, he wrote,

> The Glee Club operates on the buddy system which means that every clubber has a pal he's paired off with on the housing list. . . . The tour guide has the bus driver to toddle off with in the evening for supper. The glee club chaplain walks alone, rooms alone and smokes alone. As the lone smoker, he usually eats alone in the restaurants at the tables set with ashtrays. This means that for everyone one else in our party, gay Paree is the city of lights and laughter, but for the chaplain, it's like empty saddles in the corral where old cowpokes go to fade away.[6]

Griffin's activities with the Glee Club were curtailed in the early 1990s for health reasons. He would attend rehearsals on occasion, but he was no longer able to travel with the group. His passing in 1999 marked the loss of a great figure in the Club's history, perhaps second in memory only to Dean Pedtke. When members of the

Glee Club convened in 2000 for a reunion, they attended a memorial Mass for Griffin at Keenan-Stanford Chapel, and they planted a tree in honor of their longtime chaplain outside the residence hall.[7] Stanford Hall also adopted the "Griffin" as its mascot.[8]

Since 1994, the Glee Club chaplainship has evolved into something of a tag team of Holy Cross priests, some from the chorus's own ranks. Father Terry Linton journeyed domestically with the Club as Griffin's responsibilities receded. Father Michael Driscoll, associate professor of theology at Notre Dame, generally has been the "go-to" chaplain for European travel in the last twenty years. Fluent in French and Italian, Driscoll has great knowledge of art and architecture that has allowed for rich learning experiences on tour. Father Tom Eckert, a fluent Spanish speaker, toured Latin America with the Club in 2005. Fathers James Foster ('77), John Thiede ('92), and John DeRiso ('93), are all Notre Dame graduates who sang in the Glee Club and have more recently traveled with the Club on tours, whether domestic or international.[9]

In addition to the presence of a chaplain, the Glee Club demonstrates the Catholic nature of its university by engaging in a number of service projects that provide support to the campus and the larger community of South Bend. In 1989, *Scholastic* briefly summed up the variety of activities that consume the students outside of the rehearsal room and the concert stage: "They sing at pizza restaurants in town on various evenings, they sponsor service projects, blood drives, they rake leaves, and they sing for the nuns at SMC [Saint Mary's College]. They also hold a fundraiser for the United Way."[10] Audiences at Glee Club Christmas concerts of the last generation will remember that proceeds are directed to the South Bend Center for the Homeless. The Club has also sung informal concerts on site at the center in recent years and has made annual donations to the center in honor of director Daniel Stowe. Several times per semester in today's Glee Club, regular mini-concerts are given at retirement homes, notably the Holy Cross Village on campus and the Village at Arborwood in nearby Granger, Indiana.[11]

In earlier periods of Glee Club history, members served the community by tutoring children. In a May 1964 newsletter to the chorus's alumni, president Jim Egan ('64) noted that twenty-five singers in the Glee Club teamed up weekly with twenty-five women from Saint Mary's College as part of the Blue Circle tutoring program. The college students took a bus to Our Lady of Hungary Parish to assist the youngsters for an hour, after which the Glee Clubbers would serenade those gathered with something from their repertoire.[12] Glee Club tutors were noted into the early 1970s, then in connection with Neighborhood Youth Study Help Program for underprivileged children.[13]

A very personal service project the Glee Club undertook was assisting with the construction of the house of its director, Dean Pedtke. The Pedtke home, designed by Dean to accommodate a large family and today occupied by his daughter Dorothy, was constructed in 1947 on what had been the south twenty acres of a fifty-acre farm. When work began on the home, Glee Clubbers came out regularly on weekends to set up piles of boards and concrete blocks in convenient places around the site, to speed up the construction process. Years later, Pedtke's wife Helen distinctly recalled the young men forming an assembly line and passing cinder blocks to convenient spots near the residence. At the end of the day, Dorothy remembers, there would be a picnic at the edge of the woods for the tired Glee Clubbers.[14] Pedtke's singers also planted pine trees on both sides of the driveway. Those original trees still stand, forming a cathedral ceiling high over the drive. Even after Dean died, the Glee Club, especially under David Clark Isele, continued to use the Pedtke home for its gathering place. In gratitude for their long connection with the home, the Pedtkes have always believed that every Glee Club member should feel some ownership in the place and know that they are welcome at any time.

FRATERNITY AND DIVERSIONS

When a student is accepted into the Glee Club, one of the benefits he enjoys is a ready-made group of "brothers" united by a love of song. The young men who commit to the organization learn quickly why Clubbers and non-Clubbers alike recognize it as "the only fraternity on campus."[15] Fraternities in the true sense are, of course, more than institutions; they are societies that foster brotherhood. Since the time that director Carl Stam introduced a set of German drinking songs to the Club in the late 1980s, the singers have adopted the German word for brothers, *Brüder*, not only as a way to refer to each other but also as a term for the bonds of brotherhood they experience as young men united for a common purpose. Letters and emails from one Clubber to another often close with "Ein Bruder" ("a brother"), a meaningful signal in writing of the connection each member feels with his musical cohorts.

The most impressive display of Glee Club camaraderie comes every three years when the organization invites alumni of the chorus to return to campus for a reunion. Though about 150 alumni came to campus for the first reunion in 1963 to celebrate Dean Pedtke's twenty-fifth year as director of the Club, and as many as 250 attended each of three reunions anticipating his retirement (1972) or recognizing his contributions (1973 and 1975), his passing left a question as to whether alumni would continue to reunite in great numbers. The answer came in 1977, when a large crowd of Glee Club graduates packed historic Tippecanoe Place in South Bend. The tradition of triennial reunions is now well established.

At Glee Club reunions, former members from around the world return to campus—inevitably on a home football weekend—to share memories with classmates, rehash old songs, and participate in activities that promote fraternity.[16] The annual fall concert is characteristically billed as an Alumni Reunion concert, during which Glee Club graduates are invited on stage to sing the entire second half (from memory). The rehearsal and buffet dinner that precede the concert radiate palpable energy as one, then another, and another, alumnus spots an old singing buddy long separated from Notre Dame by time and miles. A formal banquet is usually held after the Saturday afternoon football game, followed by a Mass and a brunch on Sunday morning. Naturally, all of these events are saturated with song. About two hundred alumni returned in 1975 for the sixtieth anniversary of the Glee Club, which featured

gourmet cooking at the Pedtke home prepared by director Isele, a culinary performance he reprised on a grander scale at the Studebaker mansion two years later.[17] By one account, nearly three hundred alumni returned in 1990 for the Club's seventy-fifth anniversary, orchestrated in what would be the last year of Carl Stam's term, and an even greater number attended a reunion in 2003.[18] The Glee Club's centennial reunion in 2015 promises to be the best attended of all reunions by any measurement; more than seventy graduating classes will be represented.

Within the Club, brotherhood is cultivated on a daily basis, beginning with the simple act of sharing meals. Following weekday rehearsals, Glee Club members proceed to South Dining Hall, though they used to split time between South and North Dining Halls. At South Dining Hall, the young men are known to take their seats at the dais some call the "altar." As described in chapter 10, the group sings a short set of school songs on Fridays preceding home football games while standing on chairs. Eating together on campus extends to South Bend a few times per year. After the group's first rehearsal of the year and at other times, the Glee Club escapes to its favorite pizzeria, Bruno's Pizza, west of downtown South Bend. Like South Dining Hall, Bruno's has long tables, and the group stands on the chairs to serenade the dining public. Upon its departure, the Club also serenades the longtime owner "Rosa" (sometimes called "Mama" by the singers) with an abbreviated version of Franz Biebl's "Ave Maria."

Apart from daily interaction, the Club holds more formal events as a group and with others that advance fraternity. The responsibility of arranging these gatherings usually falls on the shoulders of the Glee

Club's vice president. As a sort of social chairman, the vice president has the duty to organize and oversee a slate of activities that fosters community within the group on a tight budget. The events have a wide range, from dances and formals to off-campus parties and special outings. Whether the occasions involve only Glee Clubbers, friends of the group, or the outside public more generally, the vice president ensures that the young men leave the planned activities satisfied.

Glee Club dances were popular from the organization's early days and were restricted to members and their dates. A band from campus or from South Bend was often hired to provide music for the event. In 1922 and in 1949, the Club reserved space in the Rotary Room of downtown South Bend's Oliver Hotel for its dances.[19] Restricting attendance was especially imperative in 1949, when membership in the Club alone exceeded one hundred students. *Scholastic* reported that the Club sang some numbers when Gene Hull's campus orchestra—the evening's hired entertainment—took a thirty-minute intermission. Guests of honor at that dance were director Pedtke and his wife Helen.[20]

A Glee Club "formal" has been an annual fixture on the social calendar since 1974. Members dress in tuxedos and also don colored silk sashes that indicate their voice part in the ensemble.[21] In addition to dance music, those invited can always expect a serenade by their hosts. A less formal dance held in the winter, "Screw Your Section-mate," is based on Notre Dame's ubiquitous "Screw Your Roommate" (SYR) dances. Following the campus tradition, in opposition to what the name seems to imply, Club members locate dates for each other, trying to match their colleagues' personalities and preferences.

Since the mid-1970s, a less formal gathering of Glee Club members and their dates has been the annual hayride, held in late September or October. Cars full of students venture to a farm in southwest Michigan to embark on a tractor-drawn hayride through the countryside at dusk. The typically crisp fall evening is filled with serenades, not just on the ride itself, but also at a campfire that is held after the ride has finished.[22]

MEMBERS ONLY

In an interview given to *Scholastic* in 1975, Glee Club director David Isele noticed that "the boys seem to realize that the harder one works, the harder one may play."[23] We have already seen how the Club "plays" with others in extracurricular activities on and off campus. Similarly, the group holds a number of members-only events outside the rehearsal room that are meant to reap the benefits of brotherhood and affirm the venerable traditions of the Club. Organized mainly by the vice president, these gatherings range from solemn to ribald in nature, favoring the latter.

Since the early 1970s, Glee Club members have kicked off the academic year with an annual members-only party known as the "Screamer." The principal idea behind the stag event is to introduce new members to the social atmosphere of the Club, one that celebrates camaraderie as much as it labors in the rehearsal room. At the Screamer, seniors are charged with introducing freshman individually to their new set of brothers on a makeshift stage.

John Murphy ('75) captured the sentiment: "Senior members take responsibility for the freshmen. We are expected to help them with adjustment and share the Club's sense of fraternity."[24]

One of the other goals of the annual Screamer is to familiarize new members with an "underground" repertoire of songs that was never intended for the concert stage. Without recourse to a musical score, Clubbers preserve these songs by oral transmission and repetition, though one could expect the music to be corrupted for this very same reason. By far, the underground piece best remembered by the singers is a once-popular country-western song "Cigarettes and Whiskey and Wild, Wild Women," recorded by the Sons of the Pioneers in 1947. Eugene Jones ('49) is credited with introducing the song to the group, and it has been passed down through almost three generations of Clubbers.[25] When performing this piece at large events, the seniors huddle together and declaim the verses of "Cigarettes," while underclassmen form a circle around them and sound the boisterous refrain.[26]

Another verse-refrain song called "In the Halls" has been circulating in the Club's repertorial underground since the University of Michigan Men's Glee Club sang a joint concert with them at Notre Dame in January 1982. (The song is known by other glee clubs as well.) At the post-concert reception, the Michigan men launched into a song called "The Halls of Michigan," which featured lewd verses improvised by soloists and a rowdy choral refrain reminiscent of a campfire song. Tom Nessinger ('82) remembers that when the Michigan group left, the Notre Dame Glee Club adopted the song and "repurposed it for our own tawdry ends."[27] Lasting as long as verses are created, "In the Halls" can persist well over an hour; for this reason, it is particularly well suited for extended bus trips. An uncatalogued Glee Club "glossary" given to rookie members benignly describes "In the Halls" as "a fantastic piece of showmanship as well as creativity." Doon Wintz ('85), however, pointedly summarized the spontaneous verses of "In the Halls" as a game of "lascivious one-upsmanship."[28]

The Screamer and similar parties are also times for new members to become acquainted with alternate lyrics sung to traditional songs, or to songs that have disappeared from the concert stage. Pedtke's "Disney Medley" and his "College Medley" of university fight songs lived in the underground during the Isele years, along with at least a dozen other favorites. Patrick Scott ('76, '79L) remembered that Isele, who was invited to the Screamer, would exit the party when the "Pedtke-era songs degraded . . . as voice parts were forgotten and words and notes elided in uncertainty."[29] The degradation of music further included the art of substitute lyrics, for example, the vulgar alternate texts sung to opponents' fight songs.

A final category of unofficial music is the Club's traditional toast for banquets, post-concert receptions, and soirees. Following an evening together, Clubbers will move about the room with a glass in hand, saluting their fellow singers with the song "A Toast to All Who Gather Here," a tune of unknown origin. It should be mentioned that Glee Club director Joseph Casasanta penned an "Irish Toast" that fell out of circulation; however, it is

"Cigarettes and Whiskey" has a fond place in my heart because we sang it the night I was accepted into the Club. During a very lonely first few weeks on campus as a scared freshman, that was the first time I felt I belonged. I never forgot that, and it was always in my mind every time we sang it.

—Brian McLinden ('82, '86MA)

preserved in manuscript in the Notre Dame Archives. Given the song's chiding of non-Domers and its blatant promotion of a drinking culture, it lacks the dignity of the current toasting song, but does shed some light on Glee Club life in the late 1920s and early 1930s, and perhaps on why Fr. John O'Hara was critical of the Club's lack of discipline at the time. "A Toast to All Who Gather Here," on the other hand, is positive and promotes fraternity: "and best of all a thousand friends like you, and you, and you."

Glee Club members have long competed against each other in several sports. The annual "Pedtke Bowl" has already been described in detail in chapter 10. Basketball and bowling have been popular among the most recent generation of members. On Sundays throughout the school year, "Glee Club Hoops" are held in the gymnasium of the Rockne Memorial. Director Stowe took part from time to time some years ago, and still is known to lace them up for a pickup game on Club tours.

Bowling was another pastime for more than a decade. In 1984, students from both the Glee Club and the Notre Dame Chorale gathered at the Beacon Bowl on South Bend's west side for some Saturday morning bowling. Glee Clubbers had been bowling with each other on Saturday mornings for at least a year prior to that.[30] This was always done in the spring, when there was no football to watch. Called "Bedhead Bowling" by 1990, the idea is for members to roll out of bed on a Saturday morning without combing their hair and head straight to the bowling lanes. The Glee Club glossary accounts for the simplicity of the event: "You will sing the national anthem before you bowl, and the bedhead commissioner will take care of the lanes, scores, and other stories that may need to be told." An alumni newsletter also notes another ritual associated with Bedhead Bowling—"the ceremonial throwing of the first gutter ball."[31]

The most dignified gathering of Glee Club members comes at an annual formal banquet, held off campus near the end of the academic year. At the 1916 banquet (the first one on record), Notre Dame's president Fr. John W. Cavanaugh was an honorary guest at the dinner.[32] Other notable guests have spoken at this annual event, including honorary Glee Club members Chuck Lennon (1995) and Fr. Theodore Hesburgh (1996). Hesburgh was present at several other banquets, including in 1971 when he was one of *thirty* guests of honor (many of them university officials) in attendance. During the banquet, the senior Clubbers are invited to address the gathered assembly. They typically highlight special moments during their time in the Club and words of wisdom to those who will continue to carry on the group's traditions. The banquet often concludes with a presentation by the incoming president of the Glee Club, in which he outlines his plans for the year to come.

In addition to an invited speaker and speeches by officers, the director, and other senior members, commemorative items are given to the singers, recognizing their contribution to the organization. In 1925, the officers of the Glee Club had a contest for members to design a pin that could be awarded to the singers.[33] In the early Pedtke years, graduating seniors were given a commemorative set of "Glee Club keys," made to fit on a tie clasp or lapel. In 1953, a decision was made to present the departing class with engraved beer mugs.[34] The tradition later became for all Clubbers to purchase a mug each year and then receive one for free in their fourth or final year. The names of the seniors are engraved on the beer stein, and sometimes a select list of tour stops or repertoire is included.

The annual banquet also features the presentation of the Daniel H. Pedtke Award, which honors members who exemplify the spirit of the Notre Dame Glee Club. The distinction is typically bestowed on two graduating seniors, and for many years it was announced by Helen Pedtke. Recipients have their names engraved on a plaque. The merit-based Pedtke Award is distinct from the Daniel H. Pedtke Scholarship. In 1977, the Pedtke scholarship fund was developed following the death of the longtime Glee Club director, with $50,000 of seed money pledged by Clubber Eugene Fanning ('53). Today, Daniel Stowe distributes around $40,000 annually from this fund to Glee Club members who demonstrate financial need. The scholarship is a non-merit based award, and the funds are spread widely to all singers that qualify.

The Glee Club is more than a musical enterprise—it is also a social one. When new members join the group, they are absorbed into an esteemed tradition fundamentally built on song, but also one built on fraternity and a shared faith that follows from the common bonds forged through music for male chorus. The friendships fostered in the organization are as strong as the memory of the music after years away from campus, and the positive moments of brotherly interaction in the ensemble endure for decades. Camaraderie, it turns out, is found less on the concert stage and in rehearsal than in the wide array of traditional activities that permeate Glee Club culture.

TWELVE

Ladies Sweet and Kind

WOMEN AND THE GLEE CLUB

When Notre Dame became a coeducational institution in 1972, traditionalists among the male students rued the invasion of their hallowed home, to which women from St. Mary's College had been only visitors. On the announcement that two historic residence halls—Walsh and Badin—would be converted to women's residences, Glee Clubber Gregory O'Toole ('74), then a sophomore in Walsh Hall, told the *Observer*, "It's generally felt by everybody that it's a rotten deal. When they had the vote for co-education, they didn't say they were going to take our halls away."[1] As it concerns music-making on campus, questions were raised, including by faculty members, about how an all-male chorus could continue at the university. What were the grounds for excluding women from the storied choral ambassadors of Notre Dame? Hadn't the Yale Glee Club just gone coed, one year after that school first admitted women?[2] These inquiries are still posed to Clubbers today, and a straightforward answer is not easy to formulate.

The Glee Club, of course, is following a tradition of male choral singing that began in the nineteenth century, one built around fraternity and a special exploitation of the male vocal range. Nevertheless, there were fears in the mid-1970s that this heritage would have to be pushed aside in the wake of women's admission to Notre Dame. Mixed choirs were inevitable, but how they would take shape was to be determined. St. Mary's College hosted three mixed ensembles in the 1970s—the Collegiate Choir, the Chamber Singers, and the Madrigal Singers. All of these groups were available to Notre Dame men. In 1973, David Clark Isele was named the

director of Notre Dame's newly created University Chorus for mixed voices at the same time that he became the Glee Club's director. The Chapel Choir at Sacred Heart Church was also a coed ensemble open to Notre Dame men and women. When another mixed ensemble known as the Polyphonic Choir failed in 1973, Isele formed the Notre Dame Chorale in the fall of 1974 and handed off the University Chorus directorship to Walter Ginter from Niles, Michigan.[3] Options abounded for women to sing at Notre Dame, yet the Glee Club still had a target on its back.

Upon Isele's departure in 1979, there were continued questions about the Glee Club's viability as a group. Glee Club alumnus Scott Sandrock ('75) wrote to members of the university's administration pleading for the Glee Club to stay intact as an all-male choir. His letter prompted a response from Notre Dame president Fr. Theodore Hesburgh, who assured Sandrock, "there is no suggestion to eliminate the Glee Club or to make it coeducational. We have the University Chorale for the latter function."[4] Although the chair of the music department, William Cerny, preferred mixed choirs to the Glee Club, he too replied to Sandrock that the group would remain an all-male organization.[5] Indeed, the Notre Dame Glee Club remains one of the few male choruses at a high profile university that retained its single gender profile in a dynamic period of American history.

Although women are not admitted to the Glee Club, they have never been far from the activities of the organization, and this observation can be substantiated in different ways. One caricature of the Club is that its singers can tap efficaciously into the special power of song to woo members of the opposite sex. The caricature is not completely unfounded, if one notices, for example, the gender makeup of campus concert audiences: invariably, young women outnumber men. A female fan culture has also been a constant. More than a few boys have joined the ranks of the Glee Club not just to reap the extraordinary music,

Ladies Sweet and Kind

fraternity, and travel privileges that the ensemble offers but also to experience the unusual sway the group has had with female students in particular. The prestige and persuasion of the Club with many college women is no late phenomenon, as evidenced by "Glee Club dances" that were held in the 1920s. A 1927 "Glee Club Dance," sponsored by the Notre Dame Club of St. Joseph Valley and the South Bend St. Mary's Alumnus Club, allowed "the Notre Dame men and the St. Mary's girls to go to a dance together and stay until one [o'clock]." Special cars were provided for transportation.[6]

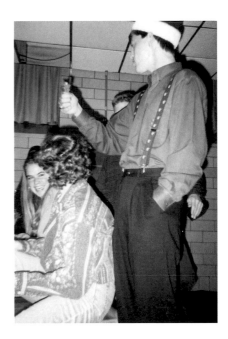

Concerts on tour were opportunities for the young men to meet women around the country, a diversion from the rough moments on the road in the company of all men. A profile of life on tour from 1953 reveals the experience with women that many Club members had on a typical gig in Chicago.

> At intermission time, most of the Club members just collapse on the nearest chair. But those with enough strength are on the loose, looking for the good-looking ushers. It's surprising how well they get to know the girls in half an hour, and quite a few dates are made for some weekend in Chicago. After the concert, the tails come off as fast as possible. There's a last-minute talk to the girls, and then it's back to the bus.[7]

In recent times, the Glee Club's practice of Christmas caroling has added a special focus on exciting the spirits of women on the campuses of Notre Dame and St. Mary's College. Clubbers make their way through the women's dorms to present a mini-concert to assembled groups of females taking a study break in a typically frenetic week of final exams. These venues are casual, and the Glee Club relishes the opportunity to have some fun with existing bonds between the sexes.

One tactic to interact with audiences during these short holiday concerts involves mistletoe. Usually, an innocent-looking freshman member of the Club will bound through the crowd dangling the sprig over the heads of various women, as the Glee Club carries on with a cheery seasonal number (like Leroy Anderson's "Sleigh Ride"). There are several

mistletoe strategies; it rarely lands above a random head in the audience. Often, it finds its way toward a woman who has attracted the interest of one or more Clubbers, or at least the mistletoe-bearer himself. Other times, it settles above the head of a girlfriend of one of the boys, which invites a kiss from that member and sometimes pecks on the cheek from his section mates. In an effort to provide a sense of equity, the mistletoe-bearing Clubber roams through the singing men during the next song, now strategically placing the sprig above selected singers, the goal being to draw audience participation. If no young women step forward, the singers standing next to the embarrassed Clubber may produce cash, credit cards, or car keys in an effort to entice involvement.[8] Then on to the next dorm. Along with impromptu singing to any group of girls or young women who will pay the slightest attention, Christmas caroling demonstrates the power of the Club's songs in action.

Mrs. Georgine R. Hill

Debbie Reynolds and Eddie Fisher with the Notre Dame Glee Club

Ladies Sweet and Kind

WORKING WITH WOMEN

The myth of the sirenic power of the Glee Club is only one aspect of the relationship of the group to women in general. The ensemble has sung benefits for women's charities and has performed concerts sponsored by many women's organizations. As mentioned in chapter 6, a small group of Clubbers helped raise several million dollars in 1989 for battered women and abused children in a New York City run-out trip, sponsored by the Archbishop of New York, John Cardinal O'Connor.[9] The Glee Club has also regularly collaborated with women's choirs since the years under director Dean Pedtke—well beyond joint ventures with the Notre Dame Chorale and St. Mary's Glee Club described earlier. The choir from Rosary College, an all-female institution in the Chicago suburb of River Forest, hosted and performed with the all-male chorus from Notre Dame several times between 1942 and 1957, as did Ursuline College in Cleveland between 1957 and 1973. The December 1949 venture to sing with the glee club of Rosary College included a joint recording session at WMAQ studios in Chicago's Merchandise Mart that was broadcast on Christmas Eve by NBC Radio affiliates around the country.[10]

Besides its choral collaborations, the Notre Dame Glee Club was often joined by female soloists on stage. In December 1923 under the baton of director J. Lewis Browne, Marjorie Berteling Galloway, Maud Weber, and Josephine Decker were likely the first women to perform with the Glee Club. Galloway appeared as a piano soloist for the evening, Weber as the accompanist, and Decker as the vocal soloist for Johannes Brahms's *Alto Rhapsody*. *Scholastic* raved that the performance of Brahms's large-scale work was "probably the most difficult ever attempted by a University Glee Club."[11] Browne also drew on soprano Sara McCabe from his church in Chicago (Old St. Patrick's Church) to provide solos in Glee Club concerts both on campus and in Chicago, where the director maintained his principal residence. A program from a 1925 concert shows the extent of McCabe's contribution. She sang six solos in the concert, appearing in both halves of the program—and this did not include encores. Her rendition of Giacomo Puccini's "Un bel di" from *Madame Butterfly* was lauded in the campus press, and she performed with the Glee Club in two pieces that Browne himself composed ("An Easter Processional" and "Come with Me to Romany").[12]

The most illustrious female soloist to join with the Glee Club in concert was radio star Kate Smith, already mentioned in chapters 9 and 10. A decade later, the Glee Club shared the stage with another female celebrity, the Hollywood actress and

Sara McCabe

singer Ann Blyth. As mentioned in chapter 7, the group performed in February 1950 at Chicago Stadium before a crowd of twenty thousand in a benefit concert that featured Blyth, Pat O'Brien, and Jimmy Durante.[13] Blyth then headed to South Bend to headline the university's Mardi Gras festivities with an appearance at the Navy Drill Hall on campus. She was greeted by a crowd of some five thousand, and again the Glee Club was invited to accompany her in song. After being showered with tokens of appreciation including a dozen roses, a gold brooch, and a blanket with a Notre Dame monogram, Blyth joined the Glee Club in singing Irish favorites "Too-Ra-Loo-Ra-Loo-Ral" ("That's an Irish Lullaby") and "When Irish Eyes Are Smiling."[14] Blyth appeared again with the Glee Club in April 1957, singing with the ensemble along with actress Erin O'Brien in the Los Angeles Philharmonic Hall as part of the Club's spring tour. This encounter with female celebrities is not surprising given the national reputation the ensemble had earned after seven consecutive yearly appearances on Ed Sullivan's *Toast of the Town*.[15]

Although the record of female contributions to Glee Club performances is clear from these examples, later cases highlight the exceptionality of women included in concerts on campus and on tour. In 1975, a university

press release titled "N.D. Glee Club Breaks Tradition" explained that the soloist for Brahms's *Alto Rhapsody*—Mary Mills from Niles, Michigan—was "believed to be the first [female to perform with the group] in the 60-year history of the University of Notre Dame Glee Club."[16] Similarly in the fall campus concert of 1996, soprano Laura Portune ('98) sang the solo in Claudio Monteverdi's *Lamento della ninfa* (*Lament of the Nymph*) backed up by the Glee Club. The yearbook proclaimed that she "was the first woman to sing with the Glee Club in its history."[17] Soprano Lauren Price ('05) also sang *Lamento della ninfa* with the Club in 2004, and cellist Noelle Thorn ('05) joined Price for performances on the group's spring 2004 tour of the country's Northwest and at the spring concert on campus.[18] Price and Thorn were indeed the first female students to both travel and perform with the ensemble on tour. They were no doubt nervous about the gender dynamics on tour, but Price in particular was relieved that the Glee Clubbers were "definitely a lot more gentlemanly than I had expected. I felt kind of like the favorite sister or cousin: somebody you could tease, but who you would still treat with respect. I couldn't have asked for anything better."[19]

GLEE CLUB MOTHER

The women discussed up to this point have either performed with the Glee Club or been wooed by the ensemble in concerts formal and informal. But there is another group of women with intimate knowledge of the Club, namely the wives, girlfriends, mothers, and sisters of members, who witness in some way the inner workings

Daniel Pedtke and daughter Dorothy Pedtke

Daniel Pedtke and daughter Cathy Pedtke

Daniel and Helen Pedtke waiting with tour bus

Daniel and Helen Pedtke

of the ensemble on and off the stage. Closer to the center of the Club's circle are the spouses of directors, especially those who have seen several classes of young men pass through the ranks of the choir. Despite her knowledge of the Club activities and personalities, Faith Fleming, wife of Daniel Stowe, has kept a low profile with members of the group over the past twenty-two years. She has a few close friends among Glee Club alumni and has traveled selectively with the group, most notably on its journeys to Guatemala and to Spain to experience the Camino de Santiago. Fleming chose to avoid becoming a mother figure to members of the ensemble, letting a parental role fall mainly to her husband. However, their daughter, Claire Stowe (born 2001), has literally grown up with the Glee Club; as a baby, she sometimes sat on a blanket in rehearsals. Claire has enjoyed opportunities to interact with Clubbers on campus and on tour and has become something of a celebrity among current members.

Doris Stam, wife of director Carl Stam, took an active role as the Club's "First Lady" once her husband established his footing with the ensemble. Traveling with the Club on a number of tours, she was a welcome yet understated companion to the Club and invaluable to the director. Friendly and tolerant of the antics of the young men, she handled her "lone female" status with good humor and aplomb. On campus, Doris was there for the Clubbers when needed and was generous with her family's time, inviting members to share an occasional meal at the Stam home. Being an accomplished soprano and musician certainly deepened the Club's affection and admiration for Doris. Mark Rolfes ('84) described her as "a perfect match for Chip, with their mutual faith, musicianship, and love for people."[20]

Without question, the most legendary woman in the inner circle of the Glee Club has been director Dean Pedtke's wife, Helen, whom he met at the College of St. Teresa in Winona, Minnesota. Though she traveled only twice with her husband and the group on tours (once to Europe in 1971), Helen was not only a maternal presence for Clubbers during the term of her husband (1938–73) but also a powerful guardian of her husband's legacy after his death in 1976 and a reminder of Club traditions to another generation of young men at Notre Dame until her passing in 2005. Known to alumni of the Pedtke era as "Mrs. Pedtke" or "Mrs. Dean," Helen made Glee Club activities a family affair, embracing members of the group from their freshman

In a 1991 Glee Club Alumni newsletter, Helen Pedtke wrote, "I'll never hear 'Passing By' done with such richness of tone and so many enthusiastic smiling faces. There are no words to describe it!"

Helen Pedtke, Maria (Casasanta) Thallemer, and Anita Casasanta

year and often opening the Pedtke house to the singers in their college years and beyond. Her three sons all attended Notre Dame, and two of them—Robert ('74, d. 2007) and Daniel ('78)—sang in the Glee Club.[21]

Picnics and football games continued at the Pedtke house after the director's death. Helen was always present to greet Clubbers with her tender smile and sometimes with a warm bowl of chili after Saturday football games on campus. She also eagerly collected photos of Glee Club alumni from the 1940s, '50s, and '60s and did well to recall their names and even occupations. While the young men were in school, Helen knew their majors and kept an eye on anyone falling off the rails while at Notre Dame. Peter Hyland ('62) was given the impression that "nothing phased her; not all of her [seven] children, not Dean's many obligations or trips, not her extended Glee Club 'family.' She always appeared to be happy to be wherever she was, doing whatever she happened to be doing. If the Club was having a blast in her yard (at the annual 'house party'), she was fine with that—apparently; she never came outside to say 'keep it down' or 'that's enough for today,' so I just assumed that as long as no one needed an ambulance, all was right with the world."[22]

The Pedtke home was not infrequently the site of post-concert events. When preparing for a reception following the 1994 Christmas concert, Helen told Glee Club president Joey Coleman that her only request in exchange for hosting the evening was that the Clubbers would sing long enough into the night to "wake the morning birdies" with their strains.[23]

Club members before 1990 never missed the chance to serenade their "second mother" on her birthday (November 27), a serenade that was sometimes phoned in from a tour stop when the group journeyed over the

Thanksgiving holiday. If Helen attended a rehearsal, Clubbers would halt their activity and sing Edward Purcell's "Passing By," which begins "There is a lady sweet and kind. . . ." She unfailingly attended Glee Club concerts on campus, often receiving an engraved invitation and always a reserved seat when she arrived.[24]

On Valentine's Day, Helen Pedtke brought in candy hearts and chocolates for the Glee Club to consume, a tradition that began in the 1990s and was revived recently by Dorothy. But Valentine's Day has also been a busy holiday for Glee Clubbers themselves. As a fundraiser, the group used to sell Singing Valentines, offering the chance for students to send a message in song to a loved one—almost always a woman—far away from campus. No matter the audience, Singing Valentines have melted the hearts of thousands by phone.

Small groups of Clubbers have also held impromptu concerts on campus, inviting a select number of women for a late night serenade near the Golden Dome. The Singing Valentines and "trouba-

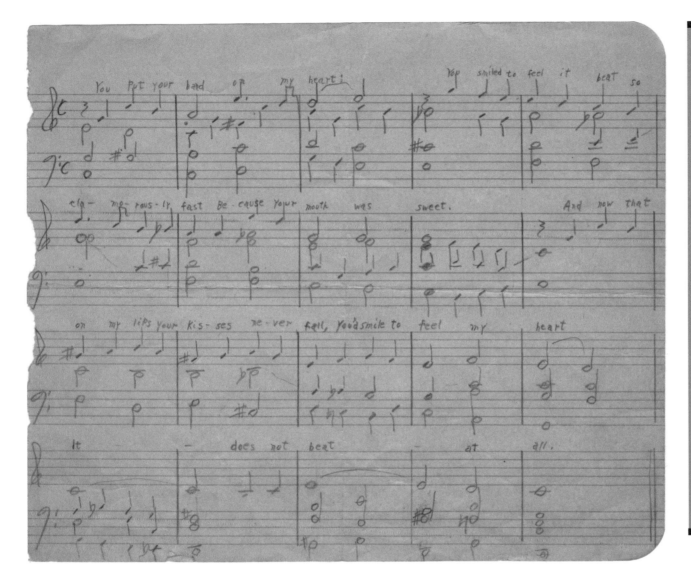

Among the artifacts pertaining to the Glee Club in the Notre Dame Archives are three undated pieces of handwritten music by Dean Pedtke that were composed for Helen. One is a song, and two are short keyboard works (one of which is titled "Helen"). All of the pieces are one page in length, and the two piano pieces are signed "Dan" by the longtime Glee Club director. The song matches Pedtke's music penmanship. The poetry of unknown origin is sentimental but ends in somber mood: "You put your hand on my heart. You smiled to feel it beat so clamorously fast, because your mouth was sweet. And now that on my lips your kisses never fall, you'd smile to feel my heart. It does not beat at all."

dour" serenades are two examples that illustrate how some of the Glee Club's lighter music is geared expressly toward a female audience. But women have actively played—and will continue to play—an important role within and around the organization. By virtue of its limited male range, the Glee Club has joined with female choirs to broaden its repertorial horizons; the group has also appeared with famous women who elevated its reputation. While women are not members of the Glee Club, they have found an amicable way into the enterprise on their own.

Postlude

THE NEXT HUNDRED YEARS

As early as the Casasanta years, *Scholastic* boasted that Glee Club had "appeared in almost every major city in the country."[1] Exposure on national radio broadcasts in the same era followed by seven consecutive yearly appearances on Ed Sullivan's top-rated television show *Toast of the Town* secured the group's reputation coast to coast. Television and movie stars appeared with the Club, and hosts in tour cities rolled out the red carpet for the ensemble in the years that followed. The proliferation of the choral arts in the United States, the splintered media landscape, and an increasingly secularized culture, however, have changed the backdrop against which the Glee Club operates today. It is hard to imagine that the Notre Dame Glee Club could regain its consistent command of the national spotlight that it enjoyed in the middle of the twentieth century. Nonetheless, it is the University of Notre Dame itself that will likely sustain both the high level of achievement and the exposure of its principal choral ambassador. On campus, the university has shown an unusually strong commitment to the arts. The DeBartolo Performing Arts Center offers first-class rehearsal and performing venues for the Club, as well as chances to collaborate with visiting artists. The worldwide reach of Notre Dame—whether as an institution or through its alumni base— continues to expand as well, which will fuel prospects for travel. The Glee Club's growing endowments will further provide opportunities for all members to share fully in all Club experiences, regardless of their personal financial situation. With these foundations in place, the Notre Dame Glee Club will be poised to carry on for decades the inimitable traditions of brotherhood and song that it has cultivated for more than a century.

CHAPTER ONE

1. Glee Club Alumni Newsletter, vol. 1, no. 1 (1963), p. 1. See Notre Dame Archives, PNDP 3251.
2. Elizabeth E. Gunn Seebirt, *Music in Indiana* (South Bend, IN, 1928), p. 36.
3. The Constitution of the Notre Dame Glee Club, Notre Dame Archives, PNDP 3250-C-2, p. 2.
4. *Dome* (1985), p. 52.

CHAPTER TWO

1. *Scholastic,* 28 November 1874, p. 123, and *Scholastic,* 5 December 1874, p. 139. Canadian organist and composer Damis Paul was a faculty member at Notre Dame and organist at Sacred Heart Church from 1870 until his death in 1913. For Paul's file, see Notre Dame Archives, PNDP 01-Pa-1.
2. *Scholastic,* 16 September 1876, p. 27. Mark C. Pilkinton has similarly addressed the early history of the Glee Club, prior to 1915. See his *Washington Hall at Notre Dame: Crossroads of the University, 1864–2004* (Notre Dame, IN: University of Notre Dame Press, 2011), pp. 62–63.
3. *Scholastic,* 19 June 1880, p. 651.
4. *Scholastic,* 20 December 1890, p. 249. One "Professor Preston" also attempted to form a glee club; see *Scholastic,* 7 March 1896, p. 370.
5. *Scholastic,* 25 May 1889, p. 624.
6. *Scholastic,* 5 October 1907, p. 63; *Scholastic,* 26 October 1907, p. 112; and *Scholastic,* 14 November 1903, p. 167.
7. *Scholastic,* 25 February 1899, p. 374, and *Scholastic,* 8 April 1899, p. 462.
8. *Scholastic,* 22 April 1899, p. 498, and *Scholastic,* 20 May 1899, pp. 560–61. These choruses were composed by the director himself.
9. *Scholastic,* 20 January 1900, p. 274, and *Scholastic,* 29 September 1900, p. 70.
10. *Scholastic,* 14 November 1903, p. 167; *Scholastic,* 24 January 1903, p. 278; and *Scholastic,* 17 April 1909, p. 477. "The regular meeting of the Glee Club was held Thursday morning in the band room. Officers for the ensuing year were elected as follows: President, G. E. Gormley; Secretary and Treasurer, J. L. Lamprey. A committee, composed of L. E. Collins, W. E. Manier and M. Shea, were authorized to purchase the latest popular songs for the club. A small fine will be imposed on all members who absent themselves hereafter without a reasonable excuse." *Scholastic,* 14 February 1903, p. 332.
11. The 1907–08 Glee Club was organized by a student nicknamed "Rosy," but it was disbanded as reported in *Dome* (1908), pp. 65, 249.
12. *Scholastic,* 24 February 1906, p. 323; *Scholastic,* 12 October 1907, p. 80; and *Dome* (1906), p. 20.
13. *Scholastic,* 19 October 1907, p. 96, and *Scholastic,* 19 October 1907, p. 96.

14. *Scholastic*, 25 November 1911, p. 156. A handwritten note, dated 14 December 1905, suggests that the Glee Club was "approved" in that year and was to be under the direction of Milton B. Griffith. See Notre Dame Archives, CHOP 13.
15. *Dome* (1909), pp. 90, 219.
16. *Scholastic*, 23 April 1910, p. 460. A program for the 1911 "Notre Dame Glee Club Annual Vaudeville & Minstrel Show" reveals a previously undiscovered theatrical talent: young Knute Rockne. Student (and later drama professor) Cecil Birder was a soloist. See Notre Dame Archives, PGCL, Concert Programs, March 30, 1911 program.
17. *Scholastic*, 15 November 1913, p. 125.
18. *Scholastic*, 17 January 1914, p. 397, and *Scholastic*, 9 May 1914, p. 647.
19. *Dome* (1916), p. 164.
20. See, for example, Frederick L. Allen, "Reforming the Glee Club," *Century Magazine* 105 (1922), p. 72.
21. *Scholastic*, 9 October 1915, p. 76.
22. *Scholastic*, 16 October 1915, p. 92. John W. Cavanaugh was president from 1905 to 1919 and is not to be confused with John J. Cavanaugh, president of Notre Dame from 1946 to 1952.
23. A well-known speaker and author in his own right, Cavanaugh booked all the entertainment for the students during his tenure. By 1914, he had accumulated a vast file on singing duets, trios, quartets, speakers, preachers, instrumentalists, poets, and travelogue lecturers, and developed some rapport with Hollywood silent film producers and the booking agencies for stage acts. See Notre Dame Archives, John W. Cavanaugh Papers, "Entertainment, 1912–19," including correspondence between Cavanaugh and Griffith Films.
24. *Scholastic*, 16 October 1915, p. 92.
25. The names of all members were published in *Scholastic*, 13 November 1915, pp. 156–57. Fifty singers were reported in the 1915–16 ensemble, though only thirty-six members are shown in the group photo in *Dome* (1916), p. 163.
26. *Scholastic*, 13 November 1915, p. 157, and *Scholastic*, 27 November 1915, p. 190. Many of the members were unaccustomed to the heavy practice schedule (six days per week), and attendance at rehearsals was a source of some concern to the young director.
27. *Scholastic*, 18 December 1915, p. 245.
28. The Yale Glee Club had been the first to tour with a mandolin group, traveling to Chicago in 1887; soon, mandolin groups began to spring up at colleges across the Midwest, including Notre Dame. By 1895, the university boasted a forty-piece mandolin orchestra. See Seebirt, *Music in Indiana*, p. 42.
29. *Dome* (1916), p. 33; emphasis mine.
30. *Scholastic*, 13 May 1916, p. 521.

CHAPTER THREE

1. *Scholastic*, 3 October 1952, p. 14.
2. *Scholastic*, 6 February 1931, p. 470.

3.   *Scholastic*, 5 October, 1934, p. 4, and *Scholastic*, 11 January 1935, p. 4.

4.   Jean Culbertson, "Singing Changes People, Notre Dame Director Says," *Clarion-Ledger Jackson Miss.* (1958). See clipping in Notre Dame Archives, UGCL 3/28.

5.   Not included in this figure is a peculiar report from the fall of 1941 in which 420 students reportedly tried out for the choir. *Scholastic*, 10 October 1941, p. 14. Only 3,200 students were enrolled at Notre Dame that year.

6.   This practice is stated in the current Glee Club constitution: "The tryout shall consist of two portions: a musical tryout with the Director and an interview conducted by no fewer than four of the executive officers of the Club." The Constitution of the Notre Dame Glee Club, Notre Dame Archives, PNDP 3250-C-2, p. 2.

7.   *Scholastic*, 12 October 1989, p. 13.

8.   See, for example, the questioning revealed in *Scholastic*, 9 September 1999, p. 18.

9.   *Scholastic*, 10 October 1941, p. 14.

10. *Scholastic*, 3 October 1952, p. 14.

11. *Scholastic*, 13 October 1933, p. 2.

12. *Scholastic*, 12 January 1934, p. 7. "Concert club" was a term used to distinguish the campus group from the "traveling club" in *Dome* (1930), p. 307.

13. *Scholastic*, 23 February 1934, p. 10.

14. *Scholastic*, 30 July 1943, p. 7, and *Dome* (1943), p. 163. The yearbook reported forty singers, and also noted, interestingly, that the ensemble made "several summer appearances" in 1943, despite the reduced ranks. Pedtke formed three different glee clubs to represent the campus's military groups, which were rapidly converted to Navy and other wartime training. Each group sang in military uniform, except the civilian club (those whose service was deferred), who wore formal attire. See the interview transcript of Daniel Pedtke by Patrick Scott, April 4, 1976, in Notre Dame Archives, CNDS (Notre Dame Students Collection), accession #2004-105, p. 11.

15. *Scholastic*, 26 May 1944, p. 4.

16. *Scholastic*, 6 October 1944, p. 4, and *Scholastic*, 29 November 1944, p. 9.

17. *Scholastic*, October 1924, issue 3, p. 72, and *Scholastic*, November 1924, issue 5, p. 139.

18. *Scholastic*, 10 October 1941, p. 14.

19. *Scholastic*, 18 September 1942, p. 29.

20. *Scholastic*, 3 May 1963, p. 41, and *Scholastic*, 21 February 1964, p. 33.

21. Glee Club Alumni Newsletter, vol. 2, no. 1 (1965), p. 3. See Notre Dame Archives, PNDP 3251.

22. Author correspondence with Daniel Stowe, 2 May 2014.

23. *Scholastic*, 18 December 1915, p. 247.

24. Extensive records of the business managers can be found, for example, in the Notre Dame Archives, UGCL 1/12–1/26.

25. Four assistant business managers are documented in *Scholastic*, 11 October 1946, p. 10.

26. *Scholastic*, 23 March 1956, p. 18.

27. See, for example, Notre Dame Archives, John W. Cavanaugh Papers, Cavanaugh to George Shanahan, 28 April 1917; Burns Papers, Rev. William A. Moloney to Burns, 7 December 1920, relaying the treasurer's explanation of why a 1919 Chicago hotel bill had not been paid. On the constitutional changes, see Notre Dame Archives, Walsh Papers, Box 35, Constitution.

28. Transcript of interview of Daniel Pedtke by Patrick Scott, April 4, 1976, in Notre Dame Archives, CNDS (Notre Dame Students Collection), accession #2004-105, p. 14.

29. *Scholastic*, 25 April 1947, p. 33.

30.   *Scholastic*, 14 October 1960, p. 14. Oliver was involved in a number of other campus music ensembles. He directed his own group and helped both with choral activities at St. Mary's and with the theater troupe at Notre Dame.

31.   *Scholastic*, 11 February 1899, p. 346; *Scholastic*, 13 January 1912, p. 221; and *Scholastic*, February 1925, issue 16, p. 487.

32.   A tryout for the Glee Club quartet is mentioned in *Scholastic*, 15 October 1925, p. 106.

33.   For an example of the wide array of entertainment offered at the intermission of Glee Club performances, see *Scholastic*, 22 January 1926, p. 426.

34.   See, for example, *Scholastic*, 1 April 1927, p. 744.

35.   *Scholastic*, 17 February 1917, p. 307, and *Scholastic*, 29 November 1929, p. 329.

36.   *Scholastic*, 5 February 1943, p. 7.

37.   *Scholastic*, 5 October 1956, p. 32; *Scholastic*, 27 September 1957, p. 9; and *Scholastic*, 4 October 1957, p. 33.

38.   *Scholastic*, 6 February 1942, p. 13, and *Scholastic*, 13 January 1956, p. 13.

39.   *Scholastic*, 17 December 1954, p. 9.

40.   *Scholastic*, 9 October 1942, p. 14.

41.   The Constitution of the Notre Dame Glee Club, Notre Dame Archives, PNDP 3250-C-2, pp. 17–18.

42.   *Scholastic*, 11 December 1959, p. 22. For the quality of incoming singers from a later period, see *Scholastic*, 25 September 1997, p. 26.

43.   *Scholastic*, 12 October 1989, p. 13. Two music majors were also reported in the following year. See *Scholastic*, 29 November 1990, p. 13.

44.   There was not always a dearth of members pursuing music majors in the Glee Club. In 1945, two of the Club's officers, Robert Schneider (secretary) and John Robert Boyes (librarian) were enrolled in the Department of Music, studying piano and music education respectively. See *Scholastic*, 30 November 1945, p. 8.

45.   *Scholastic*, 31 March 1933, p. 12, and *Scholastic*, 16 January 1953, p. 15.

46.   That the soloist had a separate (and no doubt more rigorous) audition than regular candidates is evidenced in *Scholastic*, 26 September 1930, p. 15. Publicity managers were known to put a separate photo of the soloists and a write-up about them in the press packages sent in advance of tour stops.

47.   *Scholastic*, 24 May 1929, p. 986.

48.   *Scholastic*, 7 February 1930, p. 522.

49.   Megan McSherry Breslin, "'Tony' Kopecky, 90: Banker Loved to Sing," *Chicago Tribune*, 11 December 1998, p. 16.

50.   *Scholastic*, 24 September 1937, p. 23. Pawlowski was scheduled to sing with the Polish Metropolitan Opera Company and the Polish National Broadcasting System, though there is no evidence of these performances.

51.   *Scholastic*, 3 February 1939, p. 7.

52.   *Scholastic*, 11 October 1940, p. 9.

53.   *Scholastic*, 1 December 1939, p. 17.

54.   Noland also represented Notre Dame when he sang on *The Fred Waring Show* (CBS) on 27 April 1952. The host highlighted a different university each week in his "Varsity Showcase." See *Scholastic*, 4 April 1952, p. 9.

55.   *Scholastic*, 26 October 1956, p. 32.

56.   Author correspondence with Daniel Stowe, 2 May 2014.

57.   *Scholastic*, 6 December 1946, p. 46.

58.   Author correspondence with Charles Lennon, 12 August 2014.

59.   Author correspondence with Fr. Theodore Hesburgh, via Melanie Chapleau, 7 August 2014.

60. During the Pedtke era, Durkin hosted the Club in New Jersey; for the past thirty years, he has hosted the group in Florida.

CHAPTER FOUR

1. *Scholastic*, 28 February 1891, p. 376.
2. *Scholastic*, 25 February 1899, p. 374.
3. *Scholastic*, 28 January 1899, p. 310.
4. *Scholastic*, 19 October 1907, p. 96.
5. *Scholastic*, 17 April 1909, p. 477; *Scholastic*, 29 May 1909, p. 573; *Dome* (1910), p. 210; *Scholastic*, 23 April 1910, p. 460; and *Scholastic*, 3 June 1911, p. 550.
6. *Scholastic*, 15 November 1913, p. 125.
7. *Dome* (1916), p. 343.
8. *Scholastic*, 30 September 1916, p. 28.
9. Notre Dame Archives, Cavanaugh Papers, Cavanaugh to Perrott, 9 August 1916.
10. *Scholastic*, 18 November 1916, p. 139.
11. *Dome* (1917), p. 165–66.
12. *Scholastic*, 17 February 1917, p. 307; *Scholastic*, 3 March 1917, p. 339; and *Scholastic*, 5 May 1917, p. 493.
13. Notre Dame Archives, Cavanaugh Papers, Perrott to Cavanaugh, 8 May 1917. "[A] member of the Indianapolis Knights of Columbus . . . arose and opposed my suggestion of assistance—saying that the Glee Club was not connected with the University in any way. . . . He was not in sympathy with using the University to help the Glee Club, an independent organization. As honorary president of the Glee Club . . . [please write to them] and acknowledge the Glee Club and those of us who have tried to make the thing a success." Perrott was noted as being stationed at the military base at Camp Gordon, Georgia. See *Scholastic*, 11 May 1918, p. 482. Little is known of his later life, except that he worked at the Securities and Exchange Commission in 1936. Harvard University alumni records suggest that he worked in the intelligence field and that he died in 1955. These details are courtesy of private correspondence with Patrick Scott (6 July 2014).
14. Notre Dame Archives, Cavanaugh Papers, John J. Becker, "Report of the Music Department," 19 December 1919.
15. Notre Dame Archives, Walsh Papers, Box 17, Walsh to Wilhelm Middelschulte, 8 June 1922; Burns Papers, undated memorandum (ca. 1920) regarding plans for John McCormack to perform.
16. In 1928, Becker belittled glee clubs in general as being "merely social and not musical organizations." See *Scholastic*, 10 February 1928, p. 525.
17. Don C. Gillespie, "Becker, John J.," in *The New Grove Dictionary of Music and Musicians*, 2nd ed., 27 vols., ed. Stanley Sadie (New York, 2001), 3:49–50.
18. Browne was spotted rehearsing the Club in 1927, however, despite the leadership having been passed to Joseph Casasanta. See *Scholastic*, 18 March 1927, p. 679.
19. For mentions of Browne's recitals, see *St. Paul Daily Globe*, 25 September 1892, p. 7; *Gainesville Star*, 29 December 1903, p. 1; and *San Francisco Morning Call*, 1 May 1890, p. 7.
20. "Dr. J. Lewis Browne in Jail," *New York Times*, 8 November 1907, p. 1; "Father Gunn Gives Reason for Shooting," *Atlanta Journal Constitution*, 13 November 1907, p. 1; "Recalls Nothing Said Against Father Dunn," *Atlanta Journal Constitution*, 15 November 1907, p. 7.

21. John Wanamaker was increasingly uncomfortable with Browne's alcoholism, and his struggle proved to be the grounds for his dismissal from the store and might also explain his alleged actions in Atlanta. Wanamaker wrote in a letter of 1 December 1910, "No matter how good his music is and how fine a spirit he is in when sober, I believe he is disgracing the house by his frequent sprees." See Ray Biswanger, *Music in the Marketplace: The Story of Philadelphia's Historic Wanamaker Organ* (Bryn Mawr, PA: The Friends of the Wanamaker, 1999), 74. One of Browne's organ students, Mary Vogt, also testified to his severe drinking problem. John Wanamaker ran a school for young people in the store called the John Wanamaker Commercial Institute. Wanamaker likely could not have fathomed the idea of an alcoholic leading the youth choral pageants and band-and-organ programs. (Wanamaker himself abstained from alcohol.) My thanks to Ray Biswanger for his assistance in private correspondence, 30 April 2014.

22. *Scholastic*, March 1925, p. 554. For a biography of Browne, see *American Organist* 2 (1919), p. 34, and Oscar Thompson, *International Cyclopedia of Music and Musicians*, 10th ed. (New York: Dodd, Mead, 1975), p. 302. Browne appeared at least three times with the Chicago Symphony Orchestra both before and after his time at Notre Dame. He played organ and conducted the orchestra at the organ dedication concerts at Medinah Temple on 18–20 October 1915. He also conducted two of his own works on 5 December 1931 and, less than two weeks later, he directed a chorus of high school students from Chicago, who sang the music of Palestrina and Rheinberger, as well as the spiritual "On Canaan Shore." My thanks to CSO archivist, Frank Villella, for his assistance with these details. From 1928 until his death in 1934, Browne served as director of music for Chicago Public Schools. See Notre Dame Archives, CHOP 13, and undated [1934] obituary of Browne from a Chicago newspaper. See the Daniel Pedtke scrapbook, 1922–1938, in the private possession of Dorothy Pedtke.

23. *Scholastic*, September 1923, vol. 57, no. 1, p. 50.

24. Notre Dame Archives, Walsh Papers, J. L. Browne to Walsh, 19 March 1926.

25. *Scholastic*, March 1925, vol. 58, no. 18, p. 588.

26. On the demands of the band for stipends and privileges to travel with university funding, see Notre Dame Archives, Burns Papers, Box B, undated letter from nineteen band members to Fr. James Burns. The Glee Club and band collaborated at times under Casasanta's direction. See the formal concert described in *Scholastic*, 5 April 1935, p. 8.

27. On the encores at concerts, see *Scholastic*, February 1925, vol. 58, no. 15, p. 455; for "(On) Down the Line," see *Scholastic*, 14 March 1930, p. 689.

28. *Scholastic*, 18 March 1955, p. 24.

29. *Scholastic*, 20 November 1931, p. 9.

30. *Scholastic*, 30 July 1930, p. 529.

31. *Scholastic*, 24 October 1930, p. 145.

32. *Scholastic*, 27 January 1927, p. 422.

33. In the summer of 1932, Casasanta brought these instrumentalists to Ireland to attend the Eucharistic Congress in Dublin. *Scholastic*, 14 October 1932, p. 7.

34. *Scholastic*, 9 March 1934, p. 4.

35. *Scholastic*, 8 March 1935, p. 4.

36. Notre Dame Archives, UGCL 1/3, O'Hara to Casasanta, 15 April 1937. On the size of the orchestra, see *Scholastic*, 1 October 1937, p. 12.

37. Biographical articles about Pedtke often state that he performed Tchaikovsky's Piano Concerto No. 1 in B-flat minor with the Chicago Symphony Orchestra around age 20, but no records in the very detailed programs collected in the Chicago Symphony Archives testify to his appearance. It has been discovered, however, that Pedtke played in

38. *Diapason*, 1 July 1935, p. 19. The letter from the American Guild of Organists (13 June 1936) and test results are found in the Daniel Pedtke scrapbook, 1922–1938, in the private possession of Dorothy Pedtke.

39. Notre Dame Archives, UGCL 3/28, Pedtke biography. He also studied at two other Chicago institutions (no longer in operation)—the Bush Temple Conservatory of Music and Dramatic Art, and the American Conservatory of Music. See *Scholastic*, 11 December 1959, p. 22.

40. Scholastic, 2 February 1945, p. 8. Also correspondence from the president of the College of St. Teresa, Sr. Mary Aloysius Molloy, O.S.F., to Dr. John Becker, dated May 23, 1935, in the private possession of Dorothy Pedtke.

41. Transcript of interview of Daniel Pedtke by Patrick Scott, April 4, 1976, in Notre Dame Archives, CNDS (Notre Dame Students Collection), accession #2004-105, p. 4.

42. *Scholastic*, 7 October 1938, p. 18.

43. *Scholastic*, 25 November 1938, p. 9.

44. Letter from James D. Trahey, C.S.C., to Pedtke, 22 November 1938, in the Daniel Pedtke scrapbook, 1922–1938, in the private possession of Dorothy Pedtke.

45. Letter from James D. Trahey, C.S.C., to Pedtke, 17 January 1940, in the Daniel Pedtke scrapbook, 1922–1938, in the private possession of Dorothy Pedtke. Trahey's support was especially timely because Fr. O'Hara had been consecrated two days earlier as a titular bishop and apostolic delegate to the United States Armed Forces, and Glee Club alumnus Hugh O'Donnell, a former prefect of discipline, was in line to become university president that summer.

46. Notre Dame Archives, Pedtke Papers, Pedtke to O'Hara, 6 September 1939.

47. *Scholastic*, 12 December 1941, p. 6, and *Scholastic*, 14 January 1949, p. 24. Also, author correspondence with Dorothy Pedtke, 21 August 2014.

48. *Scholastic*, 24 April 1942, p. 4, and *Scholastic*, 12 March 1943, p. 5.

49. Author correspondence with Patrick Scott, 4 September 2014.

50. *Scholastic*, 29 September 1944, p. 3; *Scholastic*, 18 January 1946, p. 7; and *Scholastic*, 11 February 1949, p. 27.

51. D. H. Pedtke, *Mass in Honor of Saint Jude* (Boston: McLaughlin & Reilly, 1957).

52. Notre Dame Archives, Pedtke Papers, Minutes of Music Faculty Meeting, 14 January 1942. Also, author correspondence with Dorothy Pedtke, 21 August 2014.

53. See, for example, Notre Dame Archives, UGCL 1/4, Secretary's Records, 1963–64.

54. Fanning also anonymously donated $50,000 of seed money for a Pedtke Scholarship Fund.

55. *Scholastic*, 14 February 1975, p. 14.

CHAPTER FIVE

1. Notre Dame Archives, UGCL 3/29.

2. Author interview with David Clark Isele, 26 March 2014. A feature on the Glee Club in *Scholastic* (14 February 1975, p. 14) suggests that the lighter material of the Glee Club was still very much programmed.

3. Author interview with David Clark Isele, 26 March 2014.

4. Ibid.

5. Audiences on this tour enthusiastically received *Red Hot Riding Hood*, especially the role of the Grandma, played by bass James Foster ('77). Jay Parks ('75) played the title character, and the "Wolfman" was sung by Paul Shay ('76).

6. Author interview with David Clark Isele, 26 March 2014.

7. "Choral Society Premieres Conductor's Original Work," *Cincinnati Enquirer*, 22 March 2001. Available at http://enquirer.com/editions/2001/03/22/tem_choral_society.html.

8. Author correspondence with Brian McLinden, 4 April 2014.

9. *Scholastic*, 29 November 1990, p. 14.

10. Brian McLinden, remembrance in "Carl Stam (1953–2011): A Commemoration," p. 10, Notre Dame Archives, PNDP 01-Sta-1. Stam performed the 360-turn at the 2006 Glee Club Reunion and one Clubber (Fr. John Thiede, S.J.) recalls the director doing this move in a formal concert.

11. Nathan Hatch, remembrance in "Carl Stam (1953–2011): A Commemoration," p. 4, Notre Dame Archives, PNDP 01-Sta-1.

12. On eating goldfish, see the Glee Club Alumni Newsletter, vol. 25, no. 2 (1988), p. 2. Issue held privately by the author. I am grateful to Robert Meffe and Doris Stam for explaining other "Stam tricks" in private correspondence. Stam used some of these same gimmicks with his youth ministry groups in Chapel Hill in the 1970s.

13. Brian McLinden, remembrance in "Carl Stam (1953–2011): A Commemoration," p. 10, Notre Dame Archives, PNDP 01-Sta-1.

14. Edward Fitzgerald, remembrance in "Carl Stam (1953–2011): A Commemoration," p. 12, Notre Dame Archives, PNDP 01-Sta-1.

15. Stam, letter to Glee Club chaplain Fr. John Thiede S.J., 19 March 2010 (author's private possession). Stam also served on the board of the Intercollegiate Men's Choruses and also led the ACDA's Repertoire and Standards committee for Music and Worship.

16. Stam, letter to Glee Club chaplain Fr. John Thiede, S.J., 19 March 2010 (author's private possession).

17. Fred Scott, remembrance in "Carl Stam (1953–2011): A Commemoration," p. 5, Notre Dame Archives, PNDP 01-Sta-1.

18. Stam, letter to Glee Club chaplain Fr. John Thiede, S.J., 19 March 2010 (author's private possession).

19. Letter to Stam from Lou Holtz, Notre Dame Archives, UGCL 1/3, "Miscellaneous Letters & Receipts."

20. *Scholastic*, 29 November 1990, p. 13.

21. From Doris Stam's speech at the 97th Notre Dame Glee Club Reunion, held in honor of Carl Stam, October 2012. Available at http://www.carlstam.org.

22. "Stam, Music Prof, Dies after Cancer Battle," from the Baptist Press web site, 2 May 2011. Available at http://www.bpnews.net/bpnews.asp?id=35194.

23. Stam, letter to Glee Club chaplain Fr. John Thiede, S.J., 19 March 2010 (author's private possession).

24. Griffin, "Is the Glee Club Damned from Here to Eternity?" *Observer*, 20 March 1992, p. 16.

25. All reflections and direct quotes from the Stowe tenure, unless noted otherwise, derive from author correspondence dated 2 May 2014.

26. Glee Club vice president Joe Dziedzic ('95) remembers the officers challenging the director about the difficulty of the Hungarian songs in particular: "In our minds, we were about college fight songs, spirituals, and drinking songs—not [Hungarian] folk songs. But you encouraged us to meet you halfway, and I'm so glad we did."

27. The orchestra in Hong Kong was led by Tsung Yeh, who has also served as music director of the South Bend Symphony Orchestra since 1988.

28. The suggestion of taking the pilgrimage route was made by Stowe's friend from Cornell University, David Yohalem, who had recently retired to Spain. "ND Glee Club Makes Pilgrimage in Spain," from the Notre Dame News web site, 17 June 2013. Available at http://news.nd.edu/news/40680-nd-glee-club-makes-pilgrimage-in-spain.

29. The Glee Club performed with other campus choirs together with the orchestra at the Gala opening of the DPAC in 2004. Other collaborations are being planned with campus choirs and orchestra.

CHAPTER SIX

1. *Scholastic*, 31 October 2002, p. 31.
2. *'Tis of Michigan We Sing*, directed by Jamie Turner, DVD (2010).
3. *Scholastic*, 22 May 1909, p. 560. See also *Dome* (1911), p. 156.
4. *Scholastic*, 23 September 1916, p. 15.
5. *Dome* (1917), p. 164
6. See, for example, *Scholastic*, 24 April 1920, p. 413.
7. *Dome* (1922), p. 204.
8. *Scholastic*, 30 April 1921, p. 427.
9. *Scholastic*, 25 February 1922, p. 420. Denny's band, at one time called the Notre Dame Collegians, served as a resident orchestra for the Hotel Oliver in South Bend. In 1924, it recorded "Dearest," "Hike, Notre Dame," and the "Victory March" on the Autograph label in Chicago, using a Glee Club quartet on the two fight songs.
10. *Scholastic*, 18 March 1922, p. 505, and *Dome* (1922), p. 201.
11. See, for example, *Scholastic*, 5 December 1941, p. 16.
12. *Scholastic*, 15 December 1926, p. 364; *Scholastic*, 1 December 1939, p. 17; *Scholastic*, 16 November 1951, p. 21; and *Scholastic*, 10 October 1952, p. 14.
13. *Scholastic*, 18 December 1915, p. 245.
14. From 1936 to 1940, the first formal Glee Club concert coincided with a themed "Music Week" on campus, which could include performances by the Moreau Seminary Choir, the band, and the orchestra. See, for example, *Scholastic*, 20 March 1936, p. 7.
15. *Scholastic*, 7 February 1930, p. 526.
16. Pilkinton, *Washington Hall of Notre Dame*, p. 264.
17. Glee Club members carry gloves to don with the tuxedoes when folders are not required. In recent years, the tendency has been to favor memorized music.
18. *Scholastic*, 16 November 1973, p. 26; *Scholastic*, 11 April 1996, p. 288. The 2003 performance was a joint concert with the all-male Cornell Glee Club.
19. Author correspondence with Daniel Stowe, 2 May 2014.
20. *Scholastic*, 4 May 1928, p. 842, and *Scholastic*, November 1924, vol. 58, no. 8, p. 232.
21. *Scholastic*, 19 June 1880, p. 651, and *Scholastic* 13 June 1908, p. 586.
22. See, for example, *Scholastic*, 11 May 1928, p. 909.
23. *Scholastic*, 23 May 1956, p. 18.
24. *Scholastic*, 27 November 1942, p. 13.
25. *Scholastic*, 17 December 1943, p. 7.
26. *Scholastic*, 14 December 1945, p. 5.
27. *Scholastic*, 3 December 1948, p. 15.
28. *Scholastic*, 12 December 1952, p. 6.
29. The 1986 and 1987 Christmas concerts were aberrations, held at the Bendix Theater at the Century Center in downtown South Bend. See *Scholastic*, 11 December 1986, p. 13.

30. *Dome* (1993), p. 317.
31. The current constitution of the Notre Dame Glee Club states that members must attend no less than one-third of all mini-concerts each semester. See Notre Dame Archives, PNDP 3250-C-2, p. 9.
32. *Scholastic*, 12 May 1933, p. 15.
33. *Scholastic*, 16 May 1930, p. 880.
34. *Scholastic*, 15 May 1953, p. 8, and *Scholastic*, 17 February 1967, p. 12.
35. Program in private possession of John Moe ('72, '75L).
36. In his remarks, President Clinton generously thanked the select members of the Glee Club. After the ceremony, Senators Joseph Biden, John Kerry, and Daniel Patrick Moynihan stopped to acknowledge the singers' contribution to the event.
37. *Scholastic*, 7 February 1920, p. 273.
38. *Scholastic*, 25 September 1953, p. 10.
39. *Scholastic*, 12 October 1989, p. 12.
40. *Scholastic*, 5 December 2002, p. 31.
41. *Scholastic*, 14 December 1956, p. 17.
42. *Scholastic*, 7 April 1917, p. 422.
43. For a press release about the 1982 joint performance at Notre Dame's Washington Hall, see Notre Dame Archives, UDIS 55/19, 3/3, 25 January 1982.
44. The glee clubs of Harvard University (1991), Ohio State University (1995–96), University of Illinois (1961, 1996), and Cornell University (2003), for example, have also partnered with Notre Dame in joint programs. Other festivals off campus that brought glee clubs together, not necessarily for joint programs, include an "Intercollegiate Festival of Song" at Purdue University (1958) and a "Songfest" at the University of Illinois at Urbana-Champaign (2006).
45. A 2005 joint concert with the chorus from the Naval Academy, sung to a full house at the DeBartolo Performing Arts Center, memorably concluded with a combined rendering of "Battle Hymn of the Republic."
46. *Scholastic*, 25 March 1960, p. 12.
47. *Scholastic*, 26 April 1946, p. 7. The symphony includes excerpts of Jefferson's speeches.
48. The Glee Club performed three pieces with the orchestra: "How Lovely Is Thy Dwelling Place," from Brahms's *German Requiem*; "The Prayer," from Wagner's *Lohengrin*; and the "Battle Hymn of the Republic." *Scholastic*, 12 March 1954, p. 12. Pedtke also brought out *The Testament of Freedom* on programs as late as the early 1970s.
49. On the last concert, see Jeremy Bonfiglio, "South Bend Symphony at Its Best in Veterans' Day Concert," *South Bend Tribune*, 13 November 2006, p. B2.
50. Claire Sobzcak, "Concert with a Cause: Glee Club Holds Benefit Concert to Help One of Their Own Battling Cancer," *Scholastic*, 21 April 2005, p. 19.
51. Andrew Hughes, "A Requiem for Today," *South Bend Tribune*, 26 September 2010, p. D1.

CHAPTER SEVEN

1. *Scholastic*, 19 February 1916, p. 341.
2. For example, *Scholastic*, 11 March 1916, p. 390.
3. The concert was held at the Murat Theater in Indianapolis. See *Scholastic*, 13 May 1916, p. 521.
4. *Scholastic*, October 1924, vol. 58, no. 1, p. 22.

5.   *Scholastic*, 23 March 1956, p. 18.

6.   *Notre Dame: A Magazine of the University of Notre Dame*, vol. 9, no. 4 (1956), p. 9. Notre Dame Archives, PNDP 83-Nd-3S.

7.   *Scholastic*, 23 March 1956, p. 19. This is an excerpt from an open letter written by Rev. Raymond O'Connor, S.J.

8.   In one of the more notable informal concerts on tour, the Glee Club sang a half-hour concert to inmates at a penitentiary while traveling through Pittsburgh in 1926. *Scholastic*, 12 February 1926, p. 521.

9.   In 2000, the Glee Club received "keys" to the city of Las Vegas. For a special proclamation about the Glee Club from the city of Bismarck, North Dakota, which declared October 22, 2002, as "A Musical Day with the Glee Club," see Notre Dame Archives, PNDP 3253.

10. *Scholastic*, 19 December 1947, p. 11.

11. *Scholastic*, 8 February 1952, p. 32.

12. Itineraries from the year 1950 until 1989, for example, are found in the Notre Dame Archives, UGCL 3/12–3/16.

13. *Scholastic*, February 1925, vol. 58, no. 15, p. 462.

14. *Scholastic*, 7 April 1917, p. 420, and *Scholastic*, 21 April 1917, p. 461.

15. *Scholastic*, May 1925, vol. 58, no. 25, p. 807.

16. *Scholastic*, 23 April 1926, p. 777, and *Scholastic*, 30 April 1926, p. 809.

17. *Scholastic*, 11 December 1936, p. 8.

18. *Scholastic*, 17 February 1950, p. 27. Proceeds from that star-studded program helped the Chicago Dominicans construct a seminary.

19. *Scholastic*, 19 March 1948, p. 8.

20. *Scholastic*, 2 December 1949, p. 18.

21. Author correspondence with Daniel Stowe, 2 May 2014. See also *Scholastic*, 28 March 1996, p. 10.

22. *Scholastic*, 28 January 1927, p. 422.

23. On the 1928 winter tour, see *Scholastic*, 20 January 1928, pp. 458–59.

24. *Scholastic*, 2 May 1930, p. 817.

25. *Scholastic*, 5 May 1933, p. 6.

26. For letters and contracts on the 1933 summer tour, see Notre Dame Archives, UVMU 2/29. See also *Scholastic*, 22 September 1933, p. 9.

27. Letter from James D. Trahey, C.S.C., to Pedtke, 17 January 1940.

28. *Dome* (1943), p. 163.

29. *Scholastic*, 15 May 1953, p. 7.

30. For a later tour of the West in 1961, director Pedtke arranged a medley of Disney songs that remained in the collective Glee Club memory for at least two decades.

31. *Dome* (1957), p. 132, and *Scholastic*, 5 April 1957, p. 31. Interestingly, on Easter Sunday in Las Vegas, the Glee Club divided into quartets and sent these small groups to sing in various parishes around the city. Also, while driving through New Mexico, the Glee Club bus (driven by Dick Aust) suffered an engine fire and had to be replaced by Greyhound in the middle of the night.

32. For the 1985 itinerary, see Notre Dame Archives, UDIS 55/19, 3 of 3.

33. Author correspondence with Aaron Trulley, 3 August 2014.

34. Author correspondence with Chris Clement, 6 August 2014.

35. They were also given New York Police Department (NYPD) and New York Fire Department (FDNY) hats.
36. Rudy Reyes, "Club Privileged to Honor Victims of September 11," Glee Club Alumni Newsletter (Fall 2002), p. 1. See Notre Dame Archives, PNDP 3251.
37. *Scholastic*, 11 March 1960, p. 18.
38. *Scholastic*, 18 March 1960, p. 5.
39. *Scholastic*, 20 May 1960, p. 13.
40. Notre Dame Archives, UGCL 3/18, "1963 European Tour Proposal."
41. Glee Club Alumni Newsletter, vol. 2, no. 1 (1965), p. 4.
42. Building on Alfred Stepan's one time gift for the Glee Club's European tour in 1971, John Moe ('72, '75L) established a European Tour Endowment Fund in 1989 for ongoing support of overseas travel. See Glee Club Alumni Newsletter, vol. 26, no. 2 (1988), p. 1. Issue held privately by the author. To this endowment, significant funds were added by the parents of Pat Deviny, a 1991 Glee Club alumnus, who died of cancer the year after his graduation. (Author correspondence with Dan Klock, 10 July 2014). This funding has been essential for keeping touring costs down for Glee Club members.
43. Author correspondence with Dennis J. ("DJ") DiDonna, 4 August 2014.
44. Author correspondence with Brian Scully, 18 July 2014.
45. *Scholastic*, 6 May 1949, p. 34.
46. *Scholastic*, 23 March 1956, p. 18. Outside of the official Glee Club soloists, Dean Pedtke was known to single out other members for solos, not letting them know until it was announced in the concert itself. Author correspondence with Dorothy Pedtke, 30 August 2014.
47. *Scholastic*, 29 April 1922, p. 651.
48. *Scholastic*, 29 April 1949, p. 28.
49. Author correspondence with Patrick Scott, 11 July 2014.
50. *Observer*, 21 October 1994, p. 10.
51. *Scholastic*, 3 June 1916, p. 572.

CHAPTER EIGHT

1. *Scholastic*, 18 December 1915, p. 245.
2. *Scholastic*, 10 October 1952, p. 14.
3. Two large files with Glee Club programs spanning a century of concerts can be found in the Notre Dame Archives, PNDP 3254-1.
4. *Scholastic*, May 1924, vol. 57, no. 9, pp. 230–31.
5. Bach's cantatas and Magnificat were performed with the St. Mary's Glee Club. See, for example, *Scholastic*, 6 May 1949, p. 12. The two ensembles performed Handel's *Messiah* in its entirety in 1957. See *Scholastic*, 25 October 1957, p. 16.
6. DVD copies of both appearances may be found in the Notre Dame Archives, AUND 30925.
7. Particularly memorable Schubert choruses undertaken by Stowe's Glee Club include "Gesang der Geister über den Wassern" and "Sehnsucht," both with texts by Goethe. Carl Stam programmed Schubert's "Die Nacht" and "Liebe," while Dean Pedtke introduced the Glee Club to a texted version of Schubert's three military marches (*marches militaires*), originally for piano four hands. See *Scholastic*, 7 June 1946, p. 10.

8. *Dome* (1965), p. 190.

9. *Scholastic*, 3 March 1939, p. 9.

10. *Scholastic*, 25 November 1938, p. 9.

11. Author correspondence with Dorothy Pedtke, 21 August 2014.

12. *Scholastic*, 23 October 1964, p. 19.

13. *Scholastic*, 14 February 1975, p. 14.

14. Pedtke had programmed such madrigals as Morley's "My Bonnie Lass She Smileth." See, for example, *Scholastic*, 12 December 1958, p. 16.

15. Author interview with David Clark Isele, 26 March 2014.

16. *Scholastic*, 18 March 1955, p. 24.

17. *Scholastic*, 14 March 1930, p. 689.

18. Author correspondence with Dorothy Pedtke, 16 September 2014.

19. Pedtke occasionally programmed Franz Schubert's famous "Ave Maria," but not nearly to the extent as the other "Ave"s.

20. The nine teams on the 1946 schedule were Illinois, Pittsburgh, Purdue, Iowa, Navy, Army, Northwestern, Tulane, and Southern California. Nebraska replaced Illinois on the 1947 schedule.

21. The Club sometimes presented the "College Medley" at formal events, for instance at the National Conference of Christians and Jews in 1951. See *Scholastic*, 16 November 1951, p. 21.

22. The dynamic annual version of the "Cavalcade" ends with "Hike, Notre Dame" as a gesture to Notre Dame fans. Student conductor Brian McLinden arranged the state song of Montana for inclusion in Isele's "Cavalcade," as a one-time addition to recognize the home state of the wife of Notre Dame's Director of Admissions John Goldrick, who hosted the Glee Club several times in private events. The curious addendum remained part of the official "Cavalcade" and has been much parodied.

23. *Scholastic*, 24 February 1939, p. 3.

24. *Scholastic*, 17 December 1946, p. 14.

25. *Scholastic*, 18 December 1959, p. 18.

26. *Toast of the Town*, April 9, 1950. A DVD copy of the original kinescope is found in Notre Dame Archives, AUND 30925.

27. *Scholastic*, 30 April 1926, p. 809.

28. *Scholastic*, 25 April 1941, p. 10.

29. Glee Clubbers James Feeney ('58) and Thomas Laboe ('58) revised the script. See *Scholastic*, 14 December 1956, p. 16.

30. *Scholastic*, 19 February 1943, p. 5.

31. *Scholastic*, 19 March 1943, p. 9, and *Scholastic*, 9 April 1943, p. 9. The campus press repeatedly mentioned that Cook did not hear the work's premiere because he was called to active duty.

32. *Scholastic*, 16 April 1948, p. 13.

33. *Scholastic*, 5 March 1948, p. 10.

34. *Scholastic*, 6 April 1962, p. 12.

35. The piece, which includes an extensive percussion contingent, was originally written for mixed voices and was premiered in 1983 at the Come Out and Sing Together Festival in New York City, the nation's first Gay and Lesbian Choral Festival.

36. The program is listed in full in *Scholastic*, 16 December 1949, p. 19. The concert was so well attended that the university's Vice President of Student Affairs Fr. Joseph A. Kehoe suggested to Pedtke that these concerts might

have to be moved from Washington Hall to the Navy Drill Hall. Uncatalogued letter from Kehoe to Pedtke, dated 20 December 1949.

37. For example, *Scholastic*, 22 November 1957, p. 26, and *Scholastic*, 11 December 1959, p. 16.
38. *Scholastic*, 14 December 1956, p. 16.
39. *Scholastic*, 18 March 1927, p. 679.
40. *Scholastic*, 11 December 1931, p. 11.
41. *Scholastic*, 24 April 1942, p. 12, and *Scholastic*, 12 June 1942, p. 2. Glee clubs from the University of Rochester and Purdue University captured first and second place, respectively, in Waring's national competition.

CHAPTER NINE

1. *Scholastic*, 13 May 1927, p. 872.
2. One of the sacred pieces was Tomás Luis de Victoria's "Ave Maria," a Renaissance motet that became a staple of Glee Club programs (along with another "Ave Maria" by Franz Xaver Witt) for at least three decades.
3. *Scholastic*, 30 November 1928, p. 335.
4. *Scholastic*, 3 February 1933, p. 15.
5. See, for example, "Glee Club at Notre Dame Cuts Sacred Music Album," *Fort Wayne News Sentinel*, 27 April 1956, p. 7, in Notre Dame Archives, UDIS 15/07.
6. All three albums recorded during the Isele years were produced by Disc Communications, Ltd., in New York.
7. Under Ring, the Glee Club released the cassette *On Christmas Night: Christmas Carols of the Notre Dame Glee Club* (1993). The group also appeared along with several other campus ensembles on the CD *One Voice, A Collection of Music from the Collegiate Choirs of the University of Notre Dame and St. Mary's College* (1993). The seven albums issued to date under Daniel Stowe are *Music from the Basilica* (1994); *From the Heart: Then and Now* (1996); *Under the Dome: The Notre Dame Glee Club* (1999); *In dulci jubilo: Holiday Music of the Notre Dame Glee Club* (2001); *Vive La Compagnie* (2005); *Beautiful Rain: The Notre Dame Glee Club* (2008); and *On the Rocky Road to Dublin* (2012).
8. *Dome* (1923), p. 187.
9. *Scholastic*, 6 May 1927, p. 841; *Scholastic*, 25 November 1927, p. 297; *Scholastic*, 13 May 1927, p. 297; and *Scholastic*, 2 December 1927, p. 328, 331.
10. *Scholastic*, 1 November 1929, p. 202, and *Scholastic*, 15 November 1929, p. 263.
11. *Scholastic*, 31 October 1930, p. 167, and *Scholastic*, 2 October 1931, p. 5.
12. *Scholastic*, 14 October 1932, p. 13; *Scholastic*, 29 November 1935, p. 5, 22; and *Scholastic*, 27 November 1936, p. 4. *Notre Dame Varieties* was a weekly campus radio program in which the Glee Club was regularly featured.
13. *Scholastic*, 27 April 1934, p. 6; *Scholastic*, 11 May 1934, p. 9; and *Scholastic*, 15 November 1935, p. 8.
14. *Scholastic*, 20 March 1936, p. 6.
15. *Scholastic*, 10 October 1941, p. 14, and *Scholastic*, 20 November 1942, p. 6.
16. *Scholastic*, 20 February 1942, pp. 5, 9. Three audiotapes of Universal Notre Dame Night survive in the Library of Congress. The 1942 recording is catalogued as #LWO 15731 76B1. The 1938 broadcast is contained in both #LWO 16675 3A1-2 and #5404 39A3, and the 1939 Notre Dame Night survives as #RWA 2871 B3-4.
17. Exceptions were performances around Christmas that aired on the NBC radio network in 1949 and 1953. See press clippings in Notre Dame Archives, UDIS 15/08. Also a concert of Christmas music aired on the federal government's *Voice of America* program on 26 December 1955. See Library of Congress, tape reel (#2005654170), preservation master (LWO 12827, reel 27), and original (RAA 42624). Programs on South Bend's WHOT were

noted in *Scholastic*, 14 December 1945, p. 5, and *Scholastic*, 21 November 1952, p. 32. An Advent Vespers program recorded with the Notre Dame Chorale in Sacred Heart Church was broadcast on WSND radio; for an audiotape, see Notre Dame Archives, ASND 8973.

18. For kinescope copies of these shows, see Notre Dame Archives, AUND 29795 and 29796.

19. Transcript of interview of Daniel Pedtke by Patrick Scott, 4 April 1976, in Notre Dame Archives, CNDS (Notre Dame Students Collection), accession #2004-105, pp. 13–14.

20. *Scholastic*, 2 April 1954, p. 12. For correspondence between Sullivan and business manager Francis Myers in 1951, see Notre Dame Archives, UGCL 1/12, Business Manager's Records, 1951–2.

21. See Notre Dame Archives, Pedtke Papers, 1955 Easter tour itinerary. Correspondence between Pedtke and Sullivan is found in Pedtke Papers, "Ed Sullivan" file. The young men even jokingly referred to *Toast of the Town* as "The Marlo Lewis Show" because of the royal treatment they received from the producer.

22. *Scholastic*, 1 April 1955, p. 18, and *Scholastic*, 9 March 1951, p. 10.

23. *Scholastic*, 9 March 1951, p. 10.

24. Author correspondence with Jerry Pottebaum, 29 July 2014.

25. Notre Dame Archives, UGCL 3/17, Ed Sullivan Show TV Appearances, 1953–62. Sullivan did promise to include the Glee Club in his 1960 Easter show (letter from 28 July 1958), but his letter from 19 August 1960 confirms that no college glee clubs, except the military academy glee clubs from West Point and Annapolis, were exempted from the strict union rules. Other university glee clubs (Illinois, Michigan, Oklahoma, Dartmouth) performed on Sullivan's show through the 1950s, though none as much as the Notre Dame Glee Club.

26. *Scholastic*, 21 October 1955, p. 13.

27. *Scholastic*, 25 September 1953, p. 10.

28. The group received $7,500 for the appearance, and the show aired 6 November 1966 with guests Polly Bergen, Jimmy Dean, and Jonathan Winters. The Glee Club also sang "This is My Country" and "When Johnny Comes Marching Home." For other logistics associated with the show on this trip to Los Angeles, see Notre Dame Archives, UGCL 1/1, Minutes of Officers' Meetings 1966, 1971, and UGCL 3/20, Andy Williams Show TV Appearance, 1966. The Glee Club also appeared on *The Mike Douglas Show* twice between 1962 and 1965.

29. For details on the event, see Notre Dame Archives, UGCL 3/21, John Davidson Show TV Appearance, 1967; Notre Dame Archives, UDIS 15/08, "Kenton Men to Appear on TV Friday with Notre Dame Glee Club"; and *Scholastic*, 13 October 1967, p. 8.

30. Narrated by Carl Stam, the video, released in 1991, was part of a series of documentaries produced by Golden Dome Productions for Today's Life Choices in association with Kentucky Educational Television.

31. In 2004, the Club appeared on *Live with Regis and Kelly* following the opening of the DeBartolo Performing Arts Center, with Regis broadcasting from the new building. On a tour of eastern cities in the fall of 1982, the Glee Club sang the school's alma mater on NBC's *Today Show* (*Dome* [1983], p. 81), and in November 1991, the group sang the national anthem on ABC's *Monday Night Football* in Minneapolis for the Bears-Vikings game (*Dome* [1992], p. 220).

32. Billy Rose, "Foy Casts Bread Upon Waters and He Got Back Shortcake," *The Terre Haute Star*, 1 February 1950, p. 8 (syndicated column, *Pitching Horseshoes*). Unfortunately, only the film of this performance, no. 2289 in the Vitaphone series, has been discovered, the audio disc having disappeared.

33. *Alumnus Magazine*, October 1933, pp. 9, 12, and file in Notre Dame Archives, UVMU 2/29. The name of the film appears in Library of Congress catalog listings for Vitaphone shorts; it was released in October 1933 and copyrighted 11 November 1933 (LP4234). Part of the Vitaphone Collection was purchased from Warner Brothers by United

Artists and stored since 1971 in the Library of Congress, Motion Pictures Division. The film has been preserved in location W, #0050390200. A digital copy is in the Notre Dame Archives.

34. *Scholastic*, 10 November 1933, pp. 2–3.
35. *Scholastic*, 27 September 1940, p. 13.
36. *Scholastic*, 4 October 1940, pp. 7, 12.
37. *Scholastic*, 24 April 1953, p. 21.
38. *Scholastic*, 17 May 1957, p. 10.

CHAPTER TEN

1. *Scholastic*, 19 January 1918, p. 220.
2. During this time, he played the position of regular end under coach Jessie Harper and assistant coach Knute Rockne for three seasons, before being called to service in World War I.
3. *Scholastic*, 1 December 1888, p. 253.
4. *Scholastic*, 2 February 1895, p. 304.
5. For a discussion of the origins of the "Fighting Irish" name, see the Notre Dame Athletics web site: http://www.und.com/trads/nd-m-fb-name.html.
6. *Scholastic*, 1 May 1931, p. 784.
7. The sheet music can be found at Johns Hopkins University, Levy Sheet Music Collection, Box 028, Item 017. For campus use of the song, see *Scholastic*, 15 May 1931, p. 851, and *Scholastic*, 9 October 1931, p. 8.
8. *Scholastic*, 4 October 1940, pp. 7, 12.
9. *Scholastic*, 6 November 1931, p. 11.
10. *Scholastic*, 5 October 1934, p. 4.
11. *Scholastic*, 25 September 1953, p. 10.
12. For the seventy-fifth reunion of the Glee Club, the group sang the national anthem at the game against Penn State (17 November 1990).
13. Michelle Pilecki, "Notre Dame Irish Won't Fight for Singers," 11 November 2009, available at http://www.huffingtonpost.com/nellie-b/nd-irish-wont-fight-for-s_b_354650.html.
14. *Dome* (1996), p. 224.
15. Author correspondence with Brian McLinden, 26 April 2014.
16. *Scholastic*, 9 October 1942, p. 10.
17. *Scholastic*, 13 November 1942, p. 5.
18. *Scholastic*, 5 February 1943, p. 7.
19. *Scholastic*, 27 September 1957, p. 9.
20. *Scholastic*, 10 November 1961, p. 15. Hilton Hill ('63), a tenor from Bermuda, sang the solo.
21. *Scholastic*, 1 November 1929, p. 202.
22. See photo caption in Lou Somogyi, "Soldier (Field) of Fortune," available at http://www.und.com/sports/m-footbl/spec-rel/100512aab.html.
23. *Scholastic*, 6 December 1940, p. 12.
24. See, for example, *Scholastic*, 11 October 1946, p. 5, and *Scholastic*, 16 October 1953, p. 8.
25. *Scholastic*, 22 October 1948, p. 12.

26. *Scholastic*, 7 October 1949, p. 26, and *Scholastic*, 29 September 1950, p. 13. In the 1960s, Pedtke Bowl also included a tug-of-war across a pond. Naturally, the losers got wet.

27. Author correspondence with Brian Scully, 28 April 2014.

28. *Scholastic*, February 1925, vol. 58, no. 16, p. 487.

29. Notre Dame Archives, UDIS 15/07, Publicity Release #3, The University of Notre Dame Glee Club, Subject: "Stage or Stadium."

CHAPTER ELEVEN

1. *Scholastic*, May 1925, vol. 58, no. 24, p. 774.

2. Notre Dame Archives, PNDP 3250-C-2, p. 15.

3. George A. Scheuer and Bernard A. Garber, eds., *Before the Colors Fade: Some Memories by Members of the Class of 1928, University of Notre Dame* (Notre Dame, 1983), p. 59. See Notre Dame Archives, PNDP 1420-1928.

4. Robert Griffin, *In the Kingdom of the Lonely God* (New York: Paulist Press, 1973; repr. Lanham, MD: Rowman & Littlefield, 2003).

5. *Scholastic*, 14 February 1975, p. 14.

6. Robert Griffin, "The Heart of the Lonely Kingdom in Gay Paree," *Our Sunday Visitor*, 8 July 1990, p. 14. Found in Notre Dame Archives, UGCL, Box 7, Folder "Newspaper Clippings, Past Pictures."

7. *Scholastic*, 5 October 2000, p. 28.

8. Anthony Macalusco, "Still Studs? Living Legends Men of Stanford Hall Adopt the Griffin as New Mascot," *Scholastic*, 1 April 1999, p. 6.

9. John Thiede is not a Holy Cross priest but rather a Jesuit priest, thus an exception to the bylaw from the Glee Club constitution. Father Driscoll is a diocesan priest as well, not a Holy Cross priest. For the 2001 tour of Asia, the *de facto* chaplains were Frs. Paul Doyle and Mark Poorman (then the vice president of student affairs), who were part of Notre Dame's delegation that met the group in China and Hong Kong.

10. *Scholastic*, 12 October 1989, p. 13.

11. Author correspondence with Brian Scully, 11 August 2014.

12. Glee Club Alumni Newsletter, vol. 1, no 2 (1964), pp. 2–3.

13. *Dome* (1971), p. 151.

14. Author correspondence with Dorothy Pedtke, 21 August 2014.

15. Glee Club Alumni Newsletter, vol. 25, no. 1, (1987) p. 1. Issue held privately by the author.

16. After the turn of the twenty-first century, a group of alumni from the 1960s decided to hold mini-reunions of members from that decade in the "off years" that did not feature an official Glee Club reunion. Andrew Reardon ('67) and Richard Leonhardt ('65) have organized these "off year" reunions. Between twenty and forty Glee Club alumni (not counting families) from the later Pedtke years have returned to Notre Dame on a football weekend or to sites of away games to recount old times and rehash repertoire that has not been transmitted to the present Club. Author correspondence with Richard Leonhardt, 4 August 2014.

17. Notre Dame Archives, UDIS 55/18, clipping 2 of 3.

18. *Dome* (1991), p. 42.

19. *Scholastic*, 4 November 1922, p. 180, and *Scholastic*, 18 February 1949, p. 11.

20. *Scholastic*, 25 February 1949, p. 13.

21. Tenor I wears purple; Tenor II, blue; Bass I, green; Bass II, red.

22. Theresa Pedtke, daughter of Dean Pedtke, met her future husband, Peter Morris ('68) on a blind date on the Glee Club hayride. Author correspondence with Dorothy Pedtke, 17 September 2014.

23. *Scholastic*, 14 February 1975, p. 15.

24. Ibid.

25. Transcript of interview of Daniel Pedtke by Patrick Scott, April 4, 1976, in Notre Dame Archives, CNDS (Notre Dame Students Collection), accession #2004-105, p. 14.

26. The Glee Club sings a variant ending in the refrain, compared to the traditional recorded versions of this piece. The verses, now easily found online, were intended to be passed down from one Glee Club vice president to his successor. Today's vice presidents are called to sing the interior verses to the song "Beer Beer Beer," honoring the fabled inventor of beer, Charlie Mopps. Like "Cigarettes," this song is not proprietary to the Club, but it is nonetheless maintained in the underground for gatherings off the concert stage.

27. Author correspondence with Tom Nessinger, 12 August 2014.

28. Author correspondence with Doon Wintz, 12 August 2014.

29. Author correspondence with Patrick Scott, 25 June 2014.

30. Glee Club Alumni Newsletter (Spring 1984), p. 3. Issue held privately by the author. The tradition was sporadically undertaken after 1997. After Beacon Bowl was closed in 2007, some attempts to revive the ritual at Chippewa Bowl south of downtown South Bend did not successfully recover the tradition.

31. Glee Club Alumni Newsletter, vol. 26, no. 4 (1990), pp. 6–7. Issue held privately by the author.

32. *Scholastic*, 10 June 1916, p. 589.

33. *Scholastic*, April 1925, vol. 58, no. 22, p. 710.

34. *Scholastic*, 15 May 1953, p. 7.

CHAPTER TWELVE

1. "Residents Are Shocked, Curious and Resigned," *Observer*, 9 February 1972, p. 2.

2. Yale University admitted women in 1969, and longtime Yale Glee Club director Fenno Heath brought women into the chorus in 1970. While president of the Intercollegiate Men's Choruses in 1968, Heath defended the significant contribution of all-male choirs to college campuses as he expressed uncertainty about their survival. See Marshall Bartholomew, "Intercollegiate Men's Choruses," available at http://www.imci.us/history.html.

3. Author correspondence with both David Clark Isele and Nancy Menk, 26 August 2014.

4. Notre Dame Archives, UGCL, Box 7, Correspondence, Letter from Theodore Hesburgh, July 25, 1979.

5. Notre Dame Archives, UGCL, Box 7, Correspondence, Letter from William Cerny, July 26, 1979.

6. *Scholastic*, 29 April 1927, p. 828.

7. *Scholastic*, 13 November 1953, pp. 17–19.

8. Author correspondence with Joey Coleman, 9 June 2014. Another account of the Glee Club's Christmas caroling on campus can be found in Kevin Coyne, *Domers: A Year at Notre Dame* (New York: Viking, 1995), pp. 157–58.

9. *Scholastic*, 12 October 1989, p. 12.

10. *Scholastic*, 2 December 1949, p. 18. Other interaction with collegiate women's choirs includes, for example, a 1994 performance in Ann Arbor with the University of Michigan Women's Glee Club.

11. *Scholastic*, December 1923, vol 57, no. 4, p. 239.

12. For a review of the 1925 performance on campus, see *Scholastic*, March 1925, vol. 58, no. 19, p. 619.

13. *Scholastic*, 17 February 1950, p. 27.

14. *Scholastic*, 24 February 1950, p. 9. Blyth followed these numbers with an unaccompanied rendition of George Gershwin's "The Man I Love."

15. *Dome* (1957), p. 132.

16. Press release in Notre Dame Archives, UDIS 55/18, dated 13 November 1975. The information in this release was picked up, for example, in "Notre Dame Concert," *Indianapolis Star*, 18 November 1975, also in UDIS 55/18.

17. *Dome* (1996), p. 224.

18. Besides the Monteverdi piece, these concerts featured Srul Irving Glick's *Five Tableaux from the Song of Songs* for cello and men's chorus, and "Elegy," from Frank Ferko's *Stabat Mater*, for soprano and men's chorus.

19. *Scholastic*, 25 March 2004, p. 29. The only spouse of a director to perform in a Glee Club concert was Doris Stam, an accomplished soprano, who sang the solo part in Schubert's "Nachthelle" when the Club toured Europe in the summer of 1987. See Glee Club Alumni Newsletter, vol. 25, no. 2 (1988), p. 5. Issue held privately by the author.

20. Author correspondence with Mark Rolfes, 27 August 2014.

21. The seven Pedtke children were: Dorothy Anne ("Dotty"), b. 1939; William Joseph ("Bill"), b. 1940; Mary Elizabeth ("Mary Beth"), b. 1941, d. 2006; Theresa Clare, b. 1948; Catherine Marie ("Cathy"), b. 1950, d. 1978; Robert Anthony ("Bob"), b. 1951, d. 2007; and Daniel Francis ("Dan"), b. 1954.

22. Author correspondence with Peter Hyland, 24 July 2014.

23. Author correspondence with Joey Coleman, 15 September 2014.

24. *Scholastic*, December 1984, pp. 16–17.

POSTLUDE

1. *Scholastic*, 26 September 1947, p. 27.

Image Credits

All photos used with permission of provider.

FRONT MATTER

CHAPTER 1

CHAPTER 2

Image Credits

34 Portrait of Samuel Ward Perrott. *Dome* (1916), p. 164. PNDP-D1916-P164. Courtesy of University of Notre Dame Archives.

35 (*top left*) Portrait of J. Hugh O'Donnell, *Dome* (1917), p. 164. PNDP-D1917-P164. Courtesy of University of Notre Dame Archives.
(*top right*) Portrait of Howard Parker, *Dome* (1917), p. 163. PNDP-D1917-P163. Courtesy of University of Notre Dame Archives.
(*bottom*) Mandolin Club, *Dome* (1917), p. 165. PNDP-D1917-P165. Courtesy of University of Notre Dame Archives.

36 Portrait of Notre Dame Glee Club Director John J. Becker, ca. 1918. GGCL 1/03. Courtesy of University of Notre Dame Archives.

37 Portrait of Notre Dame Glee Club Director Dr. J. Lewis Browne, ca. 1924. GGCL 1/04. Courtesy of University of Notre Dame Archives.

38 Portrait of Joseph Casasanta, ca. 1933. GDIS 02/17. Courtesy of University of Notre Dame Archives.

39 Portrait of Daniel Pedtke, ca. 1960s. GGCL-01-11-01. Courtesy of University of Notre Dame Archives.

40 (*left*) Daniel Pedtke conducts the Glee Club on a bus, November 1953. PNDP-S1953-1113-P017. Courtesy of University of Notre Dame Archives.
(*right*) Daniel Pedtke teaching. GNDL 13-53. Courtesy of University of Notre Dame Archives.

41 Notre Dame Glee Club rehearsal; members gathered around Director Daniel Pedtke at the organ, ca. 1960s. GGCL 1/12. Courtesy of University of Notre Dame Archives.

42 Director Daniel Pedtke conducting the Notre Dame Glee Club in concert, ca. 1970s. GGCL 1/37. Courtesy of University of Notre Dame Archives.

44 Director Daniel Pedtke, ca. 1950s. GDIS-07-Pedtke-01. Courtesy of University of Notre Dame Archives.

45 Daniel Pedtke conducting Glee Club rehearsal, O'Shaughnessy Hall, 1962. Photo provided by Phil Jones ('63).

46 Willis Nutting, prominent Notre Dame faculty member, and Daniel Pedtke, with Helen's watchgeese. Photo provided by Dorothy Pedtke.

47 Glee Club officers and Daniel Pedtke, Howard Park Tavern, South Bend, Indiana, 1963. Photo provided by Phil Jones ('63).

CHAPTER 5

48 Notre Dame Glee Club Concert, view from overhead, ca. 1960s. Photo by Robert William Simpson, *Dome* staff photographer. GGCL 1/19. Courtesy of University of Notre Dame Archives.

50 Notre Dame Glee Club Director Daniel Pedtke funeral Mass in the Basilica of the Sacred Heart, 1976. GGCL 1/07. Courtesy of University of Notre Dame Archives.

51 (*top left*) Daniel Pedtke funeral at Cedar Grove Cemetery, 1976. GGCL-01-07-06. Courtesy of University of Notre Dame Archives.
(*bottom left*) Daniel Pedtke funeral procession on Notre Dame Avenue, 1976. GGCL-01-07-03. Courtesy of University of Notre Dame Archives.
(*right*) Daniel Pedtke funeral procession on Notre Dame Avenue, 1976. GGCL-01-07-04. Courtesy of University of Notre Dame Archives.

52 Portrait of Notre Dame Glee Club Director David Clark Isele, ca. 1973–79. GGCL 1/08. Courtesy of University of Notre Dame Archives.

53 David Clark Isele at the Fall Campus Concert, Notre Dame, Indiana, 1976. Photo provided by Pat Scott ('76, JD '79).

54 Caricature of David Clark Isele by cartoonist John Fischetti, 1973. Photo provided by David Clark Isele.

CHAPTER 6

CHAPTER 7

89   (*top*) Glee Club Caricature, illustrated by Ivan Osorio ('60), from back cover of a publicity brochure for the Glee Club, ca. 1967. PNDP-3253-P-1-01. Courtesy of University of Notre Dame Archives.

       (*bottom*) Glee Club Caricature, signed by Glee Club members, 1990. Original provided by Matt Borkowski ('91/'91).

90   Notre Dame Glee Club members and children throwing rocks alongside of a train stopped on railroad tracks, ca. 1960s. GGCL 1/21. Courtesy of University of Notre Dame Archives.

91   (*left*) Loading the bus on tour, 1963. Photo provided by Phil Jones ('63).

       (*top right*) Glee Club director Daniel Pedtke gets off an airplane on tour with the Glee Club, ca. 1962. Image was published in "Notre Dame," 1962 (note: not *Notre Dame Magazine*, this is an earlier publication). PNDP-3253-03. Courtesy of University of Notre Dame Archives.

       (*bottom right*) Spring Tour, 1963. Photo provided by Phil Jones ('63).

92   Spring Tour, 1963. Photo provided by Phil Jones ('63).

93   (*left*) Itinerary for a tour of the Southwest from January 26, 1950, to February 6, 1950. PNDP-3253-02. Courtesy of University of Notre Dame Archives.

       (*top right*) Glee Club Tour itinerary, Easter Tour, 1958. Original provided by Fred Gade ('60).

       (*bottom right*) European Tour, 1971. Photo provided by John Moe ('72, JD'75).

94   Dick Aust, Indiana Motor Bus Company, New Orleans, January 31, 1964. Photo provided by Dick Leonhardt ('65).

97   The Rosary College Glee Club sings with the Notre Dame Glee Club, 1960. Photo by Charles Folak, provided by Steven Szegedi, Dominican University.

99   Notre Dame Glee Club after visiting President Coolidge at the White House, Washington, DC, January 7, 1927. GGCL-03-01. Courtesy of University of Notre Dame Archives.

100   The Notre Dame Glee Club on the exterior steps of Municipal Auditorium in San Antonio, Texas, January 7, 1928. Photo by E. Raba. GNDL 13/52. Courtesy of University of Notre Dame Archives.

102   Notre Dame Glee Club Director Daniel Pedtke and five Glee Club members outside the gates of Universal City Studios, 1966. GGCL 1/26. Courtesy of University of Notre Dame Archives.

103   Notre Dame Glee Club members playing around on a half-track at Universal City Studios, 1966. GGCL 1/26. Courtesy of University of Notre Dame Archives.

104   (*top left*) Notre Dame Glee Club members at an airport; one of them is wearing Mickey Mouse ears from Disneyland, 1966. GGCL 1/27. Courtesy of University of Notre Dame Archives.

       (*middle left*) Director Daniel Pedtke conducting the Notre Dame Glee Club in concert at Pat O'Brien's in New Orleans, 1972. Photo by Ben F. Hay, Pat O'Brien's. GGCL 1/40. Courtesy of University of Notre Dame Archives.

       (*bottom left*) Notre Dame Glee Club Director Daniel Pedtke with Glee Club members on a moving sidewalk at Universal Studios or Disneyland, ca. 1966. GGCL 1/28. Courtesy of University of Notre Dame Archives.

       (*right*) Spring Tour, Magic Kingdom Park, Walt Disney World Resort, Bay Lake, Florida, 1972. Photo provided by John Moe ('72, JD'75).

106   Daniel and Helen Pedtke meet Pope Paul VI. Photo provided by Dorothy Pedtke.

107   Alfred C. Stepan Jr. presenting a check to a Notre Dame Glee Club member while Director Daniel Pedtke, Rev. Theodore M. Hesburgh, and two other men look on, May 23, 1971. Photo by the *South Bend Tribune*. GGCL 1/39. Courtesy of University of Notre Dame Archives.

108   Daniel Pedtke enjoying an ice cream cone, European Tour, Florence, Italy, 1971. Photo provided by John Moe ('72, JD'75).

109   (*top left*) Boarding a cross channel ship from England to mainland Europe, European Tour, 1975. Photo provided by Marty Brauweiler ('78).

       (*bottom left*) European Tour, Germany, 1975. Photo provided by Marty Brauweiler ('78).

       (*top right*) European Tour, 1975. Photo provided by Marty Brauweiler ('78).

       (*bottom left*) Spring Tour, California, 1976. Photo provided by Marty Brauweiler ('78).

110   (*top left*) Glee Club members on the steps of the Piramide del Sol (Pyramid of the Sun), Latin America Tour, Teotihuacan, Mexico, 2005. Photo provided by John Paul Andree ('07).
(*bottom left*) Glee Club members playing around on the steps of a building, ca. 1973–74. GGCL 1/42. Courtesy of University of Notre Dame Archives.
(*top left*) Overlooking the city on European Tour, Florence, Italy, 1993. Photo provided by Michael Vo ('95).
(*bottom left*) Dressed for a performance of Igor Stravinsky's opera *Oedipus Rex* with the Jerusalem Symphony Orchestra, Jerusalem, Israel, 1997. Photo provided by Adam Charnley ('00).

111   Glee Club members during Asia tour, 2001. Photo by Kevin Burke. GMDG 12/22. Courtesy of University of Notre Dame Archives.

113   Glee Club members sing in Burgos Cathedral, May 2013. Photo provided by Rubén Navarro Martín.

115   (*left*) Thanksgiving Tour, 1962. Photo provided by Phil Jones ('63).
(*top right*) The Notre Dame Glee Club meets Archbishop Fulton Sheen at Rosary College, 1960. Photo by Charles Folak, provided by Steven Szegedi, Dominican University.
(*bottom right*) Tour, Niagara Falls, ca. 1962. Photo provided by Phil Jones ('63).

116   (*top left*) Spring Tour, Florida, 1972. Photo provided by John Moe ('72, JD'75).
(*bottom left*) Ticket from tour concert in Hingham, Massachusetts, 1976. Original provided by Marty Brauweiler ('78).
(*top right*) Post-concert celebration at the Hofbräuhaus, European Tour, Munich, Germany, 1975. Photo provided by Marty Brauweiler ('78).
(*bottom right*) The Bus Band, Spring Tour, 1972. Photo provided by John Moe ('72, JD'75).

CHAPTER 8

118   Glee Club members sing in Burgos Cathedral, May 2013. Photo provided by Rubén Navarro Martín.

121   Glee Club Performance Concert, ca. 1950s. GNEG 4B/15. Courtesy of University of Notre Dame Archives.

122–23 Glee Club Concert Programs through the years (some images have altered from their original form).
(*top row, 122*):
Program for Easter Tour concert, Vero Beach, Florida, 1958. Original provided by Fred Gade ('60).
Program for Easter Tour concert, Boston, Massachusetts, 1959. Original provided by Fred Gade ('60).
Program for Easter Tour concert, Asbury Park, New Jersey, 1959. Original provided by Fred Gade ('60).
Program for Easter Tour concert, Florence, Alabama, 1960. Original provided by Fred Gade ('60).
Program for Spring Tour concert, San Francisco, California, 1971. Original provided by Pat Scott ('76).
(*bottom row, 122*):
Program for European Tour benefit concert, Notre Dame, Indiana, 1971. Original provided by James Roberts ('71).
Program for Spring campus concert, Notre Dame, Indiana, 1972. Original provided by Pat Scott ('76).
Program for Spring Tour concert, Louisville, Ohio, 1972. Original provided by Pat Scott ('76).
Program for Spring Tour concert, Tampa, Florida, 1972. Original provided by Don Jacobson ('69).
Program for Spring Tour concert, Ursuline College, Pepper Pike, Ohio, 1972. Original provided by Pat Scott ('76).
(*top row, 123*):
Program for Spring Tour concert, Carson City, Nevada, 1975. Original provided by Pat Scott ('76).
Program for November concert, Detroit, Michigan, 1975. Original provided by Marty Brauweiler ('78).
Program for Spring Tour concert, Greenville, South Carolina, 1976. Original provided by Marty Brauweiler ('78).
Program for European Tour concert, Angers, France, 1978. Original provided by Marty Brauweiler ('78).
Program for National Convention of the American Choral Directors Association, Louisville, Kentucky, 1989. Original provided by Matt Borkowski ('91/'91).

(*bottom row, 123*):
Program for Cardinal O'Connor's Private Christmas Party, New York, New York, 1989. Original provided by Matt Borkowski ('91/'91).

Program for 75th Anniversary Alumni Reunion concert, Notre Dame, Indiana, 1990. Original provided by Matt Borkowski ('91/'91).

Program for Commencement concert, Notre Dame, Indiana, 1993. Original provided by Joe Dziedzic ('95).

Program for Spring campus concert, Notre Dame, Indiana, 1994. Original provided by Joe Dziedzic ('95).

Program for Spain Tour concert, Santiago de Compostela, 2013. Original provided by Daniel Stowe.

126   "Notre Dame, Our Mother" by Joseph Casasanta, signed by Glee Club members, 1990. Original provided by Matt Borkowski ('91/'91).

128   Notre Dame Glee Club Concert, Baby Medley, Spring 1975. GGCL 1/49. Courtesy of University of Notre Dame Archives.

130   (*left*) Daniel Pedtke's annotations for the performance of *Song of the Free* by Jack White and Felix Pogliano, mid-1950s. UGCL-03-37-01. Courtesy of University of Notre Dame Archives.

130–31 (*bottom*) Notre Dame's Musical Organizations (Band, Orchestra, and Glee Club) presents at the World Premiere Showing of "The Spirit of Notre Dame." With Professor Joseph J. Casasanta, Conductor. October 7, 1931. PNDP-S1943-0402-P006. Courtesy of University of Notre Dame Archives.

131   (*top*) Portrait of Kelly Cook, 1943. PNDP-S1943-0402-P006. Courtesy of University of Notre Dame Archives.

133   Fred Waring shaking hands with Notre Dame Glee Club first tenor soloist John Nolan, April 20, 1952. GGCL 1/17. Courtesy of University of Notre Dame Archives.

135   Spring Concert, Notre Dame, Indiana, 1963. Photo provided by Phil Jones ('63).

CHAPTER 9

136   Notre Dame Glee Club Concert on the *Andy Williams Show*, 1966. GGCL 1/32. Courtesy of University of Notre Dame Archives.

138   Advertisement in the *Dome* (1928) for Brunswick Music Company, featuring Glee Club song titles. PNDP-D1928-P454. Courtesy of University of Notre Dame Archives.

140   Glee Club album covers. Courtesy of University of Notre Dame Archives.

143   Notre Dame Glee Club members with Ed Sullivan behind the scenes, 1955. GGCL 1/17. Courtesy of University of Notre Dame Archives.

144   (*top*) Video still from appearance on *The Ed Sullivan Show*, April 5, 1953. Provided by Sofa Entertainment.
(*bottom*) Director Daniel Pedtke conducting the Glee Club on Ed Sullivan's television show *Toast of the Town*, April 9, 1950. Photo from *Dome* (1950), p. 371. PNDP-D1950-p371. Courtesy of University of Notre Dame Archives.

145   (*top*) Video still from appearance on *The Ed Sullivan Show*, April 5, 1953. Provided by Sofa Entertainment.
(*bottom*) Eddie Fisher performs with the Glee Club on *Coke Time* television show as part of the dedication of WNDU-TV station on campus, September 30, 1955. PNDP-D1956-P024. Courtesy of University of Notre Dame Archives.

146   (*top*) *Andy Williams Show*, Notre Dame Glee Club rehearsal behind the scenes, October 1966. GGCL 1/30. Courtesy of University of Notre Dame Archives.
(*bottom left*) *Andy Williams Show*, Notre Dame Glee Club performance, October 1966. GGCL 1/32. Courtesy of University of Notre Dame Archives.
(*bottom right*) Andy Williams signing autographs for Notre Dame Glee Club members behind the scenes, October 1966. GGCL 1/30. Courtesy of University of Notre Dame Archives.

147   Notre Dame Glee Club concert on the *Andy Williams Show*, October 30, 1966. GGCL 1/02. Courtesy of University of Notre Dame Archives.

148   Notre Dame Glee Club on the *John Davidson Show*, 1967. GGCL-01-43-01. Courtesy of University of Notre Dame Archives.

149   (*left*) Glee Club, directed by Daniel Pedtke, performing on the *John Davidson Show*, held in Stepan Center, October 1967. GPUB 18/49. Courtesy of University of Notre Dame Archives.
        (*right*) Unidentified Glee Club concert, ca. 1970s. GPUB-14-11-01. Courtesy of University of Notre Dame Archives.

150   Notre Dame Glee Club performing on the *Kennedy & Company* television show in Chicago, 1973. GGCL 1/41. Courtesy of University of Notre Dame Archives.

152   Notre Dame Glee Club with director Joseph J. Casasanta during filming of a Warner Brothers–Vitaphone short film, 1933. GGCL 1/14. Courtesy of University of Notre Dame Archives.

CHAPTER 10

154   The National Anthem performed by the Glee Club, 91st Anniversary Glee Club Reunion, Notre Dame, Indiana, 2006. Photo provided by Nathan Catanese ('07).

156   (*left*) Portrait of Rev. J. Hugh O'Donnell, C.S.C., early 1940s. GCSC-04-41-01. Courtesy of University of Notre Dame Archives.
        (*right*) Football player J. Hugh O'Donnell, full-length portrait in uniform, ca. 1915. GCLD 1/24. Courtesy of University of Notre Dame Archives.

157   Football Team in formation, 1915. Back row Arthur (Dutch) Bergman, Charlie Bachman, Stan Cofall, Jim Phelan at Quarterback. Front row Harry Baujan, Frank Rydzewski, Freeman Fitzgerald, Hugh O'Donnell, Emmett Keefe, Leo Stephan (Steve), Allen (Mal) Elward. GCLD 1/21. Courtesy of University of Notre Dame Archives.

159   Notre Dame Glee Club performs at the College Football Hall of Fame dedication, August 25, 1995. GGCL 1/59. Courtesy of University of Notre Dame Archives.

161   ND in Revue, 1993. Photo provided by Joe Dziedzic ('95).

162–63 Glee Club concert in front of Hesburgh Library prior to the North Carolina football game, October 11, 2014. Photo by Peter Ringenberg. Courtesy of University of Notre Dame Archives.

165   (*top*) Glee Club picnic at the home of director Daniel Pedtke, October 1949. PNDP-S1949-1014-P014. Courtesy of University of Notre Dame Archives.
        (*bottom*) Glee Club picnic at the home of Daniel Pedtke, October 1948. PNDP-S1948-1029-P011. Courtesy of University of Notre Dame Archives.

166   Fr. Robert Griffin presiding over Mass at Pedtke Bowl, South Bend, Indiana, 1977. Photo provided by Pat Scott ('76, JD'79).

167   Flag football game between the Notre Dame Glee Club and the Michigan State Glee Club at Spartan Stadium, East Lansing, Michigan, 2000. Photo provided by Adam Charnley ('00).

CHAPTER 11

168   Celebrating at Howard Park Tavern, South Bend, Indiana, 1963. Photo provided by Phil Jones ('63).

170   The Reverend Robert Griffin with his dog Darby O'Gill, April 27, 1982. Photo by Ron Parent. GNDM #82/019 (13/32). Courtesy of University of Notre Dame Archives.

171 "Is the Glee Club Damned From Here to Eternity?" Fr. Robert Griffin, Letters to a Lonely God, *The Observer*, March 20, 1992, p. 16.

172 The Reverend Robert Griffin, December 1981. Photo by Ron Parent. GNDM-81-049-F13A. Courtesy of University of Notre Dame Archives

173 The Pedtke home. Photo provided by Dorothy Pedtke

174 (*top left*) Notre Dame Glee Club party with beer, ca. 1947. GGCL-01-16-03. Courtesy of University of Notre Dame Archives.
(*bottom left*) Notre Dame Glee Club Alumni Reunion at Tippecanoe Place Restaurant, November 5, 1977. Photo by Pat Scott. GGCL 1/52-F29A. Courtesy of University of Notre Dame Archives.
(*top right*) Notre Dame Glee Club party with beer, ca. 1947. Photo by Bruce Harlan (119 Alumni Hall). *Scholastic* staff photographer. GGCL 1/15-04. Courtesy of University of Notre Dame Archives.
(*bottom right*) Notre Dame Glee Club party with beer, ca. 1947. Photo by Bruce Harlan (119 Alumni Hall). *Scholastic* staff photographer. GGCL 1/15-05. Courtesy of University of Notre Dame Archives.

175 (*top left*) Spring Tour, San Francisco, California, 1995. Photo provided by Joey Coleman ('95).
(*bottom left*) At a rest stop, European Tour, Ireland, 1993. Photo provided by Mike Vo ('95).
(*top right*) Glee Club Formal, South Bend, Indiana, 2007. Photo provided by Nathan Catanese ('07).
(*bottom right*) Fall Tour, 1986. Photo provided by Jim Braun ('86).

176 Daniel Stowe leading the alumni chorus, 85th Anniversary Glee Club Reunion, Notre Dame, Indiana, 2000. Photo provided by Adam Charnley ('00).

177 Collage of Notre Dame Glee Club headlines, photos, and travel ephemera, ca. 1960s. GGCL 1/23. Courtesy of University of Notre Dame Archives.

178 Friday night mini-concert at South Dining Hall, 1994. Photo provided by Joe Dziedzic ('95).

179 (*top*) Glee Club Formal, 1983. Photo provided by Mark "Chuda" Michuda ('83).
(*bottom*) Glee Club members wearing tuxedos, playing basketball, and smoking cigarettes on a break, 1955–56, from *Dome* (1956), p. 285. PNDP-D1956-p285-02. Courtesy of University of Notre Dame Archives.

180 (*top left*) Glee Club golfers at the Dunes Resort, Las Vegas, Nevada, ca. 1969. Photo provided by James Roberts ('71).
(*bottom left*) Saint Patrick's Day Parade performance, San Diego, California, 1990. Photo provided by Matt Borkowski ('91/'91).
(*top right*) Bookstore Basketball team, 1983. Photo provided by Mark "Chuda" Michuda ('83).
(*bottom right*) Glee Clubbers at a football game, Notre Dame, Indiana, 1992. Photo provided by Eileen Murphy ('95, MBA'02).

181 Glee Club Officer Election after party, Farley Hall, ca. 1969. Photo provided by James Roberts ('71).

182 Bedhead Bowling cartoon, Glee Club Alumni Newsletter, vol. 26, no. 4, 1989, p. 6. Original provided by Matt Borkowski ('91/'91).

183 Glee Club mugs through the years. Photos by Matt Cashore.

CHAPTER TWELVE

184 Glee Clubbers and their dates attending prom, Notre Dame, Indiana, 1962. Photo provided by Pete Hyland ('62).

186 Glee Club singing Christmas carols, ca. 1980s. GPUB-45-50-02. Courtesy of University of Notre Dame Archives.

187 (*top*) Caught under the mistletoe at Farley Hall, 1994. Photo provided by Eileen Murphy ('95, MBA'02).
(*bottom*) Campus Christmas Caroling at Farley Hall, 1994. Photo provided by Eileen Murphy ('95, MBA'02).

188 (*left*) Renowned Bermudan civil rights trailblazer, educator, and artist Mrs. Georgine R. Hill (mother of Glee Clubber Hilton "Buddy" Hill ['63]) performing with Daniel Pedtke at the piano, the Pedtke home on Commencement weekend, South Bend, Indiana 1963. Notre Dame, Indiana, 1963. Photo provided by Phil Jones ('63).
(*right*) Pep rally performance photo with Debbie Reynolds and Eddie Fisher on Eddie Fisher's *Coke Time* at the Old Field House, 1956. Photo provided by Gerard Pottebaum ('56).

189 Newspaper clipping advertising Sara McCabe's performance at Notre Dame, mid-1920s. UGCL-06-09. Courtesy of University of Notre Dame Archives.

190 Meal with women, St. Louis, ca. 1962. Photo provided by Phil Jones ('63).

191 (*left*) Bus hijinks, ca. 1962. Photo provided by Phil Jones ('63).
(*right*) Mixing with fans, Thanksgiving Tour, 1962. Photo provided by Phil Jones ('63).

192 (*top left*) Daniel and daughter Dorothy Pedtke at the Pedtke home on Commencement weekend, South Bend, Indiana, 1963. Photo provided by Phil Jones ('63).
(*middle left*) Daniel Pedtke and daughter Cathy Pedtke. Photo provided by Dorothy Pedtke.
(*bottom left*) Daniel and Helen Pedtke waiting next to bus. Photo provided by Dick Leonhardt ('65).
(*right*) Daniel and Helen Pedtke, April 26, 1976. Photo provided by Dorothy Pedtke.

193 Helen Pedtke, Maria (Casasanta) Thallemer, and Anita Casasanta at the 62nd Anniversary Glee Club Reunion, Tippecanoe Place, South Bend, Indiana, 1977. Photo provided by Pat Scott ('76, JD'79).

194 Quartet of Glee Club members delivering Singing Valentines, 1993. Photo provided by Eileen Murphy ('95, MBA'02).

195 Sheet of handwritten music from the Glee Club, no date. UGCL-04-02-01. Courtesy of University of Notre Dame Archives.

226 *Below*: A Notre Dame Glee Club member in a tuxedo, taking a nap on a gymnasium floor, ca. 1960s. Photo by Robert William Simpson. GGCL 1/18. Courtesy of University of Notre Dame Archives.